Interdisciplinary Instruction

A Practical Guide for Elementary and Middle School Teachers

Third Edition

KARLYN E. WOOD

State University of New York
College at Old Westbury

PEARSON

Merrill
Prentice Hall

Upper Saddle River, New Jersey
Columbus, Ohio

Library of Congress Cataloging-in-Publication Data

Wood, Karlyn E.
   Interdisciplinary instruction : a practical guide for elementary and middle school teachers / Karlyn E.
Wood.—3rd ed.
      p. cm.
   Includes bibliographical references and index.
   ISBN 0-13-114506-1
   1. Interdisciplinary approach in education—United States.   2. Education, Elementary—Curricula—United States.
3. Middle schools—Curricula—United States.   4. Curriculum planning—United States.   I. Title.

LB1570.W644 2005
   373.19—dc22

                                            2004004697

Vice President and Executive Publisher: Jeffery W. Johnston
Executive Editor: Debra A. Stollenwerk
Associate Editor: Ben M. Stephen
Editorial Assistant: Mary Morrill
Production Editor: Kris Roach
Production Coordination: *The GTS Companies*/York, PA Campus
Design Coordinator: Diane C. Lorenzo
Cover Designer: Jeff Vanik
Cover Image: Nina Vassallo
Photo Coordinator: Sandy Schaefer
Production Manager: Susan Hannahs
Director of Marketing: Ann Castel Davis
Marketing Manager: Darcy Betts Prybella
Marketing Coordinator: Tyra Poole

This book was set in ZapfIntnatl Lt BT by *The GTS Companies*/York, PA Campus. It was printed and bound by R.R. Donnelley
& Sons Company. The cover was printed by Coral Graphic Services, Inc.

Photo Credits: KS Studios/Merrill, p. 1; Larry Hamill/Merrill, p. 23; Kathy Kirtland/Merrill, p. 37; Silver Burdett Ginn, p. 57;
Anthony Magnacca/Merrill, pp. 75, 105, 133.

Pearson Education Ltd.   Pearson Education Australia Pty. Limited
Pearson Education Singapore Pte. Ltd.   Pearson Education North Asia Ltd.
Pearson Education Canada, Ltd.   Pearson Educación de Mexico, S.A. de C.V.
Pearson Education—Japan   Pearson Education Malaysia Pte. Ltd.

373.19
.W644
2005

                                                        10 9 8 7 6 5
                                                ISBN: 0-13-114506-1

To Louise, Kim, Nina, and Jennifer

*To my students and colleagues in the Teacher Education Department
at the State University of New York/College at Old Westbury*

Preface

Traditionally, instruction in U.S. schools has isolated the academic disciplines—or subject areas—from one another. In contrast, **interdisciplinary**—or **integrated—instruction** always begins with a central theme; the theme is then investigated by using any disciplines that can assist in the inquiry. The themes that students study can vary greatly; some are typical of topics usually included in a social studies or science curriculum. However, themes from other disciplines, such as literature, mathematics, and the visual and performing arts, can also become the basis of an interdisciplinary study.

Interest in the interdisciplinary method has renewed among educators. This interest has been stimulated by legislative steps taken by many state departments of education. Since the first edition of this book, nearly all states have prepared lists of content learning standards; these lists strongly suggest the need for integrated studies. Some curriculum mandates also stress interdisciplinary instruction. For example, the New York State Education Department currently requires teachers of grades 3 through 6 to develop at least one interdisciplinary project with students in their classes each year. As a result, teachers and administrators are showing more interest in interdisciplinary program designs and practical ways to plan for their implementation. Many teachers are eager to learn exactly what interdisciplinary projects should involve and how they differ from other instructional activities.

Early childhood teachers use the interdisciplinary approach as a standard method of instruction. Preschool and kindergarten teachers routinely plan their instructional programs around central themes, themes that are then used as much as feasible in teaching daily lessons and activities. Most primary grade teachers believe that they understand the method and that they have been readied for it by their college preparatory programs. Although interest in using interdisciplinary instruction in the upper elementary grades and middle school is increasing, teachers at these levels may believe they have less preparation and experience with the interdisciplinary approach than their early childhood colleagues do.

This book provides preservice and in-service elementary and middle school teachers and administrators with a handbook that introduces the interdisciplinary method and offers practical suggestions on how to plan for and implement the method in classrooms. I based this book partly on the materials that I prepared for my courses in teacher education. In the book, I have purposefully kept the theoretical chapters succinct—yet complete—so that the emphasis can be on the *thinking processes* involved in planning lessons and designing unit plans for interdisciplinary and research-oriented interdisciplinary units—two types of interdisciplinary units that are suitable for students at differing ability levels.

This book is intended for use in methods courses at both the undergraduate and the graduate levels; it is also appropriate for in-service courses in schools and teacher centers. The practical explanations and examples provided should prove especially helpful for teachers who have not previously studied interdisciplinary instruction and who want to learn how to get started.

College instructors who emphasize a constructivist approach to teaching and who advocate interdisciplinary methods in social studies, science, and generic methods courses can use this book to help their students understand both the theoretical and the practical aspects of interdisciplinary instruction. Instructors of other methods courses, such as literacy and mathematics, will find this book valuable for helping students see the relationships between these disciplines and comprehensive interdisciplinary studies.

To emphasize the planning processes and illustrate the essentials of these processes as clearly as possible, I included examples for each step in the unit planning processes outlined in chapters 5 and 6. The models in this book illustrate one way to design interdisciplinary units, although surely not the only way. The viewpoint expressed throughout this book is that no single planning format will work satisfactorily for every teacher.

▨ ORGANIZATION OF THE BOOK

The first chapter provides a theoretical framework for the interdisciplinary instruction method. In this chapter is a review of the theory supporting interdisciplinary instruction and an outline of its distinguishing features. Chapter 1 also includes the rationale for using the method with students in elementary and middle schools, outlines the requirements of teachers who plan to use it, discusses teacher collaboration, and explains the role of technology in interdisciplinary education.

New chapters 2 and 3 provide information about the lesson planning processes. Chapter 2 provides a review of several preliminary considerations in the lesson and interdisciplinary unit planning processes, including learning and development, questioning techniques, and the application of Bloom's Taxonomy. Chapter 2 concludes with suggestions for designing learning centers for student exploration and practice in connection with units of study.

Chapter 3 provides specific information on the lesson planning process. The chapter covers lesson planning formats and provides a review of a number of procedural protocols with examples for use in teaching different kinds of material.

Chapter 4 includes information on assessment. It includes information on both authentic assessment and traditional examinations. Rubrics are explained and illustrated.

Chapters 5 and 6 are specifically designed to teach the processes involved in planning interdisciplinary and research-oriented interdisciplinary units. Chapter 5 includes details of the processes involved in planning interdisciplinary units. Chapter 6 covers the research-oriented interdisciplinary unit, an alternative type of unit for students at upper elementary and middle school levels. Both chapters include a detailed unit plan outline, followed by a step-by-step interdisciplinary unit planning procedure with examples at each step. Chapter 5 includes information about the design of learning centers. Chapter 6 includes a suggestion for planning and organizing a research-oriented interdisciplinary unit to be used in a departmentalized school. Complete versions of the unit plans that are partially completed in chapters 5 and 6 are provided in the Instructional Resources section at the back of the book.

Students can use chapters 5 and 6 for reference during in-class practicum sessions. As they follow the steps to plan their own units, instructors will be able to use valuable class time to interact directly with students and critique the plans as they develop.

Chapter 7 provides a brief discussion of the process of change involved when teachers move toward an interdisciplinary program. It includes suggestions about how school systems can support teachers as they work through this process. Also included is a discussion of the need for parent and community involvement in any curricular change.

The Conclusion provides a summary of major points introduced in the book.

The new Instructional Resources section includes sample lesson plans that follow the procedural protocols discussed in chapter 3. This section also includes complete interdisciplinary and research-oriented interdisciplinary unit plan examples and 20 interdisciplinary unit plan web designs, some of which were prepared by preservice and in-service teachers.

Each chapter includes reference lists, several activity ideas, and a list of suggested readings related to chapter topics. The readings include early theoretical works for individuals who would like additional background material or who plan to undertake their own research on topics included in the chapters, as well as writings that reflect current thinking on and trends regarding these topics.

▨ NEW TO THE THIRD EDITION

- All references in the third edition were updated.
- The chapters were revised and reorganized into seven chapters to provide a logical grouping of topics.
- The appendixes of the previous editions were eliminated and replaced by the new Instructional Resources section, which includes examples of lessons and unit plans.

- The sample web designs in the second edition are now included in this new section of the book.
- Howard Gardner's ninth intelligence area was added to the discussion on multiple intelligences in chapter 1.
- "Essential questions" that are included in some lesson plan outlines were added to the lesson and unit planning discussions and examples in the book.
- Detailed discussions of procedural protocols were added in the new chapters on lesson planning.
- Information on assessment now follows the lesson planning chapters in a new chapter 4 devoted exclusively to this topic.
- Chapter 7 continues the second edition discussion on the process involved in moving toward interdisciplinary instruction.

ACKNOWLEDGMENTS

Our quest for knowledge is a lifelong pursuit in which we learn both from our experiences and from one another. Teachers often play an important role in facilitating this process. For most of us, some teachers will be especially well remembered for their positive contributions. To begin, I consider myself fortunate to have been taught by the late Myrtle Cope, an exemplary master teacher. I thank her for the early influence she had on my decision to become an elementary school teacher and for the example she provided me of the constructivist approach to education, a philosophy that continues to influence my teaching practice.

I would also like to acknowledge the late Roland Chatterton, a forward-thinking educator and pioneer in multidisciplinary education. Dr. Chatterton introduced me to interdisciplinary methodology; his patient mentoring and guidance facilitated my personal development as an interdisciplinary teacher.

I would like to thank my wife Louise for her patience and support as I prepared the manuscripts for each edition of the book. My colleagues in the Teacher Education Department at the State University of New York/College at Old Westbury provided me with their support, and I thank them for their interest and encouragement throughout the project. I am especially indebted to my colleagues Kathleen Velsor and Gareth B. Wilmott, who provided me with valuable feedback on my plans and manuscript revision drafts, and I want to thank them for their time and their many helpful suggestions. I also want to express my appreciation to my previous and present students in the Teacher Education Department at the SUNY/College at Old Westbury for permission to include several of their introductory lesson plans and unit plan web designs in the Instructional Resources section of the book.

I particularly want to thank my reviewers for their input and suggestions: Kris Sloan, Texas A&M University; Sarah J. Snider, Lincoln Memorial University; Martha M. Williams, Hampton University; Eva Weisz, DePauw University; Gail Lockhart, Eastern Illinois University; Joyce W. Frazier, University of North Carolina at Charlotte; Frank Miller, Pittsburg State University; and Dawn Foley, Arizona State University.

I would also like to acknowledge artist Nina Vassallo for the drawings she prepared for me that inspired and were adapted for the design on the cover of this book.

Finally, I would like to acknowledge my editors at Merrill/Prentice Hall: Debbie Stollenwerk for her continuous interest and her counsel; Ben Stephen for his guidance and many professional suggestions as I prepared the manuscript; Kathleen Riley King for her expertise and the recommendations she made throughout the copyediting process; and Kris Roach for her guidance and support in the final production stages of the book.

Invitation to the Reader

When I started teaching, I had little understanding of the interdisciplinary method, and I was certainly unaware of all I would have to learn during the next few years to use it in my own classroom. As a young, inexperienced teacher, I began my career in an elementary school district that was proud of its *multidisciplinary* philosophy, where teachers were expected to use a multidisciplinary approach at every level—from kindergarten through the sixth grade. I began studying the method from the outset, but not until I observed the enthusiasm of the other teachers who had been using it for some time did I become committed to developing the skills I would need to carry it out myself.

Throughout the first two years, I found multidisciplinary—or interdisciplinary—teaching far more challenging than I had ever anticipated, and I likely would have given the method up altogether if I had not been given a great deal of moral support from other teachers and administrators in my school. I learned from my colleagues how important it was to reserve extra time to plan for this kind of instruction and soon found myself spending countless hours after school on a task I found nearly overwhelming—trying to write plans for the interdisciplinary units I was teaching.

In those early experimental years, I paid little attention to planning *processes* and, instead, spent—or misspent—most of my energy searching for the best way to write a unit plan. Eventually, I realized that I needed to learn more about the planning process itself, so in time, my concentration shifted from the *writing* of the plan to the *thinking* involved in designing an interdisciplinary unit. I had discovered that the planning process was far more important than the format of the written plan. However, my attempts to locate information on the interdisciplinary approach or the unit planning process revealed that little substantive material appeared to be available. Even the most popular instructional methods textbooks in use at our local universities had little to offer on the subject.

Seventeen years later, when I began teaching education majors in college, I found that there was still a dearth of practical material written about interdisciplinary unit planning to use with my students, so, out of necessity, I began preparing my own. To develop these materials, I drew on my classroom teaching experience with the method and focused on the sequential thought processes involved in unit preparation.

Now, after using these materials for several years, I have found them to be especially helpful for students who are beginning to learn about interdisciplinary instruction and unit planning. I have noted that when the materials are used in class, I need to spend less class time explaining the planning processes and giving repetitious oral instructions about them. Instead, I have more time to work directly with students as they practice designing their own interdisciplinary unit plans.

My hope is that this book will help both preservice and in-service teachers explore interdisciplinary instruction and the planning processes involved in it. I also hope that instructors will save valuable time by using this book and will be able to use this time to help their students become better teachers.

About the Author

Karlyn Wood received his Ed.D. from Hofstra University and is Professor of Humanities in the Teacher Education Department at the SUNY College at Old Westbury on Long Island, where he teaches courses in interdisciplinary methodology and child development. He supervises and conducts seminars for student teachers and has served several terms as chair of his department. Karlyn has taught at the elementary level and has served as a district reading consultant, administrator, and coordinator for an experimental elementary program. His publications include articles in *Language Arts*, *Childhood Education*, *The Journal of Child Development*, and *The Journal of Teacher Education*. His papers have been included in *Sociological Abstracts* and ERIC documents. He belongs to the American Educational Research Association, the Association Montessori Internationale, the Association for Supervision and Curriculum Development, and Kappa Delta Pi.

EDUCATOR LEARNING CENTER: AN INVALUABLE ONLINE RESOURCE

Merrill Education and the Association for Supervision and Curriculum Development (ASCD) invite you to take advantage of a new online resource, one that provides access to the top research and proven strategies associated with ASCD and Merrill—the Educator Learning Center. At **www.EducatorLearningCenter.com** you will find resources that will enhance your students' understanding of course topics and of current educational issues, in addition to being invaluable for further research.

How the Educator Learning Center Will Help Your Students Become Better Teachers

With the combined resources of Merrill Education and ASCD, you and your students will find a wealth of tools and materials to better prepare them for the classroom.

Research

- More than 600 articles from the ASCD journal *Educational Leadership* discuss everyday issues faced by practicing teachers.
- A direct link on the site to Research Navigator™ gives students access to many of the leading education journals, as well as extensive content detailing the research process.
- Excerpts from Merrill Education texts give your students insights on important topics of instructional methods, diverse populations, assessment, classroom management, technology, and refining classroom practice.

Classroom Practice

- Hundreds of lesson plans and teaching strategies are categorized by content area and age range.
- Case studies and classroom video footage provide virtual field experience for student reflection.
- Computer simulations and other electronic tools keep your students abreast of today's classrooms and current technologies.

Look into the Value of Educator Learning Center Yourself

A four-month subscription to Educator Learning Center is $25 but is **FREE** when used in conjunction with this text. To obtain free passcodes for your students, simply contact your local Merrill/Prentice Hall sales representative, and your representative will give you a special ISBN to give your bookstore when ordering your textbooks. To preview the value of this website to you and your students, please go to **www.EducatorLearningCenter.com** and click on "Demo."

Brief Contents

Contents

Note: Every effort has been made to provide accurate and current Internet information in this book. However, the Internet and information posted on it are constantly changing, so it is inevitable that some of the Internet addresses listed in this textbook will change.

1

Interdisciplinary Instructional Theory and Rationale

▓ OVERVIEW

This chapter covers the theoretical foundations of interdisciplinary instruction. The focus of this chapter is on the following:

- The distinguishing features of the interdisciplinary approach
- A rationale for using interdisciplinary instruction at the elementary and middle school levels
- A list of the primary requirements for teachers who plan to use an interdisciplinary approach in their classrooms
- A discussion of collaborative teaching, technology, and teaching resources for the interdisciplinary approach

▓ DISTINGUISHING FEATURES OF INTERDISCIPLINARY INSTRUCTION

In their classes, elementary and middle school teachers use a variety of methods and techniques, each of which has unique characteristics. One of these techniques is **interdisciplinary**—or **integrated**—**instruction,** an educational approach that can be distinguished from other teaching methods by its special features.

How is interdisciplinary instruction distinguished from other approaches? A fundamental feature of the interdisciplinary approach is that students become involved in comprehensive instructional units of study. Such units have at least three unique characteristics:

1. During each interdisciplinary unit, students explore a specific topic or central theme.
2. Students explore the topic by using the skills and techniques—the ways of knowing—from a variety of disciplines.
3. Interdisciplinary units of study allow equal emphasis to be placed on the mastery of process and the mastery of content.

Topic-Centered Organization

Instead of being subject or discipline centered, each interdisciplinary unit has as its focus a specific topic or theme. This topic is explored by using any **disciplines**—subjects or domains—that can help the learner gain a better understanding of the topic. For example, in the primary grades, topics such as Our Family and Our Neighborhood are typically studied because they are often recommended in state curriculum guides, and they address learning standards in the social studies curriculum. However, other, less traditional topics can often afford interesting opportunities for young children to apply their inquiry skills and creativity. For example, topics such as

Changes, Environments, Flying, and How It Works can offer interesting, challenging inquiries that are feasible for early interdisciplinary studies. In addition, these topics can include concepts that address learning standards in several disciplines.

Older students can usually investigate more sophisticated, comprehensive topics such as Mediterranean Lands, The Middle East, Westward Expansion, and Our Endangered Environment. Although many of these topics are traditional social studies topics for older students, the study can develop from any discipline, subject, or domain, including the sciences, technology, children's literature, mathematics, music, and the arts.

An interesting and exceptionally well-developed example of an interdisciplinary unit that begins with the arts and evolves to include all areas of the curriculum is Spaces and Places. Pappas, Kiefer, and Levstik (1999) designed this unit for students in an upper elementary grade. Elwyn Richardson (1964), an elementary teacher in New Zealand, also used the arts as the basis for his unusual interdisciplinary program. After his students completed art projects made from raw materials from their natural rural environment, Richardson involved the students in extensive related activities in writing, reading, the arts, science, and mathematics.

Use of Academic Disciplines

While students are involved in studying holistic, interdisciplinary topics, they are being exposed to additional skills and ways of knowing inherent in the different disciplines used to investigate them. Students are encouraged to think critically about the issues inherent in their studies and to use the skills and techniques from any disciplines that can assist them in their investigation.

In interdisciplinary studies, students have many natural opportunities to observe the connections and to note relationships among the various disciplines that they use in their study. Jacobs (1989) emphasized the importance of this characteristic in interdisciplinary units and suggested that the teacher intentionally "appl[y] methodology and language from more than one discipline to examine a central theme, issue, problem, topic, or experience" (p. 8).

Emphasis on Process and on Content

Another distinguishing feature of interdisciplinary instruction is that it also involves the learning *processes*, *skills*, and *ways of knowing* that are unique to the different disciplines, subjects, or domains. In contrast, the focus of disciplinary, subject-centered instruction is almost exclusively on *content*. Such instruction is aimed largely at helping students amass facts and general information. Although no consensus exists about which focus is more important, the processes involved in inquiry and scientific investigation are especially important and useful in interdisciplinary studies.

Educators have debated for years about the importance of process versus content. For many years, interdisciplinary teachers have agreed with Dewey's (1916) advice that equal importance be attributed to content and to process. Such teachers expect their students to amass facts and develop concepts while they practice important academic learning processes that will "become the models [they will use] for later exploratory behaviors" (Gardner, 1993a, p. 31) and gain insights about and practice different ways of knowing.

At upper elementary and middle school grade levels, students undertake more complex forms of inquiry, using processes that naturally stimulate the higher level thinking and reasoning skills. Finally, besides gaining knowledge and practicing the learning processes, which are major aims in interdisciplinary instruction, students have many meaningful opportunities to practice their reading, writing, and computational skills while they are involved in authentic investigations.

▨ RATIONALE FOR INTERDISCIPLINARY INSTRUCTION IN ELEMENTARY AND MIDDLE SCHOOL

Why should interdisciplinary instruction be used at the elementary and middle school levels? Before answering this question, consider how a group of children probably receive instruction about a specific social studies topic in a school with a traditional approach to its curriculum. Observe how one group was taught about the island nation of Japan during an 8-year period:

> In the first grade, when children often study the concept of family, their teacher read stories about families from several cultures around the world; one story was about a Japanese family. A music teacher taught the children a Japanese folk song in the second grade and a traditional Japanese dance in the third grade. In the fourth grade, an art teacher helped the children experiment with origami. The children also studied geographic regions of the world that year; in that study, some discussion on islands and island nations was included. Finally, in middle school, the children studied aspects of Asian cultures, including the Japanese culture.

The sequence in the preceding description is characteristic of a traditional, or subject-centered, approach to a social topic. Instead of being provided an integrated inquiry of Japan and Japanese culture at any specific grade level, the students were offered isolated bits of information in a fragmented study that was spread across 8 years. At first, you may think it logical to approach a social study this way. We know that adults can integrate related information received about a topic during a long period. However, we also know that doing so is more difficult for very young children. Gardner (1991) suggested that the mind of a young child—5 to 7 or even 10 years old—is intuitive, resourceful, highly imaginative, and creative. However, at the same time, it is limited by a "tendency to stereotype and simplify. . . . It contains a swirl of symbols, scripts, theories, and incipient notions and concepts, which can be involved in appropriate ways but which also remain to be sorted out in a more secure manner" (pp. 110–111). Earlier, Piaget and Inhelder (1975) found that young children's thinking is often **centered;** in a young child's mind, isolated concepts and bits of information remain unrelated. In view of these limitations, an important reason for using an integrated, or interdisciplinary, method is that students who approach their studies thematically and holistically may be less likely to misinterpret and more likely to make better sense of their world.

Research on the Human Brain

Although all the implications from research on the human brain about teaching and learning may not be clear, educators are seriously studying the research. As a result, a number of authorities in the field have prepared materials based on what is known that can be especially helpful for teachers. Robert Sylwester's (1995) straightforward overview of the brain and its functions is a succinct, yet comprehensive, discussion of this important topic. In his book, Sylwester talked about the importance of helping students to make connections and find relationships between the facts they are taught and their personal experiences. He suggested that "the best school vehicle for this search for relationships is storytelling that includes such elements as conversations, debates, role playing, simulations, songs, games, films, and novels" (p. 103). He also recommended activities such as "student projects, cooperative learning, and portfolio assessments" (p. 132), all of which are included routinely when interdisciplinary units are taught.

Eric Jensen (1998) suggested the importance of interdisciplinary, holistic methods by reminding us that the brain constructs meaning better when it finds patterns. Jensen also suggested that integrated instruction may be especially meaningful to older students because they have a greater knowledge base with which to construct such patterns. However, Jensen stated more generally that interdisciplinary methods "create much more relevance and context and, more important, help students understand the connections in learning" (p. 96).

In other discussions of implications from brain research—such as those by Hardiman (2001), Lowery (1998), and Westwater and Wolfe (2000)—the need for integrated studies is also emphasized. The reason such studies are needed is that isolated learnings are difficult to process, recall, and use.

Development of Multiple Intelligences

An especially strong argument for an interdisciplinary approach evolves from Gardner's **theory of multiple intelligences.** Initially, Gardner proposed seven intelligences (1983, 1993b). An eighth intelligence was added later in Kane's (1999) analysis of additional intelligences in Gardner's theory.

Gardner proposed a ninth intelligence, **existential intelligence,** in 1999. He indicated some reluctance about including existential intelligence. Perhaps he considers it to be a *half*-intelligence because the part of the brain that deals with existential questions is not yet clear (Gardner, 1999; Smith, 2002).

Still, Gardner (1999) appears to have suggested that existential intelligence meets his eight criteria for an intelligence. He stated, "Perhaps surprisingly, existential intelligence scores reasonably well on the eight criteria. . . . Although empirical psychological evidence is sparse, what exists certainly does not invalidate the construct" (p. 64). He concluded that "existential intelligence . . . may well be admissible" (p. 64).

According to multiple intelligences theory, human beings operate in the following nine—and possibly more—intelligence areas:

1. *Linguistic, or verbal, intelligence:* The ability to use language well and to learn through verbal methods such as reading, note taking, writing summaries and reports, and conducting interviews

2. *Logical–mathematical intelligence:* Using mathematics and logic, forming hypotheses, and conducting scientific inquiries

3. *Spatial intelligence:* Detecting spatial relationships, noticing likenesses and differences visually, creating art and design, and thinking by visualizing in pictures

4. *Musical intelligence:* Using music as a tool for thinking, demonstrating feelings and attitudes with music, and associating thought with music

5. *Bodily–kinesthetic intelligence:* Using the entire body to help master or to explain ideas and concepts

6. *Interpersonal intelligence:* Understanding others, working effectively and cooperatively with other people, and sharing tasks and responsibilities

7. *Intrapersonal intelligence:* Understanding oneself and being able to analyze one's personal performance in order to grow and change

8. *Naturalist intelligence:* Recognizing flora and fauna, discriminating among them, and having a sensitivity to phenomena in the natural environment

9. *Existential intelligence:* Having interest in and raising questions about the meaning of life, death, and why things are the way they are

Gardner suggested that his "theory gives educators a way of thinking about individual gifts and how to accommodate teaching to them" (Brandt, 1988, p. 34). Thus, if students are developing in any or all of these intelligence areas, they need opportunities to grow in more than one at a time. Clearly, such opportunities will occur most naturally when educators link "the multiple intelligences with a curriculum focused on understanding" (Checkley, 1997, p. 11)—a primary focus of interdisciplinary instruction. Therefore, interdisciplinary studies in the elementary school should replace isolated, subject-centered, disciplinary instruction. Doing so will facilitate optimal development for more students.

Gardner's theory is as important for students in the middle school grades as it is for students in the earlier grades. His theory not only lends support for the interdisciplinary approach, but also is consistent with one of the eight recommendations from the 1989 Carnegie Council's Task Force on Education of Young Adolescents: to "teach a core academic program" ("The Seventh Grade Slump," 1992, p. 3). The **core curriculum** is an interdisciplinary concept that Reed and Bergmann (1995) described as "the integration of a variety of disciplines around a single core, often a theme or a problem" (p. 313). Clearly, this notion is consistent with the idea that students should have opportunities for development in more than one domain or intelligence area, which is again suggestive of the interdisciplinary method.

Although Gardner's theory is widely accepted among educators, learning theorists, sociologists, and psychologists, its acceptance is not universal. Allis (1999) cited a number of social scientists who hold more traditional views of intelligence and who disagree with multiple intelligences theory. For a comprehensive overview of multiple intelligences theory and how it is supported by research on the human brain, refer to Sylwester's (1995, pp. 108–116) clear and concise discussion.

Social Interaction

Students also need opportunities for the kind of social interaction and guidance that teachers and capable peers can provide naturally during interdisciplinary studies. Piaget (1970) believed that verbal interaction between students and teachers was necessary for youngsters to develop arbitrary social concepts. However, he did not believe that the use of direct instruction was as important in developing physical and logicomathematical knowledge. Further, he cautioned about imposing too much verbal instruction or use of demonstrations in teaching, especially with very young children, because these methods might inhibit the development of operational (generalizable, useful) knowledge.

Today, however, considerable evidence suggests that Piaget may have attributed too little importance to the value of instruction in the development of concepts. For example, the importance of verbal instruction, social interaction, and culture in promoting optimal learning is clear in Vygotsky's theory of the **zone of proximal development (ZPD;** Vygotsky, 1978, 1986). According to Vygotsky (1978), the ZPD is "the distance between the actual developmental level as determined by independent problem solving and the level of potential development as determined through problem solving under adult guidance or in collaboration with more capable peers" (p. 86).

Contemporary researchers agree with Vygotsky about the importance of culture and social interaction in the process of knowledge acquisition. For example, in Canada, Case's (1985) studies of early development support Vygotsky's theory about the impact of social interaction and instruction in early childhood on cognitive development as children mature. Case also suggested the importance of interdisciplinary instruction in promoting children's problem-solving skills "across as wide a range of culturally valued problem domains or subjects as possible" (p. 393). Also in 1985, Wertsch offered a particularly comprehensive discussion of Vygotsky's theory about the value of social interaction.

Later, in *Acts of Meaning*, Bruner (1990) discussed the importance of adult interaction and instruction in helping children make "narrative" sense of actions and ideas. Forman, Minick, and Stone (1993) also provided a compelling argument for interdisciplinary studies—what these authors refer to as **theme research projects**—in their review of Vygotsky's theory and its implications for classroom practice.

Interdisciplinary studies provide natural opportunities for the kind of instruction and teacher–student, student–student interaction that these contemporary researchers found critical for optimal learning.

Meaningful Use of Academic Skills

Another reason to use interdisciplinary instruction in the elementary grades and middle school is simply that most real problems in life are investigated or solved by using more than one discipline at a time. For example, when an individual is purchasing a new home, economics is a major factor but not the only one. Location (geography), architectural style, nearby educational facilities, and other community resources also need to be considered before a final decision can be made. Interdisciplinary instruction routinely and realistically encourages students to use the skills and ways of knowing associated with any disciplines that can be applied logically in their investigations.

Every teacher is concerned about students' academic skills and with providing sufficient practice of these skills. The exercises given to children in many schools in workbooks and on duplicated worksheets may have little or no relationship to the topics they are studying. Such exercises then simply become practice for the sake of practice. Wakefield (1993) suggested that, in contrast to this type of skills practice, "almost any subject . . . is best taught when it is needed to accomplish something else" (p. 137). The same is true for practicing academic skills.

Interdisciplinary instruction is in step with this idea because it always provides for the application of skills in meaningful contexts. As unit topics are explored, students find that they need to use their inquiry skills, need to read for information, need to write letters and reports, and need to give oral presentations in front of the class. Students use mathematical skills as they prepare charts, graphs, and maps; they make use of technology as they search for information; they follow the scientific method as they work on related science experiments and activities; they also explore drama, music, and dance and gain experience with various art media. In fact, the interdisciplinary approach can provide so many spontaneous, purposeful opportunities for students to practice their skills, prepare projects, and work with construction materials that teachers who previously used artificial duplicated materials and other conventional practice items no longer feel the need to use them.

Benefits for Children with Special Needs

Another important motivation for using the interdisciplinary method is its effectiveness as an alternative to traditional approaches for children with special needs. In 1975, Public Law 94-142, The Education of All Handicapped Children Act, was enacted, mandating that children with handicapping conditions be placed in the least restrictive instructional environment possible, preferably in regular classrooms. To comply with this regulation, classroom teachers had to begin working with children who were previously taught separately in special classes. Most of these teachers had little or no specific preparation for their new role, so they had to experiment on their own and try creative approaches and methods in order to include—not just accommodate—their new students.

Many children with disabilities still need to spend part of the school day in special assistance settings outside their regular classrooms. Their frequent absence from the classroom can make including them in the regular program of activities difficult for teachers. The flexibility afforded by the interdisciplinary method can help teachers to overcome this problem. Because interdisciplinary units are usually completed throughout a period of time, not all children in the class need to be present at the same time to participate. Those who leave the room for special help can work on unit assignments when they return or at other times during the day. Also, because students are encouraged to use a variety of resources to locate information, those who have difficulty reading for information can use alternative methods. Such methods include interviewing; studying pictures; viewing DVD or videotape programs, teacher-prepared computer or DVD presentations, films, and filmstrips; and interacting with computer software programs.

These materials and others can be selected carefully to ensure that little or no reading is required. Reports need not be limited to writing papers or answering questions from a textbook selection. Students can use alternatives, such as performing demonstrations, painting pictures and murals, and preparing dioramas and other constructions, to show the concepts they have gained.

Multiple Sources of Information

One final point supports the interdisciplinary approach: Because children use materials from many sources when they are engaged in research, ensuring that they are presented with a more inclusive view of history and historical events is easier with this approach than when they must rely on only one or two textbooks. In contrast to conventional approaches, in an interdisciplinary program no single textbook is used exclusively. Instead, classrooms are equipped with textbooks on social studies, science, language arts, and other disciplines, from many publishers. In each classroom, the available materials are written at, below, and above grade level to accommodate as many ability levels as possible. Trade books and literature related to the unit topic are borrowed from public and school libraries. Teachers ensure that a wide range of materials is available to provide children with greater access to information about the contributions of all ethnic and racial groups. Teachers can ascertain whether children's resource materials adequately address human rights issues—such as slavery, the Holocaust, the Armenian genocide and other past and continuing genocide issues—and other world problems that are sometimes given minimal treatment or neglected in a single textbook.

The significance of this kind of exposure for students is effectively dramatized in a statement by Milagros Henriquez, a graduate in teacher education, as she accepted an award for outstanding work related to multicultural education in 1995. She said, "Multicultural education is *basic* education for students in the twenty-first century." In our multicultural society, students need access to information that only a rich variety of materials can provide.

▦ REQUIREMENTS OF TEACHERS

What does interdisciplinary instruction require of teachers who use it? All teachers must plan carefully, think through any new processes, consider the logistics associated with any methodological changes, and be aware of the effects of any modifications in the instructional program. However, interdisciplinary teachers are convinced that alternative approaches to education can offer satisfactory substitutes for traditional programs. They have several concerns that are especially important for teachers who plan to explore the interdisciplinary method as an alternative.

General and Child Development Knowledge

Although teachers must encourage independence, "help the child to achieve independence, both physical and mental" (Montessori, 2002, p. 8), and avoid giving answers to students who can solve their own problems, teachers using an interdisciplinary approach must also possess a broad base of general knowledge in each major academic discipline. Teachers also need to be skilled researchers so that they can guide their students through the research processes demanded by integrated interdisciplinary studies.

Equally important, teachers need to have a thorough background in human development and be able to apply their understandings of cognitive and affective development when planning for instruction. An awareness of students' thinking and reasoning characteristics can help teachers tailor their instruction more effectively for students at different developmental levels. In her discussion of the Montessori method, Lillard (1972) explained that developing observation skills is the key to such awareness.

Gardner's multiple intelligences theory was outlined previously in this chapter to indicate how it supports an integrated approach to education. Gardner (1991) indicated that his theory has implications for instructional planning, and Armstrong (2000) provided numerous helpful suggestions for designing lessons and activities that address each of the Gardner intelligences.

Another important source for teachers who use interdisciplinary methods is the work of Brooks and Brooks (1999). This source relates contemporary developmental theory with classroom practice and offers alternatives to traditional textbook learning activities.

A Compatible Educational Philosophy

Another factor a teacher must consider when he or she is planning to use the interdisciplinary method is the compatibility between his or her educational philosophy and his or her interdisciplinary methodology. Kimpston, Williams, and Stockton (1992) discussed the relationship between specific philosophies of education and teaching methods. Their analysis indicated that the *experimentalist*—or *progressivist*—and *reconstructionist* philosophies are more compatible with interdisciplinary methods than others are. This is true mainly because both philosophies emphasize the importance of the processes involved in learning as well as the content and skills. Therefore, teachers who subscribe to these philosophies are more likely to feel comfortable with interdisciplinary instruction than teachers who do not. Explanations of experimentalism and reconstructionism can be found in most educational foundations textbooks. Duck (1994) and Ozmon and Craver (2003) have provided especially clear descriptions of educational philosophies and discussed the effects of such philosophies on teaching practice.

Planning Skills

Interdisciplinary instruction requires that teachers develop special skills in planning comprehensive instructional units. Teachers must become familiar with a number of important planning protocols, such as those used for directed instruction in reading, for helping students design experiments in science, for research, and for planning field trips. Learning how to design lessons that interest and involve students and providing adequate guidance for students as they pursue their inquiries is as important for interdisciplinary teachers as for teachers who use other methods.

In the primary grades, unit planning demands ingenuity by teachers when they are generating lessons and activities related to unit topics. Students in the intermediate grades and middle school are able to undertake more sophisticated forms of research; therefore, their teachers must have a thorough understanding of research processes. Consequently, in addition to being good organizers, teachers who use interdisciplinary methods need to be skillful planners.

Classroom Management Skills

Classroom management is a serious matter for every teacher. Orchestrating a well-run classroom requires expert organization. Planning, scheduling, assessment and record-keeping, and behavioral management skills are all directly related to success in managing a well-organized classroom. Lesson planning is discussed further in chapters 2 and 3; assessment techniques, in chapter 4; and unit planning, in chapters 5 and 6. Several suggestions for managing student behavior are outlined subsequently in this section.

Behavioral management is critical for successful interdisciplinary studies because a great deal of activity usually occurs during the development of a study. The teacher must often manage several student activities simultaneously as a unit progresses. Both formal and informal work periods are needed, so teachers need to be flexible and willing to adapt to the unique types and levels of activity that arise. At the same time, teachers need to be sensitive to the often-subtle difference between activities that are productive and those that are potentially chaotic.

Many authoritative sources are available for teachers that provide information about well-known behavioral management designs and models. Books that may be especially helpful include those by Barr, Dreeben, and Wiratchai (1983); Charles (2002); Cooper (2003); Edwards (2000); Hoover and Kindsvatter (1997); Jones and Jones (1986); Ormrod (2003); Osborn and Osborn (1989); Putnam and Burke (1992);

Queen, Blackwelder, and Mallen (1997); Senter and Charles (2002); and Valentine (1987). In each text, the authors review management models that can be used for improving student behavior and offer suggestions for effective ways to discipline students. Several suggestions included next may be especially helpful for teachers who are beginning their careers. Many experienced teachers have found that the following suggestions can help instructors improve classroom behavior and maintain a healthy emotional classroom climate for interdisciplinary instruction.

Maintain a Professional Approach to Discipline

Set an example for students by being polite to them. Discipline students privately and avoid embarrassing them. Avoid showing anger. Be brief, but firm, when administering corrective measures. A professional way to gain insights about an individual student's attitudes and feelings—and perhaps some problematic behaviors—is to ask the class to maintain journals that are used for private communication between you and each student. Johnston (1992) suggested that in these daily journal entries, "students and teacher have a context in which they can write about things that are bothering them in the classroom and they can communicate about them in a reflective way" (p. 139).

Encourage Students to Participate in Their Classroom

At the beginning of a new school year, when you hope to establish good rapport with your students, you may think you are extending a hearty welcome by preparing beautiful, artistic displays. However, students who enter a meticulous, teacher-prepared classroom may believe that the room belongs to their teacher, not them. A subtle message may be conveyed to them that they are not expected to contribute or are not invited to participate because you have prepared everything for them. They may also then not feel that maintaining it is primarily their responsibility.

Therefore, a wiser approach may be to encourage students to become involved in deciding how the room should be decorated. Students can also participate in many other decisions. Interdisciplinary units of study offer some of these opportunities. For example, students can suggest titles for their interdisciplinary units; they can prepare bulletin boards, create murals, and decide how to display their art and construction projects.

By involving students in these types of decisions, you can encourage students to accept that the classroom is truly theirs. Doing so may also motivate students to care for their classroom because they have an investment in it. In fact, students who share ownership of their classroom and the activities that go on in it are likely to assume more responsibility for how it is used (Pappas et al., 1999).

Set Standards for Appropriate Behavior

Students usually have a good general idea about what is and is not appropriate behavior. Asking them to participate in deciding on classroom rules at the beginning of a school year will ensure that they know what the rules are. Nonetheless, most students will test you to determine what is acceptable in your classroom, and they will look to you to be the key person setting behavior standards.

Be Consistent with Behavior Expectations

Students expect their teachers to be fair. In fact, children often behave inappropriately to show their resentment of teachers who are unfair.

Constantly Be Aware of Your Class

Students look to their teachers for guidance. They expect teachers to exercise authority, provide clear directions, and have reasonable expectations, both for their behavior and for academic work. To provide this kind of guidance, you must constantly be aware of everything that is happening in the room, and students need to know that you are always tuned in.

Maintain Physical Proximity with Your Students

Simply walking closer to students who are not behaving well lets them know that you are aware of what they are doing. Proximity alone can often correct a minor problem, such as occasional off-task behavior or failure to share responsibilities in a committee or cooperative group activity.

Avoid Overreacting to Problems

Try not to overreact. Not overreacting is especially important when rules are broken or when students who usually behave well suddenly present a problem. At such times, you should analyze the situation before reacting. Factors such as the weather, the day of the week, the time of day, and the time of year—particularly preholiday seasons and the months near the end of the school year—can stimulate some unusual behavior. If you keep your perspective when problems arise, you may even find that some situations offer opportunities to convey the importance of classroom rules, which will help to reestablish order.

Expect the Unexpected

Planning carefully will usually help you to be better prepared when something goes awry during a lesson or an activity (e.g., when a student responds with an unusual or unanticipated answer or when a student suddenly interrupts). At such times, it is especially important for you to be prepared for the spontaneous shifts or changes that may be necessary as a teaching session continues. Unexpected events can be disconcerting, but they can also be informative, even refreshing to both you and the students. You cannot and probably would not want to prevent surprises from ever arising during an instructional session. Therefore, you must be as ready as possible and not be discouraged when such events occur.

Try Different Approaches to Situations

In a healthy emotional classroom environment, usually only a few students need constant reminding about their behavior. Although the goal should always be to help students learn to control their behavior, you may need, at least temporarily, to accept responsibility for students who are not able or willing to control themselves.

Be Creative in Handling Annoying Behaviors

You may want to ask students who are complaining about one another to write out their complaints before attempting to make any judgments. Sometimes complaints seem less important to students after they take the time to write about them. Ellis (2002) recommended that teachers have students solve classroom management problems by applying the same inquiry skills they would use to investigate other problems. Doing so keeps the focus on "solutions rather than sources of blame" (p. 349).

▓ COLLABORATIVE TEACHING AND INTERDISCIPLINARY INSTRUCTION

Numerous opportunities are presented for collaboration among teachers who use the interdisciplinary method. Classroom teachers need to work cooperatively not only with teachers of specialties such as art, music, physical education, and special education, but also with the school nurse and others in the school environment. Specialists need to be notified before initiation of a unit so that they can plan lessons and activities that coincide with and contribute to the unit study.

This type of collaborative work among the teachers will help students discover the relevance of the social sciences, science, the arts, music, health, and other special areas to the topics being studied. Cooperation between the classroom teacher and specialists is a form of **team teaching** that can contribute significantly to the interdisciplinarity and quality of instructional units.

Observing specialty area teachers throughout time, classroom teachers develop knowledge of the processes that these specialists use with children. For example, an art teacher may reserve a class period for instructing children on a papier-mâché project. After observing the process followed by the specialist, the classroom teacher may be able to use it without help in the future.

Collaboration is not restricted to cooperative work with specialists. In some elementary and middle schools, interdepartmental teams are organized. For example, a four-teacher interdepartmental teaching team may be formed that consists of a social studies teacher, an English or a language arts teacher, a science teacher, and a mathematics teacher. The team is assigned either a block of time or separate periods in which to work with a group of students. The teachers have a scheduled time for planning in which they design the interdisciplinary units, decide how to allocate the time in their block, and determine how they will each relate lessons in their classes to the unit topic. Specialty area teachers of art and music can serve the team as consultants for these special aspects of a study. Ideally, students are included in the planning sessions as well; this kind of student participation in the planning process has been found to have considerable value in interdisciplinary instruction (Stevenson & Carr, 1993).

One way to organize a research-oriented interdisciplinary unit for instruction by a team of teachers in a departmental structure is outlined in chapter 6. Discussions on team teaching in the middle school are also available that specifically address the concerns of middle school teachers who are involved in collaborative, team-teaching arrangements (Vars, 1969, 1987; Williamson, 1993).

In schools with self-contained classes, another team-teaching structure can be arranged. This structure usually involves two or more teachers who combine their classes and work cooperatively with the same students. Under this plan, each teacher may have a special area of expertise to offer students. At times, the teachers rotate serving as the main instructor while the others assist; however, they are all involved in teaching academic skills and processes. As in the case of departmentalized plans, teachers in self-contained teams have time reserved in their regular teaching schedule to plan together and to share their knowledge of individual students' progress. Interacting in this way helps team members to keep abreast of their students' interests, strengths, needs, and limitations.

Both departmental and self-contained team-teaching arrangements are compatible with the interdisciplinary approach and are based on sound child development principles. Because team members work as a unit, instruction can be consistently and genuinely interdisciplinary rather than divided into unrelated disciplinary studies.

In contrast, some organizational structures inhibit interdisciplinary instruction because they fragment the curriculum and isolate teachers from one another. For example, totally departmentalized instruction and modified Joplin plan arrangements do not provide for genuine team teaching. In the **departmentalized** structure, students change classes for separate instruction in the various disciplines at appointed times throughout the day. The **modified Joplin plan** involves exchanging classes at a particular grade level and grouping students homogeneously for skills instruction in some subject areas during part of the day.

Both structures rarely afford teachers enough scheduled time to plan together or exchange information on the progress of individual students. The interrelationships among disciplines are obscured when reading is taught only by the reading teacher, mathematics is taught only during a mathematics lesson, and all subjects are taught in isolation.

■ TECHNOLOGY AND INTERDISCIPLINARY INSTRUCTION

Technology, both as a "new" discipline and for its many applications, is a serious subject for all teachers, including those who plan to use interdisciplinary methods. Telecommunications through the computer and interactive computer programs have become essential tools for students and teachers. Technology is cited as a discipline in most state curriculum guides and is addressed in accompanying lists of learning standards. Methods courses that combine technology with mathematics and science are now offered in colleges of education. Likewise, the emphasis of other disciplinary methods courses is on integrating technology when doing so is feasible.

Many elementary and middle schools are now connected to one another through the Internet and through networking services to colleges and universities. Elementary and middle school students design their own Web sites, where they publish and share their ideas, writing, and projects with others. Most word-processing programs can convert documents prepared by students to the hypertext markup language (HTML) format required for Web pages. Special software programs, such as Web Workshop from Sunburst Communications, are available in versions appropriate for students from Grade 2 to Grade 12. The software enables students to easily prepare their materials for posting on the Internet.

Online services devoted to educational purposes allow students to investigate topics individually, in cooperative learning groups within their classrooms, and with students in other schools. Examples of such services are NationalGeographic.com, the International Education and Resource Network, and New York Learning Link.

New York Learning Link is an example of a commercial online network for teachers and for students in kindergarten through Grade 12. The service is available throughout New York State and at selected sites in other parts of the United States. In one of New York Learning Link's most valuable services, called *classroom exchanges*, predesigned interdisciplinary problems are offered to interested classes at three general levels: Grades 2 to 4, Grades 4 to 6, and Grades 7 to 12. After a problem is outlined, students begin by working in their classrooms, using their usual resources to research the problem. Then, using the online service, they compare notes, raise questions, and discuss their ideas and findings with other classes working on the same problem.

Using computers and the Internet, students can conduct searches for information on the topics they are investigating. As an important part of the search process, students learn to locate the most reliable sources by using Web sites with Internet address suffixes such as .org (professional organizations), .gov (government sources), and .edu (educational institutions). In addition to learning the use of suffix identification, students can learn to apply a number of other criteria, such as getting in contact with the Webmaster about a document or a site they are considering using for a report. Kathy Schrock (2003) has prepared a set of other criteria that older students in the middle school can use.

Students may use Internet searches along with conventional resources, interactive CD-ROM programs, and other interdisciplinary multimedia reference resources, including the latest versions of such well-known programs as Rainforest, Oregon Trail, and the Carmen Sandiego series. While conducting their inquiries, students can develop their own time lines—in either English or Spanish—with TimeLiner, distributed by Tom Snyder Productions.

Comprehensive CD-ROM dictionaries, thesauruses, atlases, and encyclopedias are readily available. Students can also learn to prepare databases, spreadsheets, and presentations to help them organize and report the information they find by using software available from Microsoft, Corel, Claris, Lotus, and other companies.

Besides using the computer to search for and organize information, students can use word-processing, spreadsheet, and database software to take notes, write papers and letters, and draft e-mail off-line. Students can also learn to use desktop publishing facilities and presentation software, such as Microsoft's PowerPoint, to report their findings.

Resources for Teachers

Using local online services and the Internet, teachers can exchange lesson and unit plans throughout the United States and can interact with groups of teachers having similar interests. Many helpful reference materials about the Internet are available for teachers and parents. Those by Caruso (1997); Cummins and Sayers (1995); Doyle (1999); Lewin (1999); Newby, Stepich, Lehman, and Russell (2000); Ryder and Hughes (2000); and Williams (1996) are especially useful. These authors explain in detail how to access the Internet; discuss some of its valuable resources for teachers, parents, and students; and give suggestions for locating and evaluating Internet sources. Useful e-mail and Internet addresses for teachers to use are also included in the sources.

Teachers can use computer presentation software to prepare slide shows for integration with other teaching techniques. (See chapter 3 for information on preparing a computer presentation, and see the Instructional Resources section at the end of this book for a sample lesson plan that includes use of a computer presentation.)

Even in the primary grades, students and their teachers can learn to use digital cameras effectively (Pastor & Kerns, 1997). Digital and video cameras may be used to record students' projects and to develop multimedia records of oral reports and other presentations. Local telecommunications groups, such as the United Federation of Teachers' New York City Teacher Centers Consortium, give teachers access to technical and instructional assistance to help them integrate the computer and other technology in their teaching.

In addition to offering software, some companies produce interdisciplinary units for teachers to use or adapt. Good Apple, a company based in Redding, California, offers several interdisciplinary units designed specifically for young children. Likewise, The New York Times Company, located in New York City, publishes numerous instructional plans on topics suited to older groups, in middle schools and secondary schools. Sunburst Communications, in Pleasantville, New York, has produced numerous programs in nearly every discipline for students at all age levels. This company is also responsible for the well-known interdisciplinary unit called *Voyage of the Mimi*—a plan that includes guidebooks for teachers, a CD-ROM collection, and accompanying materials for students.

Educational television is also playing an important role in some areas of the United States. For example, local Public Broadcasting Service (PBS) television stations, such as WNET in New York City and WLIR in Garden City on Long Island, air numerous educational programs for students at all grade levels. The television stations broadcast these programs from 2:00 a.m. to 5:00 a.m. and have arranged copyright privileges so that teachers are free to videotape and use the programs in their classrooms. A complete guide to all programs to be aired each academic year is available from the station at a nominal cost. The guide includes a topical reference and complete descriptions of each program. Similar services are available in other cities.

The Internet, educational television, computer software programs, digital cameras, and telecommunications will supplement—not replace—other ways of teaching and learning. Teachers who plan to use interdisciplinary instruction will continue to use conventional audiovisual materials: videotape recorders, monitors, film and filmstrip projectors, overhead projectors, and audiotape recorders. Newer types of equipment, such as liquid crystal display (LCD) projectors, are rapidly becoming standard in schools as well.

▦ ACTIVITIES

1. Envision two classrooms, one in which students are following a conventional approach, studying different topics in social studies, science, music, art, and so on. In the other, students are using an interdisciplinary approach. Describe what you imagine to be distinguishing differences between the two classes and the ways they function.

2. Observe an elementary or a middle school classroom for a morning or an afternoon. Review the distinguishing features of interdisciplinary instruction presented in this chapter. During your observation, did you find evidence that the teacher is using some aspects of the interdisciplinary approach? If so, which of the distinguishing features outlined in this chapter did you find?

3. You are interviewing for a teaching position. One of the interviewers asks, "How will you plan a typical day in your classroom?" Respond to this question, attempting to include the features of interdisciplinary methodology presented in this chapter.

4. According to the text in this chapter, interdisciplinary methods place equal emphasis on process and product. Do you agree or disagree with this philosophy? Why or why not?

5. One suggestion in this chapter is that many practice exercises in workbooks and on duplicated materials are less meaningful to students than are applications during an interdisciplinary unit of study that requires the use of the same skills. Reflecting on distinctive features of the interdisciplinary method, do you think it is accurate to suggest that most conventional practice materials be eliminated if the teacher uses an interdisciplinary approach?

6. What is your philosophy of education? Write a paragraph describing it. Decide whether your philosophy is similar to the philosophies that are compatible with an interdisciplinary approach.

7. Classroom management is a concern of all teachers. Using the list of suggestions in this chapter, ask an elementary teacher which of them he or she uses. Ask for other suggestions to add to the list.

8. One suggestion in this chapter is that having a good fund of general knowledge and the ability to use technology are important for teachers who plan to use an interdisciplinary approach. Are there areas in which you feel the need to increase your general knowledge, especially of topics that are commonly taught

in the elementary and middle schools? Do your skills in the use of computers or other technology need strengthening? If so, outline several ways you may be able to improve them.

▓ REFERENCES

Allis, S. (1999, July 11). The master of unartificial intelligence: Howard Gardner's definition of "smart" still sparks controversy. *The Boston Sunday Globe*, pp. D1–D5.

Armstrong, T. (2000). *Multiple intelligences in the classroom* (2nd ed.). Alexandria, VA: Association for Supervision and Curriculum Development.

Barr, R., Dreeben, R., & Wiratchai, N. (1983). *How schools work*. Chicago: University of Chicago Press.

Brandt, R. (1988). On assessment in the arts: A conversation with Howard Gardner. *Educational Leadership*, 45(4), 30–34.

Brooks, J. G., & Brooks, M. G. (1999). *In search of understanding: The case for constructivist classrooms* (Rev. ed.). Alexandria, VA: Association for Supervision and Curriculum Development.

Bruner, J. (1990). *Acts of meaning*. Cambridge, MA: Harvard University Press.

Caruso, C. (1997, November). Before you cite a site. *Educational Leadership*, 55(3), 24–26.

Case, R. (1985). *Intellectual development: Birth to adulthood*. Orlando, FL: Academic Press.

Charles, C. M. (2002). *Building classroom discipline* (7th ed.). Boston: Allyn & Bacon.

Checkley, K. (1997). The first seven . . . and the eighth. *Educational Leadership*, 55(1), 8–13.

Cooper, J. M. (2003). *Classroom teaching skills* (7th ed.). Boston: Houghton Mifflin.

Cummins, J., & Sayers, D. (1995). *Brave new schools*. New York: St. Martin's Press.

Dewey, J. (1916). *Democracy and education*. New York: Free Press.

Doyle, A. (1999, February). A practitioner's guide to sharing the Net. *Educational Leadership*, 56(5), 12–15.

Duck, L. (1994). *Teaching with charisma*. Burke, VA: Chatelaine Press.

Edwards, C. H. (2000). *Classroom discipline and management* (3rd ed.). Upper Saddle River, NJ: Merrill/Prentice Hall.

Ellis, A. K. (2002). *Teaching and learning elementary social studies* (7th ed.). Boston: Allyn & Bacon.

Forman, E. A., Minick, N., & Stone, C. A. (1993). *Contexts for learning*. New York: Oxford University Press.

Gardner, H. (1983). *Frames of mind: The theory of multiple intelligences*. New York: Basic Books.

Gardner, H. (1991). *The unschooled mind: How children think and how schools should teach*. New York: Basic Books.

Gardner, H. (1993a). *Creating minds*. New York: Basic Books.

Gardner, H. (1993b). *Multiple intelligences: The theory in practice*. New York: Basic Books.

Gardner, H. (1999). *Intelligence reframed: Multiple intelligences for the 21st century*. New York: Basic Books.

Hardiman, M. M. (2001, November). Connecting brain research with dimensions of learning. *Educational Leadership*, 59(3), 52–55.

Henriquez, M. (Speaker). (1995). Acceptance speech at the academic awards ceremony of the Teacher Education Program at the State University of New York/College at Old Westbury.

Hoover, R. L., & Kindsvatter, R. (1997). *Democratic discipline: Foundation and practice*. Upper Saddle River, NJ: Merrill/Prentice Hall.

Jacobs, H. (Ed.). (1989). *Interdisciplinary curriculum: Design and implementation*. Alexandria, VA: Association for Supervision and Curriculum Development.

Jensen, E. (1998). *Teaching with the brain in mind*. Alexandria, VA: Association for Supervision and Curriculum Development.

Johnston, P. H. (1992). *Constructive evaluation of literate activity*. White Plains, NY: Longman.

Jones, V., & Jones, L. (1986). *Comprehensive classroom management: Creating positive learning environments* (2nd ed.). Boston: Allyn & Bacon.

Kane, J. (1999). *Education, information and transformation: Essays on learning and thinking.* Upper Saddle River, NJ: Merrill/Prentice Hall.

Kimpston, R., Williams, H., & Stockton, W. (1992, Winter). Ways of knowing and the curriculum. *The Educational Forum, 56*(2), 153–172.

Lewin, L. (1999, February). "Site-reading" the World Wide Web. *Educational Leadership, 56*(5), 16–20.

Lillard, P. (1972). *Montessori: A modern approach.* New York: Schocken Books.

Lowery, L. (1998, November). How new science curriculums reflect brain research. *Educational Leadership, 56*(3), 26–30.

Montessori, M. (2002). La maestra: Lecture 2. *Communications, Association Montessori Internationale, 4,* 6–10.

Newby, T. J., Stepich, D. A., Lehman, J. D., & Russell, J. D. (2000). *Instructional technology for teaching and learning: Designing instruction, integrating computers, and using media* (2nd ed.). Upper Saddle River, NJ: Merrill/Prentice Hall.

Ormrod, J. E. (2003). *Educational psychology: Developing learners* (4th ed.). Upper Saddle River, NJ: Merrill/Prentice Hall.

Osborn, D. K., & Osborn, J. (1989). *Discipline and classroom management* (3rd ed.). Athens, GA: Daye Press.

Ozmon, H., & Craver, S. M. (2003). *Philosophical foundations of education* (7th ed.). Upper Saddle River, NJ: Merrill/Prentice Hall.

Pappas, C. C., Kiefer, B. Z., & Levstik, L. S. (1999). *An integrated language perspective in the elementary school* (3rd ed.). White Plains, NY: Longman.

Pastor, E., & Kerns, E. (1997, November). A digital snapshot of an early childhood classroom. *Educational Leadership, 55*(3), 42–45.

Piaget, J. (1970). *Science of education and the psychology of the child* (D. Coltman, Trans.). New York: Orion Press.

Piaget, J., & Inhelder, B. (1975). *The origin of the idea of chance in children.* New York: Norton.

Putnam, J. G., & Burke, J. B. (1992). *Organizing and managing classroom learning communities.* New York: McGraw-Hill.

Queen, J. A., Blackwelder, B. B., & Mallen, L. P. (1997). *Responsible classroom management for teachers and students.* Upper Saddle River, NJ: Merrill/Prentice Hall.

Reed, J. S., & Bergmann, V. E. (1995). *In the classroom: An introduction to education* (2nd ed.). Guilford, CT: Dushkin.

Richardson, E. S. (1964). *In the early world.* New York: Pantheon Books.

Ryder, R. J., & Hughes, T. (2000). *Internet for educators* (3rd ed.). Upper Saddle River, NJ: Merrill/Prentice Hall.

Schrock, K. (2003). Critical evaluation of a Web site: Secondary school level. In *Kathy Schrock's guide for educators.* Retrieved from http://school.discovery.com/schrockguide/evalhigh.html

Senter, G. W., & Charles, C. M. (2002). *Elementary classroom management* (3rd ed.). Boston: Allyn & Bacon.

The seventh grade slump and how to avoid it. (1992, January/February). *The Harvard Education Letter, 8*(1), 1–4.

Smith, M. K. (2002). Howard Gardner, multiple intelligences and education. In *The encyclopedia of informal education.* Retrieved from http://www.infed.org/thinkers/gardner.htm

Stevenson, C., & Carr, J. F. (Eds.). (1993). *Integrated studies in the middle grades.* New York: Teachers College Press.

Sylwester, R. (1995). *A celebration of neurons: An educator's guide to the human brain.* Alexandria, VA: Association for Supervision and Curriculum Development.

Valentine, M. R. (1987). *How to deal with discipline problems.* Dubuque, IA: Kendall/Hunt.

Vars, G. F. (1969). *Common learnings: Core and interdisciplinary team approaches.* Scranton, PA: International Textbook.

Vars, G. F. (1987). *Interdisciplinary teaching in the middle grades: Why & how.* Columbus, OH: National Middle School Association.

Vygotsky, L. S. (1978). *Mind in society: The development of higher psychological processes.* Cambridge, MA: Harvard University Press.

Vygotsky, L. S. (1986). *Thought and language* (New rev. ed.). Cambridge, MA: MIT Press.

Wakefield, A. P. (1993). Developmentally appropriate practice: "Figuring things out." *The Educational Forum, 57*(2), 134–143.

Wertsch, J. V. (1985). *Vygotsky and the social formation of the mind.* Cambridge, MA: Harvard University Press.

Westwater, A., & Wolfe, P. (2000, November). The brain-compatible curriculum. *Educational Leadership, 58*(3), 49–53.

Williams, B. (1996). *The World Wide Web for teachers.* Chicago: IDG Books.

Williamson, R. (1993). *Scheduling the middle level school to meet early adolescent needs.* Reston, VA: National Association of Secondary School Principals.

▮ SUGGESTED READINGS

The following readings are included to supplement the references in this chapter.

Berk, L. E. (2002). *Infants and children: Prenatal through middle childhood* (4th ed.). Boston: Allyn & Bacon.

Brainerd, C. J. (1978). *Piaget's theory of intelligence.* Upper Saddle River, NJ: Prentice Hall.

Bright, G. D. (1987). *Microcomputer applications in the elementary classroom: A guide for teachers.* Needham Heights, MA: Allyn & Bacon.

Bruner, J. (1960). *The process of education.* New York: Vintage Books.

Burke, D. L. (1995, Fall). The future now: A child-centered school mosaic. *Kappa Delta Pi Record, 53,* 23–27.

Charbonneau, M. P., & Reider, B. E. (1995). *The integrated elementary classroom: A developmental model of education for the 21st century.* Needham Heights, MA: Allyn & Bacon.

Clark, B. (1986). *Optimizing learning: The integrative education model in the classroom.* Columbus, OH: Merrill.

Cole, H. P. (1972). *Process education: The new direction for elementary–secondary schools.* Upper Saddle River, NJ: Educational Technology Publications.

Cole, M., & Cole, S. R. (1993). *The development of children* (2nd ed.). New York: Scientific American.

Dewey, J. (1933). *How we think.* Boston: Heath.

Dewey, J. (1938). *Experience and education.* London: Collier–Macmillan.

Diem, R. A. (1989). Instructional applications for computers: The next step. *Kappa Delta Pi Record, 25*(2), 60–62.

Flavell, J. H., Green, F. L., & Flavell, E. R. (1995). *Young children's knowledge about thinking.* Chicago: Society for Research in Child Development, University of Chicago Press.

Forman, G. E., & Kuschner, D. S. (1977). *The child's construction of knowledge.* Monterey, CA: Brooks/Cole.

Fraser, H. W. (1985). Microcomputers in schools. *The Educational Forum, 50*(1), 87–100.

Frymier, J. R. (1973). *A school for tomorrow.* Berkeley, CA: McCutchan.

Furth, H. G. (1969). *Human development* (4th ed.). Upper Saddle River, NJ: Prentice Hall.

Furth, H. G., & Wachs, H. (1974). *Thinking goes to school.* New York: Oxford University Press.

Gardner, H. (1982). *Art, mind and brain: A cognitive approach to creativity.* New York: Basic Books.

Gardner, H. (1985). *The mind's new science: A history of the cognitive revolution.* New York: Basic Books.

Gardner, H., Feldman, D. H., & Krechevsky, M. (Eds.). (1998). *Project Zero frameworks for early childhood education: Vol. 1. Building on children's strengths: The experience of Project Spectrum.* New York: Teachers College Press.

Hanslovsky, G., Moyer, S., & Wagner, H. (1969). *Why team teaching?* Columbus, OH: Merrill.

Hersh, R. H., Paolitto, D. P., & Reinger, J. (1983). *Promoting moral growth: From Piaget to Kohlberg* (Rev. ed.). New York: Longman.

Holt, J. (1967). *How children learn.* New York: Pitman.

Holt, J. (1989). *Learning all the time.* Reading, MA: Addison-Wesley.

Jacob, S. H. (1982a). Piaget and education: Aspects of a theory. *The Educational Forum, 46*(2), 265–282.

Jacob, S. H. (1982b). Piaget and education: Aspects of a theory. *The Educational Forum, 46*(3), 221–238.

Jenkins, J. M. (1994). *World class schools: An evolving concept.* Reston, VA: National Association of Secondary School Principals.

Katz, L., & Chard, S. C. (2000). *Engaging children's minds: The project approach* (2nd ed.). Stamford, CT: Ablex.

Kauchak, D. P., & Eggen, P. D. (2003). *Learning and teaching: Research-based methods* (4th ed.). Boston: Allyn & Bacon.

Kindsvatter, R., Wilen, W., & Ishler, M. (2004). *Dynamics of effective teaching* (3rd ed.). White Plains, NY: Longman.

Kleiman, G. M. (1985). *Brave new schools: How computers can change education.* Needham Heights, MA: Allyn & Bacon.

Knirk, F. G., & Gustafson, K. L. (1986). *Instructional technology: A systematic approach to education.* New York: Holt, Rinehart & Winston.

Kohn, A. (2003). Almost there, but not quite. *Educational Leadership, 60*(6), 26–29.

Learning styles and the brain. (1990). *Educational Leadership, 48*(2), 4–81.

Martinello, M. L., & Cook, G. E. (2000). *Interdisciplinary inquiry in teaching and learning* (2nd ed.). Upper Saddle River, NJ: Merrill/Prentice Hall.

Mason, E. (1972). *Collaborative learning.* New York: Agathon Press.

McEwan, B. (2000). *The art of classroom management.* Upper Saddle River, NJ: Merrill/Prentice Hall.

Palardy, J. M. (Ed.). (1983). *Elementary education: An anthology of trends and issues.* Lanham, MD: University Press of America.

Peterson, D. (Ed.). (1984). *Intelligent schoolhouse: Readings on computers and learning.* Reston, VA: Reston.

Phillips, J. L. (1981). *Piaget's theory: A primer.* San Francisco: Freeman.

Phye, G. D., & Andre, T. (Eds.). (1986). *Cognitive classroom learning.* Orlando, FL: Academic Press.

Posner, M. (1994). *HEL Internet guide.* Cambridge, MA: Harvard Graduate School of Education.

Powell, R. R., McLaughlin, H. J., Savage, T. V., & Zehm, S. (2001). *Classroom management: Perspectives on the social curriculum.* Upper Saddle River, NJ: Merrill/Prentice Hall.

Ramsden, P. (Ed.). (1988). *Improving learning.* London: Kegan Page.

Sadowski, M. (1995). Moving beyond traditional subjects requires teachers to abandon their "comfort zones." *The Harvard Education Letter, 11*(5), 1–5.

Schwebel, M., & Raph, J. (Eds.). (1973). *Piaget in the classroom.* New York: Basic Books.

Seifert, K. L., & Hoffnung, R. J. (2000). *Child and adolescent development* (5th ed.). Boston: Houghton Mifflin.

Sigel, I. E., Grodzinsky, D. M., & Golinkoff, R. M. (1981). *New directions in Piagetian theory and practice.* Hillsdale, NJ: Erlbaum.

Silberman, C. E. (1970). *Crisis in the classroom: The remaking of American education.* New York: Random House.

Stensrud, R., & Stensrud, K. (1981). Discipline: An attitude, not an outcome. *The Educational Forum, 45*(2), 161–168.

Stevenson, C., & Carr, J. F. (Eds.). (1993). *Integrated studies in the middle grades.* New York: Teachers College Press.

Wadsworth, B. J. (1978). *Piaget for the classroom teacher.* New York: Longman.

Wadsworth, B. J. (1996). *Piaget's theory of cognitive and affective development* (5th ed.). White Plains, NY: Longman.

White, A. M. (Ed.). (1981). *Interdisciplinary teaching.* San Francisco: Jossey–Bass.

Woronov, R. (1994, September/October). Six myths (and five promising truths) about the uses of educational technology. *The Harvard Educational Letter, 10*(5), 1–3.

2

Preliminary Considerations in Planning for Instruction

▓ OVERVIEW

Attending to several concerns related to the teaching and learning processes can assist teachers in designing more effective lesson plans, interdisciplinary unit plans, and learning centers. The focus of this chapter is on the following:

- Concerns about learning and development
- Students' differing ways of acquiring knowledge—their unique learning and working styles
- Techniques for productive questioning and discussion
- Determination of the cognitive levels of objectives, questions, and directions by using Bloom's Taxonomy
- Design of effective learning centers for exploration and practice

▓ LEARNING AND DEVELOPMENT

Successful teachers have always attended to the literature and research on the psychology of learning and development. In her 1993 discussion of developmentally appropriate teaching practices, Wakefield offered a strong supportive argument for attending to such information. The important question is this: What are preliminary considerations about learning and development when a teacher is designing instructional plans? Following are some possible ways for teachers to respond to concerns about learning and development when they are planning lessons.

Learners Need to Construct Their Own Knowledge

Learners construct their own knowledge most efficiently both when they have opportunities to engage in direct personal experiences and through the interactions they have with other people. This principle is central to Piaget's (1963) adaptation theory, which suggests the importance of including concrete, direct experiences in learning situations. When possible, students should be given opportunities to do the following:

- Work with manipulative materials
- Conduct their own experiments
- Visit field sites where they can become directly involved with authentic materials and environments that are not accessible in their classrooms or where they can study genuine artifacts related to the topics they are studying

This initial concern also calls attention to the need for interaction with other people as students attempt to learn new concepts and compare their ideas and beliefs.

Examples of activities that encourage students to listen to others' viewpoints and to reflect on their own include the following:

- Cooperative learning projects and other group activities
- Debates and panel discussions
- Whole-class discussions
- Learning centers that involve activities requiring working with other students

New Knowledge Must Build on a Learner's Existing Knowledge Base

Kamii (1973) provided a detailed discussion of the relevance of the principle that new knowledge must build on a learner's existing knowledge base. This pedagogical principle is also based on Piagetian theory. When beginning to plan, teachers must know whether students have sufficient background knowledge for the concepts to be developed in a lesson. This determination can often be made in the lesson procedure near the beginning of the lesson by doing the following:

- Raising questions about what the students already know
- Providing a brief review of what students have learned about an ongoing study to help bridge the way to the new concepts to be taught in the lesson

These practices will also provide the teacher with information about what students know or believe they know about a topic before the lesson continues. Occasionally, a teacher may discover that the new lesson needs to be delayed until sufficient background knowledge is developed.

Intrinsic Interest Is More Effective Than Extrinsic Forms of Motivation

We know that when students are interested, learning is more easily accomplished. Observation of students and conversations with them across time can provide much information about their individual and group interests. Sometimes, a teacher can capitalize on specific interests of individual students during a study. For example, a teacher may suggest that an individual student conduct research on a subtopic of special interest that is related to a study the class is pursuing. Individuals can be invited to lead others in small-group studies and to present the results of their research to the class. Learning centers can be designed with activities that are known to appeal to students.

The Development of Concepts Is Facilitated by Unified, Integrated Studies

The principle that the development of concepts is facilitated by unified, integrated studies is supported by research on the human brain. This principle is a primary factor on which this text on interdisciplinary instruction is based and on which the planning of lessons and interdisciplinary units is structured in chapters 3, 5, and 6. Although integration of the disciplines is appropriate for students at all levels, Jensen

(1998) suggested that it may be "more useful for older students than younger ones" (p. 96). Jensen based this statement on his belief that older students will have developed a greater fund of knowledge that will help them form associations among the disciplines more easily. However, the interdisciplinary approach is also appropriate for younger children as long as they are provided with studies at their level and have adequate concrete experiences to help them detect the interrelatedness of the disciplines in these studies.

The Learning Processes—Learning How to Learn—Are Important in All Academic Pursuits

The idea that learning processes are important in all academic pursuits clearly suggests that to help students master the various processes needed for learning throughout life, teachers must plan to provide students with opportunities such as these:

- Following steps in the inquiry process as they conduct their own research on topics that are appropriate for their developmental levels
- Applying the scientific method of investigation and conducting their own experiments in science
- Practicing the various learning processes through activities provided in a learning center

Students who become skilled at the processes of learning will be better equipped to become independent learners in the future.

Students Learn in Different Ways; They Have Individual Learning Styles as They Attempt to Acquire New Knowledge

Today, any list of important teaching concerns must include attention to students' individual ways of learning. Students' learning styles have been described in different ways. Sternberg (1997) suggested that learning styles are a student's preferred ways of thinking and that these ways of thinking and learning can change with time.

Informative sources on learning styles include Howard Gardner, whose work on multiple intelligences was cited in chapter 1 (1983, 1991, 1993). Gardner, one of the foremost contemporary researchers in the field of developmental psychology, has provided us with evidence to support his theory that identifying students' individual cognitive strengths and working styles will enable more students to succeed in school. At the same time, Gardner has expressed his desire that his theory not be misinterpreted and that teachers seek appropriate applications of the theory in their classrooms (Viadero, 1995). For example, not all intelligences need to be addressed in a single lesson. Instead, lesson plans constructed across time should attempt to include opportunities for students to use their strongest intelligence areas to learn and show what they have learned.

Additional information on learning styles can be found in a collection of 23 articles on learning styles, written by an interdisciplinary group of professionals ("Learning Styles," 1990). In other works, authors have provided information about ways to diagnose students' individual styles and have suggested ways to teach students in accord with their individual styles (Dunn, 1994; Dunn & Dunn, 1992, 1993; Fizzell, 1984; Kagan, 1987; O'Neil & Spielberger, 1979; Phye & Andre, 1986).

Although **learning styles** is defined in different ways, researchers agree that this term refers to the unique, individual strengths, preferences, or approaches students use as they attempt to acquire knowledge. Thus, during the planning process, consideration must be given to practices that can help students gain knowledge in different ways. One such way is offering students choices, like the following:

- Students who are researching a topic might be given a choice between writing a conventional paper and reporting in some other way—a computer presentation, a demonstration, a performance, a panel discussion, or another project.
- In the lower elementary grades, students might paint a mural or construct a diorama to show what they have gained from a study.
- Activities in learning centers can offer many opportunities for students to apply their individual learning styles and multiple intelligences.

As mentioned previously, organizing instructional plans that can generate student interest and foster student participation is an important concern in the teaching and learning process. The questions raised during a lesson can have a considerable effect on students and their involvement during a lesson.

▓ QUESTIONING TECHNIQUES

Preparation for good questioning strategies is another important element in designing lesson plans. Teachers need to become skilled at formulating both convergent questions and divergent questions. **Convergent questions** generally require a relatively narrow range of responses from students, whereas **divergent questions** are relatively open ended and often encourage students to be creative in their answers. Models of the two question types are shown in Figures 2.1 and 2.2.

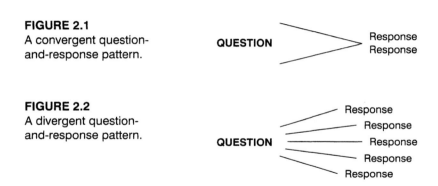

FIGURE 2.1
A convergent question-and-response pattern.

FIGURE 2.2
A divergent question-and-response pattern.

Examples (convergent questions)

Can you name two treaties that have involved European nations during the last two centuries?

Please define *amphibian*.

Examples (divergent questions)

Can you think of a way to improve our local system of mass transit?

How did you feel when you listened to the recording of "Appalachian Spring"?

Suggestions for Improving Class Discussions

The **discussion**—or discourse—during a lesson, particularly the questions that are raised, has been found critical to helping students process the concepts of a lesson (Macbeth, 2003). Therefore, preparing for class discussions, which occur frequently in teaching, is an important element in the design of many lesson plans. Plans may involve short discussions during a formal lesson in reading or another discipline, or a discussion may involve a lengthy debate about a specific issue or problem. To help students focus on a lesson topic and to ensure more productive discussions, teachers may find a few simple suggestions helpful:

- Before beginning any discussion, or raising a question that will stimulate discussion, try to ensure that students have sufficient general background knowledge about the topic.

- Before the discussion, remind students of the rules that have been established for good discussions, such as raising your hand before you answer to allow more students opportunities to contribute. Interrupting a discussion to talk about rules distracts the group from the main topic of the discussion. If possible, ignore students who call out or who make unnecessary noise when raising their hands; then immediately call on another student who has followed the rules.

- Maintain an emotional climate in the classroom that is conducive to a discussion. Students who feel safe from ridicule or sarcasm by other students or the teacher will be more willing to contribute. They will also be more willing to risk making mistakes when answering questions.

- Decide in advance how to handle students who never volunteer to participate. Sometimes, a simple nod will invite a shy student to contribute. Make decisions about whether to call on students by name if they do not volunteer. Some teachers believe that calling on students gives them a chance to participate. Other teachers believe that calling on a student by name may be intimidating and that such a practice may increase the chance that these students will not volunteer in the future. In addition, other students in the group may believe that they do not need to attend when one student is singled out for a response to a question.

- Ask only one question at a time. Silence does not necessarily indicate that students fail to understand the question. They may need a few moments to consider a possible response. Wait at least 4 or 5 seconds before restating the question or raising another.

- Ask both convergent and divergent questions. Questions that require students to recall information are easy to raise. However, it is important to plan questions that require students to think at the higher, critical-thinking levels.

- When a student responds with a vague answer to a question, ask for some clarification. Often, simply asking the student "Can you tell us more?" or "Can you give us an example?" will invite a clearer response.

- Summarize or ask students to summarize periodically during a discussion. Doing so will help to maintain focus on the main topic.

Some discussions with a class arise spontaneously during the day. Many of the preceding suggestions apply even when a discussion has not been planned. Additional information on questioning and discussion techniques can be found in many education textbooks, such as those by Cooper (2003); Orlich, Harder, Callahan, and Gibson (2001); and Ormrod (2003).

Another consideration during instructional planning concerns the difficulty of the objectives, concepts, questions, directions, and general requirements of a lesson. One useful device that can assist teachers in determining the difficulty levels of the lessons they plan is a **taxonomy**—or classification system—that was developed by Benjamin Bloom in 1956.

▓ THE USE OF BLOOM'S TAXONOMY TO DETERMINE THE COGNITIVE LEVELS OF INSTRUCTION

Teachers determine the essential questions and instructional objectives of the lessons, interdisciplinary units, and learning center activities they plan. When planning the procedure of a lesson, teachers will find that they may raise questions and give directions that are at a variety of cognitive levels. Questions may vary considerably in difficulty, from those that elicit fundamental, factual information to those requiring higher level, critical thinking by the students.

How can the levels of a teacher's objectives, questions, and directions be estimated? Bloom's Taxonomy is perhaps the most widely recognized classification system designed to help teachers determine the cognitive levels of the lessons they plan. Bloom outlined a six-level taxonomy to help teachers determine the relative difficulty of their instructional objectives. The taxonomy is also helpful for classifying questions, directions, and test items. A brief outline of Bloom's Taxonomy in the cognitive domain follows. Additional information can be found through an Internet search for "Bloom's Taxonomy." Such a search will reveal numerous Web sites with additional explanations and examples for each of the six levels of the taxonomy, as well as information on other taxonomies for the affective and psychomotor domains.

Level 1: Knowledge

Objectives and questions at level 1 require students to provide limited, memorized, factual responses. Genuine understanding may or may not be demonstrated in students' answers. Questions at this level usually require simple, convergent responses.

Examples

What is the name of the largest city on the West Coast of the United States?

What is the meaning of the word *irrigation*?

Level 2: Comprehension

Understanding is required at the comprehension level. When responding to questions at this level, students may need to explain, summarize, translate, and give examples to demonstrate their understanding.

Examples

Write a summary of the main points in this article.

Can someone explain how an irrigation system works in a desert area?

Level 3: Application

Students must use processes, problem solving, and research skills to determine their responses at the application level of the taxonomy.

Examples

Now that you have recorded the daily temperature on this graph for the past 3 weeks, what does the record appear to indicate?

Can you sort these rocks into the three classifications we just studied?

Level 4: Analysis

Analysis requires interpreting, noting inferences, thinking beyond the literal level when reading, detecting cause-and-effect relationships, and drawing conclusions. Analytic questions usually invite more divergent responses.

Examples

Let's try to determine why our experiment with plants failed.

What reasons can you give for the boy's actions in this story?

Level 5: Synthesis

Questions and directions for students at level 5 often ask for creative and divergent responses. New, or original, thinking is required to produce plans, raise hypotheses, predict, or produce original proposals, designs, art, or music.

Examples

Devise a plan that will help to minimize the environmental problems caused by the increasing number of people settling in desert areas today.

Write a poem that shows how you feel in the spring.

Level 6: Evaluation

Students make judgments at level 6. They decide ratings and express opinions based on standard or personal criteria.

Examples

Do you find that this essay on desert life includes accurate information about current problems experienced by the people who live there?

Which of these two plans to save endangered animals is better, or more likely to be effective?

▨ HOW TO PLAN LEARNING CENTERS FOR EXPLORATION AND PRACTICE

Learning centers can often be included in the design of interdisciplinary unit plans. A learning center provides students with interesting and highly motivating materials and activities for exploration and for extra practice with skills that the students have been taught. One important point to remember is that learning center activities do not replace instruction; they do not teach students something that is completely new to them.

Learning centers are especially useful for stimulating creative writing and individual work with various art media. Learning centers for younger children can also provide materials for self-exploration prior to formal instruction in areas such as science and mathematics.

Several types of learning centers are used. Simple, interactive centers can be constructed by using a bulletin board with pockets. The pockets hold written directions for tasks or problem-solving activities that the students select to work on independently. This type of learning center may be one of the easiest for students in middle schools to use. These students usually move from class to class during the day. They can take a simple task card with them to complete when they have time during another part of the school day.

Learning centers can also be displayed on an empty shelf or another flat surface in the classroom. In more elaborate centers, the materials and activities to be used are arranged on a table or a group of tables in a designated area. Space may be provided for students to work at the center, or they can be directed to take the activities from the center to their seats or another part of the room. The specific form used for a learning center always depends on its purpose and the classroom space available for its setup.

Developing a learning center requires a considerable amount of planning and preparation. Following nine steps in designing a learning center will help to ensure its effectiveness:

1. Decide on its purposes; determine if the center activities will be primarily for exploration or for practice.

2. Decide on a title for the center. When the learning center is used with an interdisciplinary unit, the title can be the unit topic or a related topic.

3. Determine the specific activities to be included. They can be a variety of interdisciplinary tasks, explorations, problems to be solved, construction activities, science experiments, readings, research, writing, and other activities that relate to the center's purposes and are appropriate for the students who will use it.

4. Prepare task cards. **Task cards** provide specific directions needed to complete each activity. The sample task card shown in Figure 2.3 has directions for a group of fourth-grade students who are studying a research-oriented interdisciplinary unit on deserts in the United States.

5. Provide space for and assemble the equipment and materials needed for the activities. Art supplies; science equipment; computers and computer software; DVD programs, videotape programs and viewing equipment; tape recordings; filmstrips; textbooks and trade books; charts and diagrams; picture collections;

FIGURE 2.3
Sample task card for a desert collage.

Desert Collage

In this activity, you will make a collage to show what you learned from watching a video on the Mojave Desert.

Directions:

1. Use the videotape recorder and television monitor to watch the tape entitled "The Mojave Desert."

2. Using materials from our scrap box, prepare a collage that shows something specific you believe you learned from the video program.

3. Take a sheet of construction paper from the supply section in the learning center. Write your name on the back of the paper. Paste, glue, tape, and other supplies for your work are kept in our supply closet. Take paint and paint brushes if you want to use them.

4. Be prepared to explain your collage during one of our regular "forums" at the end of each day this week.

duplicated worksheets; and any other items that may be needed should be supplied at or near the center.

6. Prepare a schedule—a sign-up sheet or teacher-prepared list—to ensure that all the students will have an opportunity to use the center during a certain time period.

7. Develop a record-keeping device for assessing students' use of the center activities and for monitoring their participation. A simple checklist of students' names and learning center activities is usually adequate for this purpose. See Figure 2.4 for a sample checklist.

8. Designate a place where students can leave their completed work.

9. Decide how to introduce the learning center to the class. Most students thoroughly enjoy using learning centers, and they may want to begin as soon as they see it appear in the classroom. A thorough introduction can clarify routines and guidelines for using the center and help to deter problems that can arise from misuse of the activities or materials. A set of directions should be prepared for students to read before they work with any of the learning center activities. Figure 2.5 shows an example of a directions poster.

Clearly, learning centers can be especially effective for providing elementary students with opportunities to work independently on new skills that have been taught and on tasks related to their interdisciplinary units. More comprehensive discussions of learning centers are available in books by Fredericks and Cheesebrough (1993, pp. 186–193),

FIGURE 2.4
Sample checklist for a learning center.

Check (X) the activities you have completed.										
Learning Center Activities	1	2	3	4	5	6	7	8	9	10
Name										
Kim	X			X		X				X
Ryan		X		X	X					
Shannon	X		X							X
Nina	X							X		
Michael			X	X		X		X		
Katherine	X			X		X				X
Azim	X				X		X			X
Tamika	X		X				X			
Maria		X		X			X			X
Emily						X		X		X

FIGURE 2.5
Example of a directions poster.

> **Using the Desert Learning Center**
>
> 1. Study all the choices you will have before beginning to work on any activity.
> 2. Choose an activity, and carefully follow the directions on the task card included with that activity.
> 3. If the task requires another person to participate, you may ask someone who is not busy to work with you.
> 4. When you finish the activity, find your name on the record sheet, and check the box for the activity you completed.
> 5. Remember to replace all materials and to keep the learning center neat and orderly for others to use.

Isbell (1995), McClay (1996), and Opitz (1994). Earlier handbooks by Fisk and Lindgren (1974) and Kaplan, Kaplan, Madsen, and Gould (1980) also offer teachers two of the more comprehensive presentations on this topic. For teachers who want to develop a learning center for a single discipline, Poppe and Van Matre's 1985 manual is helpful.

ACTIVITIES

1. Observe in an elementary or a middle school classroom for a morning or an afternoon. Listen to the questions the teacher raises during this time, and write down as many of the questions as you can during the observation. Later, try to determine the level of each question by using Bloom's Taxonomy. Decide if each question is convergent or divergent.

2. Review state and local lists of learning standards. Using Bloom's Taxonomy, try to estimate the levels of any 10 learning standards on the lists.

3. Select a topic from those included in a local or statewide curriculum guide or a social studies textbook for an elementary or a middle school grade. Develop plans for three or more activities to include in a learning center devoted to that topic. Prepare the task cards for these activities.

REFERENCES

Bloom, B. S. (1956). *Taxonomy of educational goals, by a committee of college and university examiners*. New York: Longmans, Green.

Cooper, J. M. (2003). *Classroom teaching skills* (7th ed.). Boston: Houghton Mifflin.

Dunn, R. S. (1994). *Teaching young children through their individual learning styles: Practical approaches for grades K–2*. Boston: Allyn & Bacon.

Dunn, R., & Dunn, K. (1992). *Teaching elementary students through their individual learning styles: Practical approaches for grades 3–6*. Boston: Allyn & Bacon.

Dunn, R. S., & Dunn, K. (1993). *Teaching secondary students through their individual learning styles: Practical approaches for grades 7–12.* Boston: Allyn & Bacon.

Fisk, L., & Lindgren, H. (1974). *Learning centers.* Glen Ridge, NJ: Exceptional Press.

Fizzell, R. (1984). The status of learning styles. *The Educational Forum, 48*(3), 303–312.

Fredericks, A., & Cheesebrough, D. (1993). *Science for all children: Elementary school methods.* New York: Harper Collins.

Gardner, H. (1983). *Frames of mind: The theory of multiple intelligences.* New York: Basic Books.

Gardner, H. (1991). *The unschooled mind: How children think and how schools should teach.* New York: Basic Books.

Gardner, H. (1993). *Multiple intelligences: The theory in practice.* New York: Basic Books.

Isbell, R. (1995). *The complete learning center book.* Beltsville, MD: Gryphon House.

Jensen, E. (1998). *Teaching with the brain in mind.* Alexandria, VA: Association for Supervision and Curriculum Development.

Kagan, D. (1987). Cognitive style and instructional preferences: Some inferences. *The Educational Forum, 51*(4), 393–403.

Kamii, C. (1973). Pedagogical principles derived from Piaget's theory: Relevance for educational practice. In M. Schwebel & J. Raph (Eds.), *Piaget in the classroom* (pp. 199–215). New York: Basic Books.

Kaplan, S. N., Kaplan, J. B., Madsen, S. K., & Gould, B. T. (1980). *Change for children: Ideas and activities for individualizing learning.* Glenview, IL: Scott, Foresman.

Learning styles and the brain. (1990). *Educational Leadership, 48*(2), 4–81.

Macbeth, D. (2003). Hugh Mehan's learning lessons reconsidered: On the differences between the naturalistic and critical analysis of classroom discourse. *American Educational Research Journal, 40*(1), 239–280.

McClay, J. L. (1996). *Learning centers.* Westminster, CA: Teacher Created Materials.

O'Neil, H. F., & Spielberger, C. D. (1979). *Cognitive and affective learning strategies.* New York: Academic Press.

Opitz, M. F. (1994). *Learning centers: Getting them started, keeping them going.* New York: Scholastic.

Orlich, D. C., Harder, R. J., Callahan, R. C., & Gibson, H. W. (2001). *Teaching strategies: A guide to better instruction* (6th ed.). Boston: Houghton Mifflin.

Ormrod, J. E. (2003). *Educational psychology: Developing learners* (4th ed.). Upper Saddle River, NJ: Merrill/Prentice Hall.

Phye, G. D., & Andre, T. (Eds.). (1986). *Cognitive classroom learning.* Orlando, FL: Academic Press.

Piaget, J. (1963). *Judgment and reasoning in the child.* Totowa, NJ: Littlefield, Adams.

Poppe, C. A., & Van Matre, N. A. (1985). *Science learning centers for primary grades.* West Nyack, NY: Center for Applied Research in Education.

Sternberg, R. J. (1997). *Thinking styles.* New York: Cambridge University Press.

Viadero, D. (1995, November 8). Expert testimony. *Education Week*, pp. 33–34.

Wakefield, A. P. (1993). Developmentally appropriate practice: "Figuring things out." *The Educational Forum, 57*(2), 134–143.

▨ SUGGESTED READINGS

The supplemental readings listed next provide additional background material on the topics covered in this chapter, including Bloom's Taxonomy and questioning techniques.

McNeil, J. D., & Wiles, J. (1990). *The essentials of teaching: Decisions, plans, methods.* New York: Macmillan.

Paris, S. G., Olson, G. M., & Stevenson, H. W. (1983). *Learning and motivation in the classroom.* Hillsdale, NJ: Erlbaum.

Ramsden, P. (Ed.). (1988). *Improving learning.* London: Kegan Page.

Wilen, W. W. (Ed.). (1987). *Questions, questioning techniques, and effective teaching.* Washington, DC: National Education Association.

3

Lesson Planning for Interdisciplinary Instruction

▓ OVERVIEW

This chapter provides a discussion of essential lesson planning processes. The focus of this chapter is on the following:

- Formats used to prepare written lesson plans
- Determination of learning standards, instructional objectives, and essential questions during lesson and activity planning
- The elements critical to planning a procedure for any lesson
- Protocols used to design lesson plan procedures

▓ LESSON PLAN FORMATS

Because lesson planning is such an important part of a teacher's work, designing successful plans for lessons and other classroom activities—including those used to introduce interdisciplinary units—is one of any teacher's most serious concerns. At first, new teachers may feel the need to follow detailed planning formats for their lessons, and they often find daily lesson planning time consuming and difficult. As they gain experience, teachers usually modify their planning strategies to fit their needs and teaching styles; however, most teachers continue to consider, at least mentally, the critical elements in the lesson planning process.

Several formats are available for designing successful lesson and activity plans. Most formats are similar; all include sections for listing learning standards, objectives, materials, and procedures. Many contemporary lesson plan formats also include essential questions. However, the procedure section is often handled differently. In some lesson plans—such as those included in books by Cooper (2003), Kellough and Kellough (2003), and Reiser and Dick (1996)—the procedure is divided into separate tasks. In general, these plans usually specify areas such as the anticipatory set, motivation, application, guided practice, and follow-up activities. Formats of this type are well suited for planning skills-oriented lessons; however, they may not be as practical for planning lessons in areas such as history and literature, for planning field trips, or for encouraging students to conduct their own research and experiments.

In other formats, the procedure is not divided. Formats such as those found in books by Borich (2004); Post, Ellis, Humphreys, and Buggey (1997); and Roberts and Kellough (2004) are more easily adapted for most types of instruction.

The format used to plan introductory lessons for interdisciplinary units is found in chapter 5, and the formats for research-oriented interdisciplinary units in chapter 6. These lesson plans include nine sections: topic, level, estimated time, learning standards, general objectives, essential questions, behavioral objectives, procedure, and materials. The lesson plan topic, grade level, estimated time, and materials need little explanation. However, more information about learning standards, general objectives, essential questions, behavioral objectives, and the procedure is given next.

■ LEARNING STANDARDS, INSTRUCTIONAL OBJECTIVES, AND ESSENTIAL QUESTIONS

Interdisciplinary unit plans and lessons include learning standards, which are long term (i.e., require considerable time to meet), and two levels of instructional objectives: (a) those that are long term and (b) those that are short term (i.e., can often be accomplished in a single lesson or activity). Both unit plans and lesson plans include lists of learning standards and *general* objectives (long-term goals) and essential questions. Lesson plans also include specific, short-term, *behaviorally* stated objectives or a separate assessment section.

Learning standards and *general* objectives are broad-based, long-term goals toward which a unit or a lesson can contribute in some ways. Learning standards and general objectives both focus on student behaviors; in fact, when these standards and objectives are written, they appear to be similar. An interdisciplinary unit usually addresses a number of learning standards and general objectives. However, because a single lesson or activity plan is short term, situation specific, and much narrower in scope than a unit, it can address relatively few (often only one) learning standards and general objectives.

Learning Standards and General Objectives: Long-Term Goals

Before the advent of learning standards, teachers usually included general objectives in their instructional plans. Although both are long term and suggest purposes that are addressed in an interdisciplinary unit, they differ substantially. **Learning standards** are developed at national, state, and local levels by groups of professionals; they communicate clearly and provide for a degree of uniformity from teacher to teacher and school to school. Using learning standards, teachers can help to ensure that students are introduced to similar content regardless of where they attend school.

General objectives differ from learning standards in that they are written by individual teachers for a particular group of students. General objectives vary considerably from one teacher to another. Even when the same topic is studied and the same materials are used, teachers may emphasize different content and skills in their units.

Minimally, interdisciplinary unit plans should include the learning standards that they address. Teachers can add general objectives if they find that their units also address long-term goals that are not included in lists of learning standards adopted by their schools.

When deciding on the learning standards and general objectives to include in a plan, teachers need to consider three categories: content (or cognitive), attitudinal (or affective), and process objectives. Examples of each category appear next. (*Note:* The sample learning standards provided in this book are similar, but not identical, to those found in lists available from many professional associations and state departments of education.)

Examples

Students understand basic geographic features of the earth. (*Content learning standard or general objective*)

Students gain an understanding of the ways in which their government functions. (*Content learning standard or general objective*)

Students maintain a healthy self-concept. (*Attitudinal learning standard or general objective*)

Students develop a positive attitude about failure in scientific experimentation. (*Attitudinal learning standard or general objective*)

Students apply the scientific method when experimenting in science. (*Process learning standard or general objective*)

Students are proficient in using the research process. (*Process learning standard or general objective*)

In addition to learning standards, other standards categories, such as performance, curriculum, and delivery standards, may be included in national, state, and local standards lists. Sweeny (1999) explained the differences in these categories, indicating that **performance standards** describe "how well students must know and do specific assessment tasks" (p. 64). Teachers can use the performance suggestions to help assess students' progress toward meeting content learning standards. **Curriculum standards** are written for teachers to "define how teachers will reach desired results" (p. 64) and what teachers will need to teach. **Delivery standards** outline what teachers "must know and do if students are to perform at the desired level" (p. 64).

Subdivisions of learning standards—or **benchmarks**—also accompany most national, state, and local lists:

Examples

The following two examples of benchmarks are related to New York State Social Studies Standard 1: "Students will use a variety of intellectual skills to demonstrate their understanding of major ideas, eras, themes, developments, and turning points in the history of the United States and New York" (Learning Standards, 1996, p. 1).

Benchmark (elementary level): Students will "explain those values, practices, and traditions that unite all Americans" (p. 2).

Benchmark (intermediate, or upper elementary, level): Students will "interpret the ideas, values, and beliefs contained in the Declaration of Independence and the New York State Constitution, and United States Constitution, Bill of Rights, and other important historical documents" (p. 4).

Benchmarks narrow the scope of broad-based learning standards, but the preceding examples clearly reveal that even benchmarks may still be so general that they do not substitute for the essential questions or short-term objectives that are needed for lesson planning. Therefore, teachers need to tailor their essential questions and short-term objective statements to the specific contexts of their lessons and activities.

Essential Questions

Essential questions are included in many lesson plans. "Questions define tasks, express problems, and delineate issues" (Elder & Paul, 2002, p. 3). They reflect the process of inquiry, which always begins with questioning. Essential questions can be added to or even substitute for the behavioral objectives in a lesson or an activity plan.

Lessons are planned to help students find answers to questions at all levels of Bloom's Taxonomy—often in more than one discipline. Raising the essential questions to be addressed in a lesson is also a logical way of expressing its purposes and main objectives. Several examples of essential questions follow:

- Why is knowing how to use a compass important?
- What factors contribute to changes in the seasons?
- How do import quotas affect our economy? What are some advantages and possible disadvantages?
- What are some effective ways to keep our neighborhood clean?

Additional information on essential questions and numerous examples can be found on the Internet by searching for "essential questions." Other examples of essential questions can be found in the lesson and unit plan examples given in subsequent chapters and in the Instructional Resources section at the back of this book.

Behavioral Objectives: Short-Term Goals

Short-term objectives usually conform to the format and terminology associated with *behavioral* objectives. Following are three questions that may help teachers to formulate short-term behavioral objective statements for their lesson and activity plans:

1. What should the students learn (gain) from this lesson? What standard or standards are being addressed? What is the purpose of this lesson?
2. How will the students show that they have met the standard being addressed? Are there specific performances that will help students to master the standard?

What will they have to be able to do to demonstrate this? (These performances are indicated by verbs describing observable behaviors to be demonstrated by students. *Note:* An Internet search for "behavioral objectives" will locate lists of verbs that are appropriate for describing observable behaviors at all six levels of Bloom's Taxonomy.)

3. How well are the students expected to master this learning? How well will they need to perform what they are required to do? What is the standard that needs to be reached?

A behavioral objective statement is written in a single sentence that states (a) for whom the lesson is planned, (b) the behavior that will indicate that students have met the standard addressed by the lesson, (c) the special conditions (if any) under which this behavior should be performed, and (d) how well the students must perform to meet the standard successfully. Examples of three behavioral objectives follow:

1. *After a trip to the zoo* (describes a condition), *the children* (tells for whom the objective is intended) *will each complete a drawing of one animal observed at the zoo and dictate a sentence for each picture that includes at least one fact learned about the animal as a result of the field trip* (explains the specific behaviors to be demonstrated by the children). The degree of acceptable performance for this objective for kindergarten or early first-grade level is implied to be 100 percent.

2. *Given a compass and five written directions to follow* (the conditions), *each student* (for whom the objective is intended) *will accurately follow four of the five directions* (the behavior to be demonstrated and degree of acceptable performance; upper elementary grade level).

3. *After completion of a unit called* Emerging African Nations (the condition), *the students* (for whom the objective is intended) *will pass a comprehensive unit test on major concepts developed in the unit* (the behavior to be demonstrated) *with at least 75 percent accuracy* (the degree of acceptable performance; middle school level).

Teachers who include essential questions can use, as a substitute for behavioral objectives, an assessment section that describes how the lesson will be assessed.

Sources on Learning Standards and Instructional Objectives

Many excellent sources are available for more information on learning standards and instructional objectives: Cooper (2003); Dembo (1994); Dick and Carey (1996); Gronlund (1991); Harris and Carr (1996); Kibler, Cegala, Barker, and Miles (1981); Mager (1997); Schmoker and Marzano (1999); Sweeny (1999); and Zook (2001). Descriptive documents on standards are also located on the Internet at the Mid-continent Research for Education and Learning Web site: http://www.mcrel.org.

LESSON PLANNING PROCEDURES

Critical Elements in a Lesson Plan Procedure

The procedure sections of the lesson plans in chapters 5 and 6 and the Instructional Resources section of this book are not segmented into several subdivisions, such as motivation, development, and so on. However, these lessons do include the elements that are needed in the procedure of any lesson plan. When planning the procedure, teachers must try to visualize what will occur at each step. One way to do this is to imagine recording the lesson with a video camera and to attempt to anticipate student responses and reactions as the lesson proceeds. Recognizing possible student behaviors—their reactions, interpretations, and potential misinterpretations—before teaching the lesson can help to allay some of the fears about what to do if the unexpected occurs.

Other elements are fundamental in planning any lesson or activity, regardless of the discipline. Addressing the following critical elements should help to ensure a greater degree of success when a lesson plan is taught.

Provide a Clear Introduction to the Lesson, and Help Students to Focus Their Thinking on the Lesson Topic

The lesson should be clearly introduced in some way; this can often be accomplished informally and creatively. The introduction should help students to focus on the topic of the lesson. A brief statement such as "Today, we are going to begin to study more about the planet Mars" or another explanation should let students know what the lesson will be about or what the activity will involve.

Help Students Make Connections to What They Already Know About the Lesson Topic

Early in the procedure, students need to form a connection between the new concepts or skills to be developed in the lesson or activity and the knowledge they possess. Possible ways to accomplish this include (a) reviewing what has been studied or learned previously about the topic, (b) reminding students about what they know about the topic, and (c) asking students what they know about the new topic. Occasionally, the teacher may need to provide a preliminary experience or an entire lesson to help prepare students for new concepts and to develop adequate background information for the new lesson.

Stimulate Thinking with Questions and Other Techniques That Cause Conflict in Students' Minds

Students construct their own knowledge; this construction process cannot begin (neither will students become interested in learning anything new) until they first realize that something is of importance to them that they do not know. This constructivist viewpoint strongly suggests that motivation must develop from within. Therefore, instead of assuming the role of motivator, teachers need to help the students become aware of the need to develop some new knowledge or a new skill. In each lesson procedure, the teacher must introduce cognitive conflict to help students realize that there is something they do not already know; then the process of acquiring this new knowledge can begin. The teacher can introduce cognitive conflict in a number of ways, including the following four:

1. Asking a critical question—the essential question—relating to the concept(s) to be developed in the lesson
2. Having students observe a discrepant event—something they will have difficulty explaining immediately
3. Raising questions before and after students study some visual material—a computer presentation, videotape, film, or filmstrip—or as they observe a demonstration performed by the teacher
4. Instructing students to read for certain purposes or listen to material read by the teacher so that they can find answers to specific questions

Follow Appropriate Methods, Techniques, and Protocols

The method, approach, or technique used to structure the lesson procedure should be appropriate for the objectives of the lesson. (A discussion of several common protocols is presented subsequently in this chapter.)

Assess the Objectives of the Lesson

An important step in the procedure is assessing the behavioral objectives of the lesson. In lesson plans in which essential questions replace behavioral objectives, the techniques that will be used to assess these questions need to be explained in a separate assessment section of the lesson plan. The assessment step is usually located near the end of the lesson.

Bring Closure to the Lesson

At the end of the procedure, the design should include a way to bring the lesson or activity to closure and a way to summarize what students have gained from their instruction. Such closure can be accomplished by (a) reviewing with students what they have learned, (b) having one student or several students summarize what they believe they have learned, or (c) holding a discussion about the students' different projects—pictures, murals, dioramas, papier-mâché or other art constructions, drama or dance performances—that reflects the concepts they have gained.

Include Notes About Possible Student Reactions and Responses

At various steps in the lesson procedure, the teacher should note anticipated student responses or reactions. For example, if a question is raised, students' possible responses can be noted. Although information of this kind is not typically included in the lesson plan procedure, it may help to minimize some problems that can arise from unexpected reactions.

Other Considerations for Planning the Procedure

In addition to the considerations just discussed, the following are important to consider:

- **Address the principles of learning, and consider students' learning and working styles.** The teacher should consider students' different learning and working styles in the procedure of the lesson. The teacher should consider students' multiple intelligences, interests, and talents, and when feasible attempt to address them.
- **Include sufficient detail.** All steps in the procedure should be well detailed and clear enough so that another teacher can follow the plan.
- **Sequence the steps in a logical order.** The sequence of the procedure should be clear, logical in order, and easy to follow.

Summary

In summary, attention to the preceding critical elements and other considerations for designing a lesson procedure should help to ensure a greater degree of success when the lesson is taught. Productive instructional sessions are more likely to occur when the procedure in a lesson plan does the following:

- Provides a clear introduction to the lesson and helps students focus their thinking on the lesson theme
- Helps students make connections to what they already know about the lesson topic
- Stimulates thinking with questions and other techniques that cause conflict in students' minds
- Follows appropriate methods, techniques, and protocols
- Assesses the objectives of the lesson
- Brings closure to the lesson
- Includes notes about possible student reactions and responses

Finally, lessons are more likely to be successful when lesson plans attend to students' different working and learning styles, provide enough detail, and are carefully sequenced.

▓ THE USE OF PROTOCOLS FOR PLANNING SOME PROCEDURES

Many lessons and activities that are taught in elementary and middle schools can be planned by following established protocols. A **protocol** is a "set" procedure that has been found to work well in practice. In other professions, practitioners use protocols regularly. For example, in the medical profession, surgeons follow protocols for surgery, and in the legal profession, lawyers and judges have set procedures for many deliberations.

In teaching, we have also learned that some specific procedures—or protocols—work better than others for certain types of lessons. Eight of these protocols are outlined next:

1. **The scientific method:** For having students experiment in science
2. **The directed reading activity (DRA):** For many lessons in reading
3. **The survey, question, read, recite, review (SQ3R) technique:** For independent study of a reading selection
4. **Directed listening:** To help students attend and gain more during a listening activity
5. **Directed viewing:** For when visual materials are used
6. **The know, want to know, learned (KWL) technique:** For establishing purposes and organizing for any kind of research
7. **A field trip protocol:** To help students gain as much as possible from off-campus excursions
8. **A protocol for skills instruction**

The Scientific Method of Investigation: A Protocol for Some Lessons in Science

The scientific method is a logical choice when a lesson involves students in experimentation. In the procedure, students are guided to follow these five steps:

1. Observe a phenomenon.
2. Suggest hypotheses for the phenomenon.
3. Design a method of testing the hypotheses.
4. Observe the results.
5. Draw conclusions relative to the hypotheses.

The lesson plan that follows is an example of a lesson in which the procedure follows the scientific method of investigation. It is a lesson that provides students with an opportunity to discover that the length of a pendulum is the only variable affecting its swing rate. (*Note:* Sample lessons for other protocols reviewed in this chapter can be found in the Instructional Resources section at the back of this book.)

The Pendulum Problem: A Sample Lesson Plan Following the Scientific Method of Investigation

Topic: The Pendulum

Level: Grade 3 or 4

Estimated Time: 20–30 minutes

Learning Standard: Students will prepare and conduct research and record observations and measurements.

General Objective: Students will use the scientific method of investigation to solve problems.

Essential Question: How can the swing rate of a pendulum be changed?

Behavioral Objective: After experimentation with a pendulum, students will state in their discussion that the length of a pendulum affects its swing rate.

Procedure

1. Set up a simple pendulum before the lesson.

2. Swing the model pendulum, and ask the students if this reminds them of anything they have seen before.

   Students may be reminded of swings on the playground and clocks that they have seen. Some students may suggest that it is like a "pendulum." However, because other students may not be familiar with the word pendulum, *you may need to clarify its meaning.*

3. While the pendulum is swinging, tell the students this: "Today, we are beginning a new unit in which we will be involved in completing several investigations. The first will be a study involving a pendulum."

4. Ask the students if they can think of a way to determine how fast the pendulum is swinging.

   Timing and counting will probably be suggested.

5. Because the students will not know how to count pendulum swings to determine the swing rate, demonstrate how to count the swings—one swing for each back-and-forth movement. Decide on how long to time the pendulum swings. Have one student keep time while others count silently; then, record the basal swing rate on the board.

6. Say, "I wonder if there is a way to make the pendulum swing faster." List the students' suggestions—their hypotheses—on the board under the basal swing rate.

   The students may suggest pushing it harder, starting it from a higher position, adding or subtracting weights, and perhaps lengthening or shortening the pendulum.

7. Ask how they can determine if any of their ideas will make the pendulum swing faster.

The students should suggest that they will need to try each suggestion—to experiment.

8. Provide time for experimentation. Ideally, the pendulum should be set up in a corner of the classroom where all students will have an opportunity to experiment during several days. A schedule, either a sign-up sheet or a list of names, should be posted near the pendulum. Students will need to work in pairs to test their hypotheses—one child to time the swings and one to count. The students should record their hypotheses and the results of each test in their notebooks or on a specially designed worksheet. If you decide that the experimentation should be completed as a whole-class activity (for safety or other reasons), some students should be invited to assist with timing and counting. Others should be reminded to observe carefully.

9. After the experimentation is completed, engage the class in a discussion. Ask, "What have you found causes the pendulum to swing faster?"

   The response should include the idea that only shortening the pendulum will increase its swing rate.

10. Collect any student records—notebooks or worksheets—of their experimentation.

Optional Follow-Up Questions

Indicating each of the hypotheses—on the board—that failed to increase the swing rate of the pendulum, ask the following five questions:

1. Can anyone explain why you thought that would work? (This question helps the students to analyze their thinking about each hypothesis.)
2. How do you suppose we could correct a clock with a pendulum that is too slow?
3. If you want your backyard swing to swing faster, what would you have to do to it?
4. Do you think there is any other way to make a pendulum swing faster?
5. What will we have to do to make the pendulum swing slower?

Materials

A simple pendulum (Use a stick, a ruler, or an unsharpened pencil taped securely to a tabletop so that it overhangs the top by about 6 inches; a 30-inch length of string tied and wrapped several times around the end of the stick; a large paper clip, opened and attached to one end of the string; several weights, such as metal washers of equal size and weight, placed on the open end of the paper clip; and several additional weights for experimenting.)

Masking tape

A timer with a second hand

A Protocol for Directed Reading Instruction

The directed reading activity, DRA, and the directed reading–thinking activity, DRTA (Stauffer, 1969), have been used successfully by elementary school teachers for instruction in reading for many years. According to Heilman, Blair, and Rupley (2002), this protocol is followed in commercial reading textbook series. It is a logical approach to use for many reading activities. The four steps in the protocol involve the following:

1. **An introduction to the selection to be read:** Students are helped to make a connection between what they will be reading and their current background knowledge. New vocabulary and concepts are introduced.

2. **Silent reading of the selection or part of the selection:** The teacher—or the teacher and the students together—set specific purposes for reading the selection (or part of the selection if the reading is divided into two or more sections). The teacher may raise a specific question that can be answered only after the selection is carefully read, the students may set their own purposes by deciding what they would like to find in the reading, or the students may predict what they believe will occur in the selection and then read to determine whether their predictions are accurate.

3. **Discussion of the material that has been read:** The teacher raises questions about the selection after students have read silently, or students discuss what they discovered about their predictions. Students can be asked to read parts of the selection orally during the discussion to support their answers. Having students read the entire selection orally is not usually necessary after they have read it silently. To do so prolongs the activity and, because it may interrupt the flow of a narrative, can lessen student comprehension and interest.

4. **Follow-up skills and enrichment activities:** Practice with skills on worksheets or in workbooks may be helpful for some students after the reading. However, other activities, such as some creative writing activities, outlining, preparing a dramatization, or writing a report, may be more appropriate and engender greater student interest.

See the sample lesson plan called *The Louisiana Purchase* in the Instructional Resources section at the back of this book. It is a lesson in which the procedure follows the DRA protocol to assist students in reading a selection.

SQ3R: The Survey, Question, Read, Recite, Review Protocol for Independent Reading

A technique related to the DRA is SQ3R. Students learn to apply the steps in the protocol independently because the teacher is not present. SQ3R resembles a DRA without the teacher. The five steps in SQ3R are as follows:

1. **Survey.** Students learn to look over the selection they will be reading and try to recall what they know about the topic. Titles, headings, subheadings, illustrations, photographs, captions, and introductory paragraphs are examined.

2. **Question.** The teacher is absent, so students raise specific questions to guide their reading. They can learn to turn boldface headings into questions to help with this step.

3. **Read.** Students read the selection, keeping in mind the questions they raised.

4. **Recite.** Students try to answer their questions after reading. They prepare notes for later review.

5. **Review.** Students check their notes to review what they gained from the reading material.

A Protocol for Directed Listening

A directed listening protocol is also similar to directed reading. It provides direction for students when material is read to them or when they are listening to recorded material. To follow this protocol, the teacher does the following:

- Helps students make the necessary cognitive connection with the topic of the material they will hear
- Clarifies new concepts or vocabulary included in the listening activity
- Provides, or elicits from students, the purposes for listening to help students attend to the material they will be hearing
- Holds a discussion following the listening to determine what students have gained from it

See the lesson plan called *An Eskimo Story* in the Instructional Resources section of this book for an example of a procedure that follows the directed listening protocol.

A Protocol for Directed Viewing

A directed viewing protocol is similar to directed reading, but it provides direction for students when they are watching a DVD or videotape program, a computer presentation, a film, or a filmstrip for some specific information. To follow this protocol, the teacher must do this:

- Help students make the necessary cognitive connection with the topic of the material they will be viewing
- Introduce new concepts or vocabulary that will be in the visual material
- Set specific purposes for viewing to direct students' attention and help them focus on the visual presentation
- Conduct a discussion with the students to determine what they have gained from the viewing activity

See The Space Age, a lesson plan in the Instructional Resources section of this book, for a sample lesson plan using the directed viewing protocol.

KWL: The Know, Want to Know, Learned Protocol

The know, want to know, learned (KWL) technique was initially designed to assist students with reading comprehension (Ogle, 1986). Today, it is also commonly used to help students organize for research. Before the lesson, the teacher prepares three large charts or sections of chalkboard, each of which has one of the letters *K*, *W*, and *L* at the top. Students' responses will be recorded under each letter. The charts form the three columns needed for the protocol. The charts or board sections must be large enough to be easily read and to accommodate all student responses. The KWL protocol includes the following five steps:

1. Ask students to list what they know about a topic, and write their ideas in the *K* column. Ogle (1986) suggested that two steps be included in the *K* section. First is a brainstorming step to determine what the students think they know. To stimulate student thinking during this initial brainstorming,

   > . . . ask volunteers after they have made their contributions, "Where did you learn that?" or "How could you prove that?" By not simply accepting the statements that students offer but probing to make them think about the sources and substantiveness of their suggestions, you challenge both contributors and the rest of the class to a higher level of thinking. (p. 566)

   Second is to help students find common categories among the information they have listed. For example, if several students have suggested different foods an animal eats, "foods" would be a common category, a category in which students have included more than one item in the *K* section.

2. In the *W* section, students are asked to list what they would like to learn as they research the topic. The students set the main purposes of their study. As students contribute to the *K* and *W* sections during the initial lesson, the teacher should write the contributions on the chart, using complete sentences.

3. Students copy the first two sections for reference as they conduct research to determine whether what they thought they knew about the topic in the *K* section is accurate and to find answers to questions in the *W* section of the chart.

4. Time is provided for the students to gather information, to find answers to their questions, and to locate support for the information recorded in the *K* column. This step will require a number of active research periods.

5. As the students gain information, they enter it in the third—what was learned, or *L*—section. The information included in this section helps students to realize what they learned and what they were unable to learn relative to the questions they raised initially. The students can then try to decide where to search for additional information.

A sample lesson plan called *Dolphins*, which follows the KWL protocol, can be found in the Instructional Resources section at the back of this book.

A Protocol for Organizing Field Trips

A logical protocol for taking a field trip conforms to the research process. Similar to the KWL procedure, this protocol also involves three phases—preparation for the trip, the field excursion, and a follow-up session. The three phases are explained next:

Phase I: Before taking a field trip, students plan their excursion with guidance from their teacher. The KWL technique may be helpful to use for this discussion. Questions about what students would like to learn at the field site are elicited from students and recorded for reference during the trip. Each student should have a copy of the questions raised during the discussion to take along on the field trip.

Permission slips are distributed with instructions for returning them before the day of the trip. Several parents are usually invited to assist on the day of the trip.

Phase II: On the day of the field trip, students attempt to gain answers to their questions and to learn other related information while at the field site. They use their lists of questions at the site and note answers to their questions.

Phase III: Finally, when students return to their classroom, they discuss and record what they gained from the trip. This discussion is guided by the initial questions they raised. Some questions may not have been answered; other information that was not planned for can be included during the discussion.

The teacher then assists the students in summarizing what they learned from their field trip. This summary may take the form of an outline that students then copy for their records.

The introductory lesson plan for a sample unit plan called *Spring* provides an example of the initial phase in the field trip protocol. It is found in the Instructional Resources section at the back of this book. This lesson prepares students for a walk in the neighborhood to look for signs of spring.

A Protocol for Skills Instruction

Skills instruction can follow a fairly traditional outline. A five-step lesson plan (Hunter, 1982) is especially appropriate for teaching skills lessons. The protocol for the lesson includes the following five elements:

1. An *anticipatory set*, during which the teacher sets the purpose for the lesson, introduces students to the concepts that the lesson will include and helps students to make the needed connections between their present skills and the new skill to be developed.

2. The *presentation* of the lesson, in which the teacher uses various techniques to present a model of the skill to be developed. The teacher demonstrates the skill for the students.

3. *Guided practice*, in which students are assisted with practice applications of the new skill.

4. *Independent practice*, in which students practice the new skill they have just been taught. Following the lesson, additional practice is assigned.

5. *Closure*, in which students are helped to summarize what they learned about the new skill and its applications during the lesson.

See the sample lesson plan called *Learning How to Outline* in the Instructional Resources section at the back of this book for an example of a skills lesson that follows this protocol.

Formats for Other Procedures

Procedures suitable for demonstrations, applications, and practice sessions can involve combinations of the preceding protocols. For example, a lesson might begin with a directed listening protocol, having students listen to a short selection or book. The listening activity may lead to the preparation of a KWL chart to introduce some research the students will be undertaking. Follow-up activities might make use of additional protocols.

THE DESIGN OF LESSONS THAT INCLUDE TEACHER-PREPARED COMPUTER PRESENTATIONS

The use of computer presentation software by teachers and students at all levels of education is increasing. Some teachers are recording instructional DVD presentations that serve as an alternative to computer presentations. The following general suggestions may be helpful to teachers who have not previously designed presentations for instruction. Experimentation will help define the optimal layouts and effects, including the background color or texture; fonts and text styles; use and arrangements of pictures, drawings, and clip art; inclusion of sound elements and movies; animation; and transitional effects.

Design Elements

Background Color or Texture

A liquid crystal display (LCD) projector is used with a computer or DVD player to project a finished presentation. To maintain adequate contrast between the background and the foreground in the projected slide show, you must usually keep the background color or texture of the presentation slides very light. A pale yellow or blue, or a light marble texture, provides a pleasant contrast and makes text and pictures easy to see when the presentation is projected. Dark background colors can also be effective, but they should be used with white or very light text colors.

Text

The text needs to be large enough for students to read easily when it is projected on a screen. Therefore, use at least a 28-point font for computer presentations. Larger sizes are often better. You may need to use sans serif fonts for clarity of the text when it is projected with some LCD projectors because serif details are often lost, which leaves letters partly blank. Serif details are easily projected with more powerful projectors.

Use only one or two fonts in a single presentation; doing so helps students maintain their focus on the content and purpose of the presentation instead of being distracted by changing font styles. Instead of underlining, use boldface and italics to highlight because underlining cuts through the lower portion of descending letters.

Finally, try to minimize the amount of text on each slide. Use narration along with the presentation so that only the major points are written on the slides; otherwise, some students may try to write everything they see on the screen instead of becoming involved in the discussion of the main points of the presentation. In some cases, you may want to provide students with a script of the text that is displayed during the presentation.

Inserts

Choose pictures, drawings, clip art, and sound effects that are consistent with the theme of the presentation. Keep each slide clean and uncluttered to avoid distracting students from the purpose of the presentation. Add sound effects sparingly and only for emphasis, and include videos only to strengthen important points.

Animation

Words can appear all at once or letter by letter; pictures can fade in, dissolve, or fly from any part of the screen, and objects can swirl around. The temptation may be to use too many of these effects. Use animation discretely and for emphasis, not to startle or distract students.

Transitions

Use only one transitional effect from slide to slide in a presentation. Many effects are pleasant, including dissolve, vertical bar, and fade techniques. However, too many different effects can distract students from the purpose of the presentation.

Sample Lesson Plan with a Computer Presentation

A sample lesson plan that includes the use of a computer presentation can be found in the Instructional Resources section at the back of this book. The lesson is designed to introduce an interdisciplinary unit of instruction called *Endangered Animals*.

▓ SUMMARY

This chapter covered a general overview of lesson plan formats, learning standards, essential questions, instructional objectives, critical elements in the procedure, and lesson planning protocols for teachers who are beginning to plan for interdisciplinary instruction. Chapters 5 and 6 elaborate on the unit planning processes for two types of units: interdisciplinary and research-oriented interdisciplinary units.

▓ ACTIVITIES

1. Review state and local lists of learning standards. Using Bloom's Taxonomy, try to estimate the level of any 10 learning standards on the lists.

2. Some educators argue that meticulous and detailed planning for teaching can detract from a teacher's spontaneity and creativity during instruction. Do you agree or disagree? Why or why not?

3. Study the sample lesson plans referred to in this chapter that are in the Instructional Resources section of this book. The plans follow the different protocols discussed in this chapter. Locate the critical elements in the procedure sections of these plans. Decide which of the plans best meets the list of critical elements outlined in this chapter. Revise the procedures for the plans that need improving.

4. Use the key words *lesson plans* for an Internet search to locate two lesson plans. Examine the procedure sections of the plans to determine how well they meet the critical elements outlined in this chapter. Next, decide whether each plan follows an appropriate protocol. Finally, revise a plan that you believe needs improving.

5. Using the list of critical elements to be included in a lesson plan procedure, develop a procedure, on a topic of your choice, that includes these elements. Indicate places in the procedure where you have provided for them.

6. Use one of the protocols discussed in this chapter to prepare a complete lesson plan on a specific topic.

▓ REFERENCES

Borich, G. D. (2004). *Effective teaching methods* (5th ed.). Upper Saddle River, NJ: Merrill/ Prentice Hall.

Cooper, J. M. (2003). *Classroom teaching skills* (7th ed.). Boston: Houghton Mifflin.

Dembo, M. H. (1994). *Applying educational psychology in the classroom* (5th ed.). New York: Longman.

Dick, W., & Carey, L. (1996). *The systematic design of instruction.* New York: HarperCollins.

Elder, L., & Paul, R. (2002). *A miniature guide to the art of asking essential questions.* Dillon Beach, CA: Foundation for Critical Thinking.

Gronlund, N. E. (1991). *Stating objectives for classroom instruction* (4th ed.). New York: Macmillan.

Harris, D. E., & Carr, J. F. (1996). *How to use standards in the classroom.* Alexandria, VA: Association for Supervision and Curriculum Development.

Heilman, A. W., Blair, R. R., & Rupley, W. H. (2002). *Principles and practices of teaching reading.* Upper Saddle River, NJ: Merrill/ Prentice Hall.

Hunter, M. (1982). *Mastery teaching.* El Segundo, CA: Instructional Dynamics.

Kellough, R. D., & Kellough, N. G. (2003). *Middle school teaching: A guide to methods and resources* (4th ed.). Upper Saddle River, NJ: Merrill/Prentice Hall.

Kibler, R. J., Cegala, D. J., Barker, L. L., & Miles, D. T. (1981). *Objectives for instruction and evaluation* (2nd ed.). Boston: Allyn & Bacon.

Learning standards for social studies. (1996). Albany: The University of the State of New York/The State Education Department.

Mager, R. (1997). *Preparing instructional objectives: A critical tool in the development of effective instruction* (3rd ed.). Atlanta, GA: Center for Effective Performance.

Ogle, D. M. (1986). K-W-L: A teaching model that develops active reading of expository text. *The Reading Teacher, 39,* 564–570.

Post, T. R., Ellis, A. K., Humphreys, A. H., & Buggey, L. J. (1997). *Interdisciplinary approaches to curriculum: Themes for teaching.* Upper Saddle River, NJ: Prentice Hall.

Reiser, R. A., & Dick, W. (1996). *Instructional planning: A guide for teachers* (2nd ed.). Boston: Allyn & Bacon.

Roberts, P. L., & Kellough, R. D. (2004). *A guide for developing interdisciplinary thematic units* (3rd ed.). Upper Saddle River, NJ: Prentice Hall.

Schmoker, M., & Marzano, R. J. (1999, March). Realizing the promise of standards-based education. *Educational Leadership, 56*(6), 17–21.

Stauffer, R. G. (1969). *Teaching reading as a thinking process.* New York: Harper & Row.

Sweeny, B. (1999, Winter). Content standards: Gate or bridge? *Kappa Delta Pi Record, 35*(2), 64–67.

Zook, K. B. (2001). *Instructional design for classroom teaching and learning.* Boston: Houghton Mifflin.

▊ SUGGESTED READINGS

The supplemental readings listed next provide additional background material about lesson planning as discussed in this chapter.

Burns, D. E., & Purcell, J. H. (2001). Tools for teachers. *Educational Leadership, 59*(1), 50–52.

Carin, A. A. (2001). *Teaching science through discovery* (9th ed.). Upper Saddle River, NJ: Merrill/Prentice Hall.

Elements of effective instruction: The Madeline Hunter model. (n.d.). Retrieved from http://www. humboldt. edu/ ~tha1/hunter-eei.html#eei

Guskey, T. R. (2001). Helping standards make the grade. *Educational Leadership, 59*(1), 20–27.

Kindsvatter, R., Wilen, W., & Ishler, M. (2004). *Dynamics of effective teaching* (3rd ed.). White Plains, NY: Longman.

Lesson design and performance models. (n.d.). Retrieved from http://www.foothill.net/ ~moorek/lessondesign.html

McNeil, J. D., & Wiles, J. (1990). *The essentials of teaching: Decisions, plans, methods.* New York: Macmillan.

Paris, S. G., Olson, G. M., & Stevenson, H. W. (1983). *Learning and motivation in the classroom.* Hillsdale, NJ: Erlbaum.

Penta, M. Q. (2002). Student portfolios in a standardized world. *Kappa Delta Pi Record, 38*(2), 77–81.

Peterson, R., Bowyer, J., Butts, D., & Bybee, R. (1984). *Science and society: A source book for elementary and junior high school teachers.* Upper Saddle River, N J: Prentice Hall.

Ramsden, P. (Ed.). (1988). *Improving learning.* London: Kegan Page.

Reigeluth, C. M. (1987). *Instructional theories in action: Lessons illustrating selected theories and models.* Hillsdale, NJ: Erlbaum.

Sava, S. G. (1975). *Learning through discovery for young children.* New York: McGraw-Hill.

Torbert, W. R. (1972). *Learning from experience: Toward consciousness.* New York: Columbia University Press.

Wadsworth, B. J. (1978). *Piaget for the classroom teacher.* New York: Longman.

Weinland, T. P., & Protheroe, D. W. (1973). *Social science projects you can do.* Upper Saddle River, NJ: Prentice Hall.

Wilson, M., & Tienken, C. (2001). Using standards to improve instruction. *Kappa Delta Pi Record, 38*(2), 82–84, 88.

4

Assessment in Interdisciplinary Instruction

▓ OVERVIEW

This chapter covers several techniques for assessing the work students produce during their unit studies. The focus of this chapter is on the following:

- The purposes of assessment in the instructional process
- Authentic assessment techniques
- The use of rubrics to grade individual students' papers and projects
- The role of examinations in the assessment process
- Suggestions for writing valid and reliable test items

▓ ASSESSMENT IN THE INSTRUCTIONAL PROCESS

Assessment is always an essential component of interdisciplinary instruction. Although educators agree that some form of assessment is needed, not all agree on the best ways to evaluate student progress. Ellis (2002) urged teachers to become familiar with several approaches to evaluation because experience has not proved that one is better than another. Sternberg (1999) added that "different kinds of assessment . . . complement one another. . . . There is no one 'right' kind of assessment" (p. 51). Perhaps, as Guskey (2003) suggested, those that are "best suited to guide improvements in student learning are the quizzes, tests, writing assignments, and other assessments that teachers administer on a regular basis in their classrooms" (p. 7).

The Purposes of Assessment

A critical part of teaching lessons and comprehensive interdisciplinary units is assessing the results of instruction to determine the students' achievement of the objectives established at the outset. Achievement can be assessed at many points in the instructional process. Following are brief explanations of two general assessment categories, summative and formative evaluation; the use of student assessment techniques for assessing teaching effectiveness; and diagnosis in the assessment process.

Summative Evaluation

Traditionally, we think of using various assessment measures at the end of instruction. The techniques often used at this point include final examinations or various kinds of reports. Assessment of achievement at the conclusion of instruction is referred to as **summative assessment.** We anticipate that the same material will not be evaluated again.

Formative Evaluation

Assessing student progress during the teaching process and while concepts are still forming is an ongoing kind of assessment. Techniques that can serve as **formative measures** include reviewing with students, raising a question about some material that has been taught, giving a short quiz, and observing the ways students work on various tasks.

Teaching Effectiveness

Another purpose of assessment is for individual teachers to address their personal effectiveness. Teachers often use the results of both summative and formative evaluation techniques to judge their teaching. However, the use of examinations and other student products needs to be combined with informal observations before any tentative conclusions can be drawn.

Diagnosis

Both summative and formative assessment techniques are used in the ongoing diagnosis of students' areas of strength and relative weakness.

▨ AUTHENTIC ASSESSMENT

For years, teachers have collected representative examples of students' work in folders to use when they are preparing reports and conferring with parents. Students, as well as teachers, should be involved in assembling these collections of authentic materials, which represent the work produced by students in their day-to-day activities. Whenever students take part in selecting the samples, they are encouraged to become actively involved in their assessment. For the most part, the teacher assembled work folders of the past; students only contributed the products but did not have a direct part in the selection. An authentic assessment technique that does involve students in the selection process is the **portfolio.**

Portfolios can be exceptionally useful authentic assessment tools because they indicate concretely what students are gaining from their work in school. In addition, portfolios provide a vehicle for reflection and interaction between students and their teachers. A portfolio also adds concrete evidence that can be combined with more objective techniques such as examinations.

A portfolio is referred to as an **authentic assessment** device because it includes examples of students' work and surveys of their interests, feelings, and attitudes. It can often indicate growth in areas for which examinations are ineffective. When students are responsible for maintaining their portfolios or parts of their portfolios, they can follow their own development. If they are asked to provide notations on the materials that they include in their portfolios, the process becomes even more reflective for them. It encourages them to use important strategies such as "questioning, discussing, guessing, proposing, analyzing, and reflecting" (Shores & Grace, 1998, p. 11).

A portfolio prepared by the student—or the student and the teacher—can include many kinds of materials that are useful in the overall assessment process. Johnston (1992) explained that a student portfolio is analogous to an artist's portfolio because the student has the opportunity to include "work that she sees fit to display and talk about to others" (p. 129). The following list indicates some of the more common materials found in student portfolios:

- Examples of students' work and work in progress, such as samples of creative and practical writing, records of experiments, pieces of creative work in the arts and music, and photographs of projects completed or in progress
- Notes and memos
- Student observations and analyses of what was gained from instruction; what has been understood and not understood
- Teacher observations
- Surveys of feelings and attitudes
- Individual interest surveys
- Journals kept by students that include personal reflections and evaluations of their work in the class
- Self-evaluations prepared by students
- Journals kept by teachers, reflecting on individual progress
- Teachers' anecdotal records
- Records of individual pupil–teacher conferences
- Formal and informal quizzes, tests, and examinations
- Recordings—audio- or videotapes—of oral readings, reports, or recitations

Selecting materials for a portfolio needs to be a thoughtful process. Materials selected should provide for balance, with examples that represent the learning processes as well as student products. Work samples need to include products that are in progress as well as those that are complete (Pappas, Kiefer, & Levstik, 1999). The teacher should develop some criteria for guiding students in the selection of the samples they want to include, for determining how the materials will be evaluated and weighted in the overall assessment process, and for deciding on the role of others, including parents, in evaluating a student's progress with time (Borich, 2004).

Preliminary research on the portfolio technique indicates that portfolios have a positive effect on the improvement of instruction and an impact on the insights that students develop about their academic strengths and weaknesses (O'Neil, 1993). Additional discussions and explanations about authentic assessment and portfolio evaluation can be found at numerous Web sites, such as Houghton Mifflin's Education Place at http://www.eduplace.com. Comprehensive explanations can be found in the works of Charbonneau and Reider (1995); Darling-Hammond (1994); Darling-Hammond, Ancess, and Falk (1995); Ellis (2002); Engel (1994); Grosvenor (1993);

Lescher (1995); Orlich, Harder, Callahan, and Gibson (2001); Viadero (1995); and Wasserstein (1994).

■ THE USE OF RUBRICS TO GRADE REPORTS AND PROJECTS

While studying an interdisciplinary unit, students are usually required to prepare reports and projects of different kinds. The teacher's evaluation of these student products should be as thoughtful and objective as possible. Although subjectivity cannot be eliminated entirely, using clearly defined criteria in the evaluation process can help to minimize it. One of the more effective techniques that teachers have found for this purpose is to prepare sets of **rubrics,** or criteria.

In some school systems, sets of rubrics are available for teachers to use to assess student products in various disciplines or subject areas. An example is *The Rubric Bank,* by Chicago Public Schools (2000), which can be found at the Web site listed in the References. To study the Chicago rubrics and numerous other examples of rubrics and the different ways they can be prepared, refer to *Kathy Schrock's Guide for Educators* at the Web site listed in the References (Schrock, 2004).

One example of rubric construction, a set of criteria combined with a rating scale, is shown in Figure 4.1. In the example, the rubrics for evaluating student reports on endangered animals are delineated. The rubrics indicate that each report must provide information about why the animal is endangered and include two suggestions for possible ways to correct the problem. The reports must be evaluated for their organization, clarity of the introduction and conclusion, and overall quality of writing. Each criterion standard is also rated with a range of points to be used for determining grades for the papers.

The example shown in Figure 4.1 is an application of rubrics. As mentioned previously, a set of rubrics is simply a set of criteria—a scoring tool—prepared before an assignment and used to evaluate a completed student product (written or oral report, art project, construction, or other). Usually, rubrics indicate quality gradations for each criterion included. The student's products are then examined for compliance with the criteria. Some teachers first arrange the products as they assess them in three or more groups; the individual products are then studied a second time to ensure consistency in application of the rubrics. An alternative method some teachers use involves collecting samples of student products first, then developing rubrics for those and future products of the same type. However, when rubrics are prepared after students complete their work, the teacher cannot inform the students in advance of the criteria that will be used to assess their products.

Rubrics provide several advantages, especially for assessing projects and papers. Not only do they help to ensure a fairer, less subjective grading process, but Goodrich (1997) found that using rubrics may also "improve student performance, as well as monitor it, by making teachers' expectations clear and by showing students how to meet these expectations" (p. 14). Rubrics provide teachers with a standard to apply in their grading and may help to reduce the amount of time teachers must spend making decisions as they grade student products.

CRITERIA	QUALITY (points)		
	Excellent (5–4)	Fair (3–2)	Needs Improvement (1–0)
Introduction • Topic is clearly indicated. • Purpose is stated. • Introduction is succinct and clearly written. **Body of Paper** • Main reasons why the animal is endangered are stated. • Two ways to help correct the problem are included. **Conclusion** • Discussion refers to the purpose stated in the introduction. • Discussion provides a complete summary for the paper. **Writing** • Syntax and grammar are clear and correct. • Spelling and punctuation are accurate.			

Total Points for Report: _____

Rating: Excellent: 40–45
Good: 31–40
Needs Improvement: 0–30

FIGURE 4.1
Rubrics combined with a rating scale for a written report on endangered animals.

Ideally, rubrics also provide students with a clear set of expectations in advance and offer students the opportunity to evaluate their work before submitting it to the teacher for a grade. In an experimental writing program, Porcaro and Johnson (2003) found that requiring students to use rubrics in the form of writing checklists motivated the students to "look critically at their work" as they edited their papers (p. 78).

■ EXAMINATIONS

Most examinations are designed to measure verbal and/or logical–mathematical achievement; therefore, paper-and-pencil tests are useful for only part of the total evaluation process. Also, any single test provides only a sample of all the questions— the test items—that are possible to include because all tests are limited in length for practical purposes. Nonetheless, both standardized tests and informal, teacher-made examinations are evaluation tools that most teachers use.

Test Scores

Several scores are used in grading examinations. The **raw score** is the number of test items a student has answered correctly or the number of points earned on an examination. For example, if a student answers 22 items correctly on a 30-item examination, the student's raw score is simply 22. The raw score is the easiest score to determine, but it is not useful for making comparisons with scores on other examinations because the number of items may not be equal.

The raw score can easily be converted to a more useful score, the **percentage score.** This score is computed by dividing the number of items the student has answered correctly by the total number of items on the examination. The student who answered 22 items correctly on the 30-item examination will earn a score of .73, or 73%. The percentage score is one of the most frequently used scores because it allows teachers to compare and note progress on different examinations.

Percentile scores are frequently used scores that are reported in standardized examination manuals. A **percentile score** expresses the rank, or placement, of an individual student in a theoretical group of 100 students. For example, a student whose percentile score is 78 achieved a higher score than 77 students in the theoretical group; a percentile score of 46 would indicate that the student achieved a lower score than 54 students in the group.

The **grade equivalent score** is also reported for standardized examinations. This score expresses a student's raw score as a grade and month equivalent. It comprises a whole number representing the grade level and a decimal number to indicate the month in the 10-month academic year. For example, a grade equivalent score of 5.3 indicates that the student has earned a score equivalent to that of a student who has completed 3 months in the fifth grade.

Testing Concerns

In interdisciplinary instruction, the teacher must determine whether students have gained specific facts or concepts as a result of their study. A conventional examination can be helpful for assessing the degree to which the students have developed many of these concepts. Preparing such examinations so that they yield dependable information about student achievement is never easy, though, primarily because tests can be effective instruments only if they are both valid and reliable.

Validity

Is the test assessing what it is intended to assess? Is the main question raised when you are determining the validity of an examination? Test validity depends on several factors. First, all test items—the questions—included on the examination must address the objectives for which the test is written. For example, if a teacher intends to prepare a test that will help determine whether students have gained specific concepts from a unit called *The Middle East*, the test items must address only these concepts. No test is perfectly valid because various factors, such as readability and clarity of the test items, affect the validity of an examination.

One serious factor that influences the validity of a test is its readability. Written tests involve the need to read with full comprehension. If a test is designed to assess students' conceptual knowledge rather than their ability to read the words and understand what the test is asking of them, the readability of the questions on the test must be at a comprehension level that is low enough for the students to read independently. Otherwise, the test may be measuring the students' reading ability instead of their concept mastery.

Validity can also be affected by preparation. Students need to have been provided with adequate instruction—readings and other assignments—that prepare them for the questions they are asked.

Reliability

Test reliability is also a major concern. The teacher must ask "Is the result of this examination a reliable estimate of what students have gained from their study?" when he or she is determining the reliability of any examination. A test cannot be reliable if it is not valid to begin with; it cannot be reliable if the directions for the test or any part of it are unclear to students. The teacher should explain the directions in advance to ensure that students understand them. The same directions should also appear on the test paper so that students can refer to them when necessary.

Reliability can also be affected by the length of the test and the amount of time allotted for students to complete it. In general, a test will be more reliable if it includes a larger sampling of students' knowledge. This is accomplished by having enough test items and by allowing students sufficient time to complete these items. For example, except for some essay examinations, a test with only a few test items inadequately samples what students may have gained from their work. Of course, the length of a test must be reasonable for the amount of time allowed to complete it. Teacher-prepared examinations should be designed so that all students can complete them without the pressure of time constraints. Only speed and accuracy tests need to be restricted to severe time limits.

Teachers can determine the reliability of the standardized tests they administer by noting the **standard error of measurement (SE),** a statistic that is determined during the standardization process and reported by the publishers in each test manual. The *SE* expresses a range, or band, of error that should be considered in the interpretation of an individual student's test score. For example, suppose a fourth-grade student achieves a grade equivalent score of 4.5 on a test that has an *SE* of 2.3 grades. If an equivalent test were to be administered, the student might achieve a grade equivalent score that is either 2.3 grades lower or 2.3 grades higher than the 4.5 on the original test. The range that the original 4.5 grade equivalent score suggests is a grade equivalent score that is between 2.2 and 6.8. This range of error is considerable, yet typical of that for many standardized tests.

A relatively simple statistic, the **split-half correlation,** can be computed for informal tests. Determining this statistic involves three steps. First, while marking the test results, the teacher must keep an account of the number of students who passed each item on the test.

Example (25 Students)

Item Number	Number Passed
1	22
2	19
3	21
4	15
5	24
6	17
7	19
8	25
9	12
10	26

Second, the test is split in half between the odd-numbered and even-numbered items. The total number of students who passed the odd-numbered items and the total number who passed the even-numbered items are computed. In the example, the total number of students passing the odd-numbered items is 98, and 102 students passed the even-numbered items. The third step is to divide the smaller (odd total) by the larger (even total) to determine the reliability coefficient, a percentage. For the example test, the result is about .96, or 96%. The percentage indicates an estimate of the extent to which the teacher can rely on each students' final score as an accurate indicator of the students' mastery of the test content.

During the administration of an examination, two additional factors can affect the results of the examination: guessing and cheating. Although guessing may be thought to be a serious concern, it usually is not. Consider a multiple-choice test with four answer choices. If a student has no idea which of the four choices is correct and guesses wildly, the chance of choosing the right answer is only 25 percent. If 10 questions are on the test, the chance of guessing all answers correctly is a negligible 2.5 percent. Most tests have more than 10 items, and most students try to the best of their ability to determine the correct response to each question. Therefore, guessing is probably not a serious problem affecting the reliability of most test results.

Several precautions will help to minimize the possibility of cheating during the administration of an examination. Teachers should ensure that the test is given in an atmosphere that is businesslike. Students need adequate seating with enough space between their desks. Teachers should supervise their examinations because students need the security of knowing that their teacher is available to respond to questions. Directions should be reviewed carefully with students before the test begins, even though the directions are included on the test papers. Some tests include several pages. Students should be asked to check that they have the entire test in case a page was missed during collation.

To ensure greater test reliability, teachers should use clear and unambiguous language to construct test items. Also, the questions should be constructed so as to discriminate accurately between students who know and those who do not know the information required for a correct response.

Construction of Reliable Test Items

The test items that teachers prepare fall into two general categories:

1. **Supply-type items:**   Students provide the answers, as in sentence completion, fill-in, short answer, and essay items.
2. **Objective-type items:**   Students are provided with choices from which to select their responses, as in true–false, multiple-choice, and matching formats.

To ensure greater validity and reliability, teachers must take special care when preparing test items of both types. By following several general guidelines for writing items in the various formats, teachers can help to ensure that their questions are clear and that each test item addresses the objectives for which the test is being designed.

Nearly every educational psychology textbook and some generic methods texts include information on test-item construction. Thorough explanations can be found in books by Cangelosi (1990); Cooper (2003); Dembo (1994); Hoy (2003); Meisels, Harrington, McMahon, Dichtelmiller, and Jablon (2001); and Orlich et al. (2001). An Internet search for "constructing test items" will yield a list of many other texts and excellent checklists for preparing test items in different formats. Following are some suggestions for test-item construction with examples for preparing items in each testing format. Using these simple guidelines can help to ensure better validity and reliability of an examination.

Short answer or fill-in item suggestions:

- Maintain uniformity in the length of all blanks on a completion test to avoid suggesting the length of different words. Make all blanks long enough for the longest answer.

- Include only one blank per test item to avoid the possibility that, in addition to testing for its intended objective, the test will be testing for **closure** (the ability to bridge gaps left in a sentence and to expand on the author's message) or for the ability to use context clues during reading.

Examples

(Poor)   A _____ is used in a house to help prevent the _____ of the electrical wiring.

(Better)   The overheating of electrical wiring in a house may be prevented if _____ are installed.

- Use one blank, even for names with two words, such as *Los Angeles* and *New York*. Two separate lines may suggest the correct answer.
- Construct the test item so that the blank appears either at or near the end of the statement. If the blank appears early in the sentence, students will need to rely heavily on closure and context clues to determine the meaning of the needed word. Unless the test is meant to determine the student's ability to use context clues, locate the blank near the end of the statement.

Examples

(Poor)   _____ is the most important product in Brazil.

(Better)   The most important product in Brazil is _____.

- Include a word or phrase that indicates the category to which the answer must belong. For example, if a statement calls for the name of a country, the student will know that unless a country is named, the answer cannot be correct. Giving a direct indication of the kind of information that must be included in the blank for a fill-in response helps to lessen ambiguity and the possibility of multiple correct answers.

Examples

(Poor)   When did the English first arrive in North America? _____

(Better)   In what year did the English first arrive in North America? _____

- Avoid copying material directly from sources that students have used for their information. Quoting text material for an informal test not only models plagiarism but also encourages students to memorize the text instead of developing genuine concept comprehension.
- Check all test items on a test to determine if one of the questions gives students an answer to another item.
- Always use clear syntax, correct grammar, and accurate punctuation when writing test items.

Essay item suggestions:

- Phrase essay questions so that they clearly indicate the task. Be precise about what and how much information is expected in the response.

- When a test includes several essay items, suggest time allotments for each item to help students budget their time.

- In general, do not offer choices on essay examinations. If each essay item addresses an important objective, little reason exists to tell students that only "three of five" items need to be answered. Any item that is not important should not be included on the exam. However, when the purpose of the test is to determine whether students can write a well-developed essay, students may be given a choice of topics.

- Develop grading criteria—or rubrics—before administering the test. Prepare an outline of what is expected for a complete answer to each essay question and decide how to weight each essay item before beginning the grading process.

- Use a consistent scoring method: rubrics, a rating scale, rubrics combined with a rating scale, or holistic scoring. Teachers who use **holistic scoring** assign a single numerical score, often using a 10-point scale, in assessing the overall quality of a work. Establish a policy for handling other factors, such as any irrelevant information that students include, and the mechanics of spelling, handwriting, punctuation, grammar, and syntax.

- Read all students' responses to one essay question before reading others; that is, read all student responses to the first essay question, then continue to read all responses to the second, and so on. Comparing all responses to the same essay question may help you to maintain a more even scoring of the responses, especially when you are using a holistic grading method.

Examples

(Poor)   Discuss what you have learned about the British Parliament and the United States Congress.

(Better)   Describe two major differences and one similarity between the British Parliament and the United States Congress.

True–false item suggestions:

- Keep the wording succinct and clear in true–false items.

- Avoid broad statements and words, such as *always, never, all, may, seldom, usually,* and so on.

- Use negatives sparingly at all grade levels. However, when you do use them, always draw attention to them with underlining, italics, or bold type. Completely avoid negatives in examinations for children in the primary grades because very young children have considerable difficulty with reversals in thought.

- Avoid ambiguity in the statement. A true–false item should be unequivocally true or false.
- Keep the items as uniform in length as possible.
- Try to balance the numbers of true and false items. When an overbalance of either exists, students may be led to believe they must have answered some questions incorrectly.

Examples

(Poor)   _____ Birds eat more than mammals.

_____ Martha and George Washington had two children.

(Better)   _____ Considering body weight, birds eat more than mammals do.

_____ Martha and George Washington raised two children.

Multiple-choice item suggestions:

- A multiple-choice test item comprises two parts: a stem and several answer choices. The stem should present enough information so that the answer choices can be relatively short. If students have to read lengthy choices after reading the stem, the questions may actually be testing students' short-term memory. Unless this is the purpose of the test, this memory factor may interfere with the validity of the item.
- Use negatives sparingly, and highlight them if they are used. Avoid negatives in tests for children in the primary grades.
- Avoid determiners, such as *all*, *some*, *often*, *usually*, and so on.
- Use special alternatives such as *all of the above* and *none of the above* sparingly.
- Try to keep the answer choices similar in length to avoid suggesting that any particular answer is the correct one.
- Make sure that all the answer choices are somewhat feasible while ensuring that only one correct answer exists.
- Ensure that all answer choices are grammatically consistent with the stem of the item.

Poor Example

An example of:

A. an animal that is a mollusk is a whale.

B. an animal that is a mollusk is a clam.

C. an animal that is a mollusk is a crab.

D. an animal that is a mollusk is a lobster.

Better Example

An example of a mollusk is a:

A. whale.

B. clam.

C. crab.

D. lobster.

Matching items suggestions:

- Each matching item comprises a set of premises and response choices listed in two columns. The matching set should be relatively short. Requiring students to search through too many choices for an answer may test their short-term memory as well as their knowledge of the material for which the test is intended. This will lower the validity of the test. Try to limit any matching set to seven or fewer premises. Prepare more than one matching set if more items need to be tested.

- The material being tested in a single matching set should be as homogeneous as possible. For example, if the testing is about simple machines, avoid other topics.

- Include as much material in the premises as needed, but keep the length of response choices relatively short to avoid testing short-term memory instead of content.

- Include one or two extra response choices to avoid the certainty that a student who has one answer wrong will have another wrong.

- Place the entire matching set on one page.

Poor Example

Column A	Column B
_____ 1. Thermometer	A. An instrument that measures humidity
_____ 2. Barometer	B. An instrument that measures rainfall
_____ 3. Wind vane	C. An instrument that measures wind direction
_____ 4. Rain gauge	D. An instrument that measures air pressure
_____ 5. Hygrometer	E. An instrument that measures temperature

Better Example

Column A

_____ 1. An instrument that measures wind direction

_____ 2. An instrument that measures temperature

_____ 3. An instrument that measures humidity

_____ 4. An instrument that measures rainfall

_____ 5. An instrument that measures air pressure

Column B

A. Thermometer
B. Barometer
C. Wind vane
D. Humidifier
E. Hygrometer
F. Telemeter
G. Rain gauge

▓ CONCLUSION

Traditionally, examinations and quizzes have been used more than any other assessment tool. However, most paper-and-pencil tests are limited to assessing students' verbal and logical–mathematical achievement. To limit evaluation to formal and informal tests fails to recognize the value of the evaluation *process* for both students and teachers (Wexler-Sherman, Gardner, & Feldman, 1988), and it leaves the responsibility for evaluation solely on the shoulders of teachers, with students playing a passive role (Johnston, 1987).

As mentioned in chapter 3, behaviorally stated instructional objectives have also been used for many years in lesson and activity plans. Behavioral objectives are useful for short-term purposes in lesson planning and for measuring progress in the development of specific skills. Although using behavioral objectives can help in determining whether a lesson has been effective in some ways, teachers should still consider them as only a small part in the overall assessment process.

If we consider the importance of assessing individual student progress in domains other than linguistic and logical–mathematical, neither examinations nor behavioral objectives are totally adequate. For example, a teacher may believe that interdisciplinary unit activities should foster cooperation and help promote interpersonal skills among students. To evaluate progress in these areas, the teacher must directly observe students. Using a test would not be a logical choice. By the same token, testing is not helpful for determining students' interests and attitudes or feelings about their progress. Realistically, examinations rarely invite students to participate in evaluating their own work. There is an option, however: authentic assessment.

░ ACTIVITIES

1. Not all student products are easy to assess fairly and consistently. When rubrics are used, art projects, oral reports, and written reports can be assessed more consistently. Prepare a set of rubrics to use in the assessment of one or two of such student products.

2. Visit an elementary or a middle school teacher. Ask what topics his or her students are currently studying. Select one topic, and gather information on this topic. Use only the books and other materials that are available to the students in the class. Prepare a list of five behavioral objectives or essential questions (see chapter 3) for the concepts students would have access to in the study. Next, prepare at least five test items designed to test students' mastery of these concepts. Try to use at least three of the formats reviewed in this chapter when preparing the test items. Finally, check the items to determine whether they follow the guidelines for the formats of your questions.

3. Review the information and suggestions provided in this chapter for preparing test items in different formats. Locate an informal, teacher-made test that has been given to students in an elementary or a middle school. Study each item on the test to determine whether the item reflects the criteria outlined in this chapter for its particular format.

░ REFERENCES

Borich, G. D. (2004). *Effective teaching methods* (5th ed.). Upper Saddle River, NJ: Merrill/Prentice Hall.

Cangelosi, J. S. (1990). *Designing tests for evaluating student achievement.* New York: Longman.

Charbonneau, M. P., & Reider, B. E. (1995). *The integrated elementary classroom: A developmental model of education for the 21st century.* Needham Heights, MA: Allyn & Bacon.

Chicago Public Schools. (2000). *The rubric bank.* Retrieved from http://intranet.cps.k12.il.us/Assessments/Ideas_and_Rubrics/Rubric_Bank/rubric_bank.html

Cooper, J. M. (2003). *Classroom teaching skills* (7th ed.). Boston: Houghton Mifflin.

Darling-Hammond, L. (1994). Setting standards for students: The case for authentic assessment. *The Educational Forum, 59*(1), 14–21.

Darling-Hammond, L., Ancess, J., & Falk, B. (1995). *Authentic assessment in action: Studies of schools and students at work.* New York: Teachers College Press.

Dembo, M. H. (1994). *Applying educational psychology in the classroom* (5th ed.). New York: Longman.

Ellis, A. K. (2002). *Teaching and learning elementary social studies* (7th ed.). Boston: Allyn & Bacon.

Engel, B. S. (1994). Portfolio assessment and the new paradigm: New instruments and new places. *The Educational Forum, 59*(1), 22–27.

Goodrich, H. (1997). Understanding rubrics. *Educational Leadership, 54*(4), 14–17.

Grosvenor, L. (1993). *Student portfolios.* Washington, DC: National Education Association.

Guskey, T. R. (2003). How classroom assessments improve learning. *Educational Leadership, 60*(5), 6–11.

Hoy, A. W. (2003). *Educational psychology.* Boston: Allyn & Bacon.

Johnston, P. (1987). Teachers as evaluation experts. *The Reading Teacher, 40,* 744–748.

Johnston, P. H. (1992). *Constructive evaluation of literate activity.* White Plains, NY: Longman.

Lescher, M. L. (1995). *Portfolios: Assessing learning in the primary grades.* Washington, DC: National Education Association.

Meisels, S. J., Harrington, H. L., McMahon, P., Dichtelmiller, M. L., & Jablon, J. R. (2001). *Thinking like a teacher.* Boston: Allyn & Bacon.

O'Neil, J. (1993, September). The promise of portfolios. *Update, 35*(7), 1–5.

Orlich, D. C., Harder, R. J., Callahan, R. C., & Gibson, H. W. (2001). *Teaching strategies: A guide to better instruction* (6th ed.). Boston: Houghton Mifflin.

Pappas, C. C., Kiefer, B. Z., & Levstik, L. S. (1999). *An integrated language perspective in the elementary school* (3rd ed.) New York: Longman.

Porcaro, J. J., & Johnson, K. G. (2003, Winter). Building a whole-language writing program. *Kappa Delta Pi Record, 39*(2), 74–79.

Schrock, K. (2004). Teacher helpers: Assessment & rubric information. In *Kathy Schrock's guide for educators.* Retrieved from http://school.discovery.com/schrockguide/assess.html

Shores, E. F., & Grace, C. (1998). *The portfolio book: A step-by-step guide for teachers.* Beltsville, MD: Gryphon House.

Sternberg, R. J. (1999). Ability and expertise. *American Educator, 23*(1), 10–13ff.

Viadero, D. (1995, April 5). Even as popularity soars, portfolios encounter roadblocks. *Education Week,* pp. 8–9.

Wasserstein, P. (1994, Fall). To do or not to do portfolios: That is the question. *Kappa Delta Pi Record, 31*(1), 12–15.

Wexler-Sherman, C., Gardner, H., & Feldman, D. H. (1988). A pluralistic view of early assessment: The project spectrum approach. *Theory Into Practice, 27,* 77–83.

▩ SUGGESTED READINGS

The supplemental readings listed next provide additional background material on assessment as discussed in this chapter.

Arter, J. A., & McTighe, J. (2001). *Scoring rubrics in the classroom: Using performance criteria for assessing and improving student performance.* Thousand Oaks, CA: Corwin.

Eby, J. W., & Martin, D. B. (2001). *Reflective planning, teaching, and evaluation: K–12* (3rd ed.). Upper Saddle River, NJ: Merrill/Prentice Hall.

Jacobs, H. H. (1997). *Mapping the big picture: Integrating curriculum and assessment, K–12.* Alexandria, VA: Association for Supervision and Curriculum Development.

Popham, W. J. (2002). *Classroom assessment: What teachers need to know* (3rd ed.). Boston: Allyn & Bacon.

5

Designing Interdisciplinary Units

▓ OVERVIEW

This chapter covers an eight-step procedure for planning interdisciplinary units for students at all grade levels. Examples are provided for each step in the procedure.

The focus of this chapter is on the following:

- An introduction to interdisciplinary unit planning and a practical design that may be especially helpful for teachers who are learning to plan interdisciplinary units
- The relationship of child development in early and middle childhood to the design of interdisciplinary units of study
- A review of two developmentally appropriate methods for selecting topics for interdisciplinary studies
- An outline for a complete interdisciplinary unit plan
- A description of eight steps in the unit planning process, along with explanations and examples at each step for designing an interdisciplinary unit called *Spring* for children in second grade

---

Interdisciplinary units of study can be used in teaching at all levels of the elementary school and the middle school. As students mature, their changing developmental abilities allow them to undertake studies that are increasingly sophisticated. Therefore, teachers or teaching teams can use another type of interdisciplinary unit that involves more advanced research opportunities—the research-oriented interdisciplinary unit—for these students. This type of interdisciplinary unit may occasionally be planned for some students in upper primary and intermediate classes. However, its design is most appropriate for students in the upper elementary grades and middle school, who are usually more experienced and proficient in their research skills and who can read for information independently.

▓ INTRODUCTION TO INTERDISCIPLINARY UNIT PLANNING

Planning interdisciplinary units requires considerable time and skill. Poorly planned units generally resemble an assortment of loosely connected lessons that lack a central topic. Jacobs (1989) referred to this kind of unit planning as the **potpourri approach.** Teachers are likely to be disappointed with the results of units that are unfocused; they may even be discouraged from undertaking interdisciplinary studies as a result.

In addition to requiring unit planning skills, interdisciplinary units make use of every instructional mode: working with the whole class, small cooperative groups, and individuals. Therefore, developing techniques for working with each of these modes is important.

When teachers begin to plan and teach interdisciplinary units, two questions usually arise: Where can I find ideas for the topics to be taught at my grade level? and How can I design and develop the unit plan?

Selecting Interdisciplinary Topics

Teachers who are new to the interdisciplinary method will want to know how to select suitable topics, sometimes referred to as **themes,** for their units. Teachers may find useful two developmentally based approaches to this task that publishers of elementary textbooks follow and that are evident in state curriculum guides and lists of learning standards.

In the first approach, the **expanding environments**—or **widening horizons— approach,** topics are ordered according to students' developmental levels. Young children initially study topics that are within their personal experience and about which they have considerable prior knowledge. In the primary grades—for example, in social studies—topics begin with the study of self and family; later, children study their school and neighborhood. Older students study regions, states, nations, and cultures in the Eastern and Western Hemispheres. To use the widening horizons approach in selecting social topics for a particular grade level, teachers can usually rely on those listed in state curriculum guides and textbooks in science, social studies, and other disciplines.

Some educators have criticized the exclusive use of the widening horizons approach for selection of topics for interdisciplinary units. For example, Ravich (1988) contended that by following the widening horizons approach, teachers limit students to simple, familiar topics that may fail to challenge or motivate them. This concern is reasonable today when, even before they enter school, many young children are exposed to a wide range of information through the television and other media. However, if teachers keep this possible limitation in mind when selecting their topics, the widening horizons approach can still provide a useful general guide.

The second approach to selecting topics involves the development of concepts. In Bruner's (1963) **spiral curriculum,** children may be exposed to the same concepts and basic ideas at each grade level. Bruner (1963) stated, "A curriculum as it develops should revisit these basic ideas repeatedly, building upon them until the student has grasped the full formal apparatus that goes with them" (p. 13). Each year, new and more complex aspects of these concepts and ideas are introduced as children become developmentally ready to understand them. For example, the concept of *community* can be taught at each grade. As children become intellectually ready, they are exposed to more sophisticated meanings of this concept. Bruner's approach is compatible with and complements the expanding environments approach. Whereas the latter approach centers on the selection of topics, the spiral curriculum approach involves developing fundamental key concepts.

Both the expanding environments approach and the spiral curriculum approach to the selection of topics for different grade levels take important child development characteristics into consideration. In addition to students' developmental abilities, other factors are important in the selection of topics—factors such as their academic skills, especially skills in reading, writing, and research. Students' interests and their ability to work together also need to be kept in mind.

Several practical matters also influence the selection process. The availability of adequate supplies of appropriate learning resource materials for a topic is critical. In addition to books, other media resources should be used to investigate most topics. These resources include relevant children's magazines, newspapers, computer software, teacher-prepared presentations, DVD and videotape programs, films, filmstrips, and networking facilities. Teachers must ensure that their students have the equipment, technology, and materials needed for related research, constructions, art projects, and science experiments. A detailed description of the thinking process that a group of teachers may experience as they work together to select a unit topic is given in Perkins's interesting and informative scenario on this important task (Jacobs, 1989, pp. 67–76).

Once a topic is chosen, the teacher must decide on the type of unit plan to be designed. The planning of interdisciplinary units is explained in this chapter, and research-oriented interdisciplinary units are discussed in chapter 6. Each of the two unit types has attributes tailored to students' having different developmental and academic skills abilities. Therefore, once the topic is selected, the teacher must determine which type of plan is more appropriate for the topic and the students for whom the study is being planned. The remainder of this chapter provides a description of the first type—the interdisciplinary unit—and outlines an eight-step process that can be used to plan it.

Designing the Interdisciplinary Unit Plan

Most teaching methods textbooks include unit plan outlines. However, perusal of these textbooks, including books on the teaching of science and social studies, reveals that, among the different authors, no consensus exists about a unit plan format. For example, the emphasis in one text may be on unit objectives, another may mainly list resources, and still another may suggest that units are simply a collection of lesson plans.

The unit plan format recommended in this book is primarily a description of ideas for possible lessons and activities related to a central topic to be studied by a group of students. This design is similar to the topic studies described by Charbonneau and Reider (1995) and the unit plan model discussed in Jacobs's text (1989). Each time the same unit is retaught, complete plans for the lessons and activities that are used can be added to the initial unit plan design. Thus, the unit plan is perceived as a dynamic, constantly changing, ever-developing record.

Whenever a teacher or a teaching team designs an *initial* unit plan—one not taught before—they need not write detailed plans for all the lessons and activities suggested in the plan. The reason for delaying the detailed planning of most lessons is simply to conserve a teacher's planning time. Often, after the unit is introduced, the teacher may decide that some lesson or activity ideas are not appropriate for a particular group of students. Even though complete lesson plans need not be prepared initially, brief descriptions of these lessons or activities should be included in the unit plan. Such descriptions include the general idea and purpose of each lesson or activity idea. The descriptions should provide just enough information about the idea so that the teacher can prepare more complete lesson and activity plans if and when they are needed as the unit progresses.

At first, only one lesson or activity, the one that will introduce the unit, needs to be prepared in detail: the introductory lesson. In this lesson, students will begin responding to the unit topic, and their special interests and needs will begin to surface. Students' reactions during the first lesson can facilitate the teacher's deciding which possible lesson and activity ideas in the unit plan are most appropriate to include as the study progresses. Then, only the lessons and activities selected to be taught will need to be planned completely.

Therefore, in its initial design, an interdisciplinary unit plan needs to have only one fully developed lesson plan—the one that will be used to introduce the unit. Nevertheless, planning an introductory lesson should follow the same guidelines that are needed for designing lessons or activities for other purposes. These guidelines were discussed in chapters 2 and 3.

■ DESIGN OF INTERDISCIPLINARY UNITS FOR EARLY CHILDHOOD

Piaget (1955, 1966, 1970, 1973, 1974, 1976) often stressed the importance of recognizing that at all age levels children's thinking characteristics have a significant effect on the kinds of academic work that they can do. Piaget's research also led him to conclude that the thinking and reasoning of children in the primary grades was dominated by **preoperational thought**—a pattern of thinking that is egocentric, centered, irreversible, and nontransformational (Phillips, 1981; Piaget & Inhelder, 1969). For many years, Piaget's unchallenged research led us to believe that all young children were highly egocentric and that their thinking was extremely centered during the early childhood years.

Since Piaget completed his work, contemporary researchers (often referred to as **neo-Piagetian** and **post-Piagetian** researchers) found that Piaget had underestimated the abilities of children in the preschool and early elementary years (Flavell, 1985). These researchers found young children to be less egocentric than Piaget believed. Also, Piaget never considered the impact of social interaction as seriously as Vygotsky (1986) and the post-Piagetians did. Several post-Piagetians have been cited in support of interdisciplinary instruction (Bruner, 1990; Case, 1985; Checkley, 1997; Forman, Minick, & Stone, 1993; Gardner, 1991, 1993; Wertsch, 1985).

Although Piaget's work can still provide us with important information about children's intellectual development, one fact is clear: Contrary to Piaget's belief, children's intellectual development appears to proceed continuously, and their cognitive development is influenced considerably by their culture and by instruction. Santrock (2003) affirmed this notion: "Most contemporary developmentalists agree that children's cognitive development is not as grand stage–like as Piaget thought" (p. 383).

Information is processed, and learners improve steadily in their ability to absorb and store knowledge from their environment (Berk, 2002).

Involving Students in the Unit Planning Process

Although the teacher takes the major responsibility for planning interdisciplinary units for students at all levels, children should always be offered opportunities to participate in the design of their studies and to have their questions, suggestions, and special interests incorporated as an interdisciplinary unit develops. Once a topic is selected, the teacher guides the planning process with the students so that several disciplines are integrated in the study. Students are then helped to note the relationships of the various disciplines to the central topic of their unit. Although the teacher's long-term goal is to help the students become independent in the planning process of their studies, the teacher should proceed slowly until the children have developed adequate skill in doing so. Gardner (1995) emphasized this idea:

> The educator of the future needs to walk a fine line—always encouraging the youngster to stretch, praising her when she succeeds, but equally important, providing support and a non-condemnatory interpretative framework when things do not go well. Eventually, aspiring creators can supply much of this support, scaffolding and interpreting framework for themselves. (p. 15)

In early childhood, children's perceptions may be influenced by some of the traditional Piagetian characteristics, such as having difficulty reversing thought patterns and following transformations. Their sense of time, history, and relationships develops slowly, and some lingering egocentricity may interfere with their participation in cooperative group activities (Flavell, 1985; Furth, 1971; Wadsworth, 1996). As they mature, students in the upper elementary grades and middle school are not limited in these ways.

Encouraging Students to Develop a Variety of Abilities

All children are unique in their mental makeup, learning styles, and abilities. Gardner's (1993) proposition that "people have different cognitive strengths and contrasting cognitive styles" (p. 6) suggests that children should have opportunities to develop simultaneously in more than one cognitive area. Therefore, if teachers consider children's multiple intelligences, young children should be encouraged to undertake inquiries and to use reporting methods that do not always exclusively depend on their linguistic ability. Using music, art media, movement, natural exploration, and thoughtful questioning to investigate and to demonstrate mastery of concepts can supplement or even replace traditional book learning at times.

For many young children, inquiries that rely exclusively on reading can be difficult, mainly because relatively few resources are available on some topics for them to read independently. Instead, early childhood classrooms should offer an environment with a rich and abundant supply of materials and learning activities, similar to the

Montessori *prepared environment*, a major component of the Montessori method (Lillard, 1972; Montessori, 1964). This type of environment allows children to become active participants in their learning (NCSS Task Force, 1989) and to become increasingly more involved with the learning materials and activities in the environment (Standing, 1957). When young children are developing concepts, activities involving hands-on learning are more helpful to them than are abstract materials, which generally rely on linguistic and mathematical abilities. Providing concrete opportunities is especially important for the inclusion of children with special needs.

Children who have specific talents—artistic, musical, physical, linguistic, mathematical, and so on—should be challenged to undertake forms of inquiry that use their special abilities. In all grades, children who can read for information and prepare written reports should be encouraged to do so. Some students, even in the lower elementary grades, may also be able to complete research-oriented interdisciplinary studies similar to those described in chapter 6 as an alternative. As an interdisciplinary unit reaches its conclusion, a culminating activity should be planned to help the students summarize the major concepts they gained from their study.

▓ An Interdisciplinary Unit Plan Outline

The eight-step procedure explained and illustrated subsequently in this chapter provides the information needed for a teacher to design an interdisciplinary unit plan. Most unit plan formats include learning standards, objectives, procedures to be followed, important materials, and evaluation techniques to be used for assessment. Some include essential questions. Figure 5.1 shows an outline for an interdisciplinary unit plan, with headings for each major section. This basic outline can be used to design interdisciplinary unit plans for students at all grade levels: primary, upper elementary, and middle school. The planning task and the specific kinds of information to be included under each heading in the unit plan outline are as follows.

Topic

State the topic of the unit.

Title

The title of a unit can be the same as the topic being studied. However, often a more interesting idea for the unit title can be used. List any title suggestions and possible ways to involve students in deciding on a title for their unit.

Level

State the grade or grades for which the unit is intended. Although only the grade level needs to appear in this section, you should consider the students' background and readiness for the unit, their social and developmental characteristics, and their academic abilities when you are making decisions about the appropriateness of any unit topic.

FIGURE 5.1
An interdisciplinary unit plan outline.

Topic:
Title:
Level:
Estimated Unit Length:
Learning Standards:
General Objectives:
Essential Questions:
Web Design of the Unit:
Introductory Lesson Plan:
    Topic:
    Level:
    Estimated Time:
    Learning Standards:
    General Objectives:
    Essential Questions:
    Behavioral Objectives (or Assessment Techniques):
    Procedure:
    Materials:
Descriptions of Lessons and Activities:
Unit Assessment Methods and Techniques:
Unit Materials:

Estimated Unit Length

Estimate the amount of time needed to teach the unit. Units for early childhood may range from a few days to one or more weeks. In the upper elementary grades, most interdisciplinary studies take at least 3 or 4 weeks; many require more time.

Learning Standards

Learning standards are gleaned from lists at the national, state, and local levels. Include the standards that the interdisciplinary unit addresses in significant ways.

General Objectives

In addition to important learning standards, general objectives can be listed that reveal other content, concepts, skills, affective goals, and learning processes that you hope to promote throughout the study with a specific group of students.

Essential Questions

Essential questions that define the main objectives of the study can be listed to guide unit development. In this section, state only the major questions. More specific essential questions will be included in the lesson and activity plans as the unit develops.

Web Design of the Unit

Design a **web**—a detailed graphic outline—that suggests possible lessons, interdisciplinary activities, and skills to be taught during the unit. Use interconnecting lines to show ways in which these ideas relate to the various disciplines and to one another. The web design should indicate that provisions have been made for students' differing cognitive strengths, multiple intelligences, and working and learning styles. An optional introductory statement may accompany the web design to provide other teachers with a rationale for teaching the unit, to show the major concepts the unit is intended to develop, and to indicate that the unit is interdisciplinary.

Introductory Lesson Plan

The following lesson plan outline is used to plan the introductory lesson for the unit. This lesson is the first taught in the new unit. The same lesson plan outline can be used for other lessons and unit activities. Other lesson planning formats can also be substituted, such as those outlined by Ellis (2002), Kauchak and Eggen (2003), and Roberts and Kellough (2004); the MI (multiple intelligences) lesson plan (Armstrong, 2000); or the "new style" lesson plan recommended by McNeil and Wiles (1990).

Topic:

State the unit topic and the main topic of the lesson.

Level: State the age levels or grades for which the lesson is designed.

Estimated Time: Estimate the amount of time needed for the lesson or activity.

Learning Standards: Include one or more learning standards from national, state, or local sources that the lesson will address.

General Objectives: List one or more general objectives that the lesson will help to develop for a specific student group.

Essential Questions: List the main question or questions that suggest the main purpose or purposes of the introductory lesson. Many lessons address only one major question. Any essential questions that are listed should be capable of being assessed in the lesson.

Behavioral Objectives (or Assessment Techniques): State the specific objectives that need to be assessed in the procedure of the lesson. Optionally, you may prefer to eliminate behavioral objective statements and list the assessment techniques that will be used to assess the lesson.

Procedure: Prepare a sequential list of steps detailing the procedure for the lesson. Although using a list is recommended, you may prefer to write the procedure in paragraph form. Consider students' individual strengths and limitations with regard to their academic skills and MIs. Attend to the critical elements outlined in chapter 3 when planning the procedure of the lesson.

Materials:

List the principal materials needed for the lesson.

Descriptions of Lessons and Activities

In this section of the unit plan, you expand on the idea suggestions found in the unit plan web design. Write a paragraph describing each lesson and activity idea listed in the web design. Add details that may affect the plan that were not in the web design description because of space limitations. For example, include special student information and a statement to explain the main purposes for including it in the unit. Finally, list in brackets the multiple intelligence areas the lesson or activity mainly addresses.

Unit Assessment Methods and Techniques

The behavioral objectives or assessment techniques stated in individual lessons and activities will help to assess the effectiveness of these lessons and activities. However, other, more comprehensive measures are often used for the unit as a whole. List the assessment methods, including authentic techniques, examinations, and observations, that will be used in the overall unit assessment.

Unit Materials

List major materials needed for the unit. Two lists should be prepared: (a) one to be used with students and (b) one that provides background resources for the teacher. Addresses of Internet resources, lists of teacher-prepared computer presentations, computer software, videotaped programs, films, filmstrips, and other media can be included for reference. Some materials rapidly become outdated, and new ones may become available. Therefore, when the unit is first planned, a simple list indicating the types of texts, trade books, and other materials will suffice until the unit is under way.

■ AN EIGHT-STEP PROCEDURE FOR DESIGNING AN INTERDISCIPLINARY UNIT PLAN

Interdisciplinary units are appropriate for students at all elementary and middle school grade levels. Primary-grade teachers find interdisciplinary units especially well suited to the developmental characteristics and academic abilities of their young children. Teachers of students in the upper elementary grades and middle school can teach interdisciplinary units, or they can use a modification of the interdisciplinary design that involves considerably more reading-related research activities: a research-oriented interdisciplinary unit. (The design of a research-oriented interdisciplinary unit plan and the steps involved in developing it are covered in chapter 6.)

The following eight-step procedure details how to develop material needed for a complete interdisciplinary unit plan. Each step is illustrated with examples. This planning procedure is intended for preservice and in-service teachers who are learning to design interdisciplinary units. The process outlined in this chapter is used to develop an initial unit plan, one that has never been taught. An initial unit plan will become more complete with time; it should be modified and updated each time it is taught to a new group of students.

One recommendation is that individuals who have not previously studied interdisciplinary unit planning follow each step in the sequence outlined in this chapter. Later, once the eight-step process is mastered, it can easily be modified to suit the teacher's personal teaching style and planning needs. The sequence presented conforms closely to conventional practice, with the following exceptions: (a) the step for listing learning standards and general objectives of the unit appears later in the sequence instead of being at the beginning of the process, and (b) in the introductory lesson plan, writing formal (behavioral) objectives is placed after designing the procedure in lessons and activities.

A reason exists for these changes in sequence. Traditionally, teachers have been taught to begin planning by stating their objectives and then to plan a procedure to meet these objectives. However, beginning the planning process with formal standards and objective statements may inhibit some teachers' natural creativity. In fact, the entire planning process may become regimented by these standards and objectives.

As long as the purposes for teaching the unit are considered at the outset, the more formal, behaviorally stated objectives for the lesson can be delayed until later in the planning process. Therefore, the actual writing of the unit learning standards, general objectives, and behavioral objectives for the initial lesson plan appears later in the planning process in this eight-step procedure than in conventional practice. Teachers who prefer to write their behavioral objectives before any other planning step should do so, so long as their creativity in planning the procedure is not restricted.

Although standards and objectives statements do not have to be written before planning a procedure, the teacher should have some potential standards and objectives in mind for the unit before beginning to plan. Some of these objectives may be to develop concepts, provide students with opportunities to practice the learning processes, and help students gain further insights about the different ways of knowing associated with the various academic disciplines.

After the teacher selects a topic and has some learning standards and objectives in mind, the eight-step process can begin. Several of the eight steps listed next can be completed quickly; two require more time.

1. Consider the students' developmental abilities, cognitive strengths and limitations, learning and working styles, knowledge, and experiential background for the topic to be studied.

2. Brainstorm for possible procedures—the lessons and activities that will address the different disciplines and students' MIs. Prepare a graphic web design, showing

the basic ideas for teaching skills and other lessons, field trips, science inquiries and experiments, research, and related activities.

3. Prepare a complete plan for the introductory lesson or activity that will be used to introduce the unit.

4. Write brief descriptions of other lessons and activities. (The descriptions substitute, temporarily, for complete plans that can be developed later if the ideas are used once the unit begins.)

5. List the learning standards, general objectives, and essential questions for the unit.

6. List tentative assessment methods and techniques for the unit.

7. List the major unit materials required for students and resource materials for the teacher.

8. Decide on the unit title, or develop a method of involving the students in selecting a title.

If a unit plan is to be shared with other teachers, an introduction, a one-paragraph statement, can be inserted after the unit plan web design. This statement should explain the purpose of the unit and summarize the interdisciplinary procedures suggested in the web design.

Each of the eight steps to be followed during preparation of an interdisciplinary unit plan is explained next, and several examples are provided at each step. As an illustration, material for a primary-level unit plan on the topic *Spring* is generated as the steps are explained. This particular topic was selected because it offers young children a number of opportunities to have direct experiences related to the concept and the processes of "change," an important concept in social studies and science curricula. At each step in the eight-step procedure, only a few examples from the *Spring* unit are shown; however, the complete sample unit plan for the *Spring* topic can be found in the Instructional Resources section at the back of this book.

Step 1: Considering Students' Developmental Abilities and Background for the Topic

Considering students' developmental abilities and background for the topic may be the most important step in the planning process. Whenever successful teachers plan, they attend to the critical match between the cognitive abilities of students in their classes and the new facts, concepts, and generalizations to be developed in their units. Estimating students' thinking and reasoning levels prior to teaching helps to minimize the chance that students will meet with frustration.

Piaget estimated that young children in the primary grades are still primarily egocentric and that their thinking patterns are totally preoperational. However, as mentioned previously, evidence from post-Piagetian research reveals that Piaget may have underestimated these children's cognitive abilities. Even before the second or early third grade, some students develop more sophisticated thinking and reasoning skills, especially if they have bad adequate instruction and opportunities to interact with adults and competent peers.

Nevertheless, students in the primary grades need to have direct, hands-on experiences. These concrete experiences can easily be brought to primary-level interdisciplinary units. Young students can conduct their own inquiries and experiments in science and use concrete materials to develop concepts in many interdisciplinary studies. They develop their spatial abilities by working with art media and producing art to show some of the concepts they are gaining. Typical art activities include completing various projects, painting murals, and working with other art media, such as papier-mâché, play dough, and clay, to form artifacts, dioramas, and other constructions.

Teachers can also provide concrete experiences for young students by organizing field trips, especially to places where the students are permitted to interact physically with real objects as well as to observe. Music is also a pathway to learning for many children, and teachers can offer opportunities to learn about the world through singing, experimenting with simple musical instruments, and listening to recordings. The only techniques that are not defendable, from a developmental view point, include substituting teacher demonstrations and lectures and whole-class, oral reading from textbooks for concrete learning experiences.

Development in the affective and psychomotor domains should also be considered. Knowledge of students' individual feelings, attitudes, temperaments, and the ways in which they interact with one another are valuable when teachers are planning unit activities. Information about motor coordination, health, and physical development is also critical, particularly when a teacher is planning outdoor activities or field trips or is planning to prepare food.

Equally important is to learn as much as possible about the students' experiential and knowledge background for the topic to be studied. New information in a study can be assimilated only if it builds on the students' existing knowledge base. To prevent student frustration and failure, the teacher must ensure that the students have a foundation for any new material they are expected to assimilate.

Knowing students' developmental and academic abilities is more difficult during the early months of a school year than it is later. However, this step cannot be avoided whenever a new unit is being planned, and in the early months, the teacher should estimate as well as he or she can students' readiness for the units he or she plans to teach.

Following is a description of the second-grade class for which the interdisciplinary unit called *Spring* is designed in this chapter. Note that the description includes information about the children's previous study and background for the new unit. Their thinking, academic abilities, social characteristics, special needs, and talents are also outlined.

The students in this heterogeneous group of second graders are mainly preoperational in their thinking and reasoning abilities. They will need concrete experiences whenever possible to help them develop concepts in their unit on spring. Some students in the group can read for information; however, most have not yet developed independent reading levels adequate for many of the books and other resources available on this topic. Socially, members of the class get along well with one another, although occasional conflicts and minor behavioral problems occur. Four students have special needs: one is physically handicapped, and one has been diagnosed with a specific learning disability; another has a special talent for mathematics and another for art. Others have strength in music. This year, the class has completed a unit on the concept of a neighborhood. *The focus of this unit was on learning about the local neighborhood, and their most recent interdisciplinary unit, Our School, expanded their knowledge of concepts related to the neighborhood. It is early spring in an elementary school in the northeastern United States, and many students have indicated their interest in the weather changes they have noticed.*

Step 2: Brainstorming for Possible Procedures and Preparing a Graphic Web Design

Teachers will recognize the brainstorming and web design step as another critical one in planning for unit instruction. Because the intent is to develop *interdisciplinary* plans, designing a web showing anticipated disciplines and activities can help to ensure the interdisciplinarity of a plan. A web design can be prepared by hand or with a computer by using drawing software or drawing tools available in some word-processing programs. Software is also available that is specifically designed for web construction, such as Inspiration, from Inspiration Software, Inc., Portland, Oregon. The design can be charted in a number of ways.

One approach is to construct a **unidirectional web,** one that begins with the topic at the center of the web design. All brainstormed ideas related to the topic are then listed in a radiating pattern outward from the center, as shown in Figure 5.2. Pappas, Kiefer, and Levstik (1999) and Stephens (1974) used variations of this web arrangement for their interdisciplinary web designs.

Unidirectional web designs often fail to designate the disciplines involved in the study. Unless the disciplines are included in the web design, some important disciplines or study areas may be overlooked. As a way to avoid this possibility, once the topic is centered in the web design, names of the major disciplines, as well as the

FIGURE 5.2
A unidirectional "idea" web design.

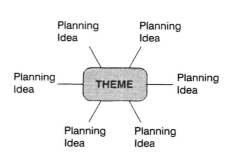

brainstormed ideas, can be pictured surrounding the topic. The design can then be completed with brief statements about the central idea of each brainstormed idea. Additional lines can then be constructed to indicate graphically the teacher's interdisciplinary thinking and to show more of the interrelationships among the activities, lessons, and disciplines involved in the study. As a result of adding the names of disciplines and interconnecting lines, the web design shows branching and becomes a **multidirectional web** design. This multidirectional design has the appearance of a true web. See Figure 5.3 for a multidirectional web design showing both disciplines and planning ideas radiating from the central topic, with connections to one another.

In their books, Charbonneau and Reider (1995) and Jacobs (1989) showed examples similar to the multidirectional construction, and the examples in this book are all multidirectional web designs. These examples accomplish the major purpose of constructing a web design: to help the planner consider the interrelatedness of lessons and activities in the unit and to chart interdisciplinary possibilities for the study. After some experience with either design, teachers will find that each design type—unidirectional and multidirectional—offers some unique advantages and that the designs can easily be modified to suit personal preferences.

Before beginning to brainstorm, the teacher should prepare three lists: (a) a list of disciplines, (b) a list of interdisciplinary areas of concern, and (c) a list of instructional media, strategies, and techniques. The lists will assist in the brainstorming process and

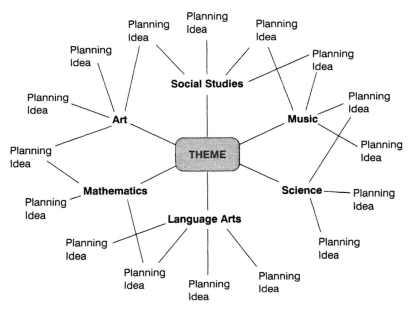

FIGURE 5.3
A multidirectional interdisciplinary unit planning web design.

TABLE 5.1

Brainstorming Lists

Disciplines	Areas of Concern	Media, Strategies, and Techniques
Anthropology	Career education	Art projects
Economics	Citizenship	Audio recordings
Geography	Civics	Charts and graphs
History	Consumerism	Computer programs
Language arts	Current events	Constructions
Listening	Ecology	Demonstrations
Reading	Family living	Dioramas
Speaking	Future studies	DVD programs
Writing	Global studies	Experiments
Mathematics	Health	Field trips
Performing arts	Human behavior	Films
Dance	Human rights	Filmstrips
Drama	Internet	Group discussions
Music	Learning and working styles	Internet resources
Psychology	Multicultural studies	Interviews
Science	Political science	Multimedia
Sociology	Space exploration	Murals
Technology	Substance abuse	Presentations
Visual arts	Values clarification	Reports
		Research
		Skills lessons
		Software
		Surveys
		Time lines
		Video programs

help to ensure that the unit is interdisciplinary and comprehensive. An example of each type of list is shown in Table 5.1.

At first, the inclusion of abstract areas—such as political science, global issues, and future studies—for children in the primary grades may seem questionable. However, young students have a natural curiosity about people in other parts of the world and often express concern about the natural disasters, conflicts, and environmental problems they hear about. Although such students may have some difficulty comprehending global issues, teachers can supply explanations and offer to discuss these issues, using terms that the children can understand. These explanations may help allay the fears that young children sometimes develop about world problems.

In the primary grades, students also enjoy thinking about both the past and the future. All history is in the past, which sometimes makes it a difficult subject for the very young to fully comprehend. Nevertheless, early childhood teachers can include aspects of history in their interdisciplinary units. Today, we know that by selecting a variety of materials—not only textbooks—and by providing opportunities for children to use a variety of media and their individual working styles, we can help them to master some concepts once thought to be beyond their understanding.

In the primary grades, students can usually relate better to historical events and concepts when they are discussed by using terms such as *long ago* and *a long time before we were born*. These are terms with which the students can relate to personally and that have special meaning for them.

The concept of *future* is also problematic for young minds. Still, young students are naturally interested in what the future will be like for them; they can and should be encouraged to think about it.

Both the past and the future become more meaningful when students use learning aids, such as time lines, to plot historical events. Time lines can easily include each student's birth date as a meaningful personal reference point for the historical events that are studied.

Some disciplines and interdisciplinary areas overlap or include similar material. For example, human relations and conduct are components of both psychology and sociology. Human relations and values clarification issues are both included in multicultural studies. Many teachers may believe that other important categories or items should be added to the lists in Table 5.1. These lists can always be modified to meet individual teachers' purposes, special interests, and concerns.

During brainstorming, the web design should be sketched to record the ideas that are generated. As explained previously, the web design is a simple drawing showing the disciplines along with ideas for lessons and activities that will potentially become part of the unit work. It shows at a glance what may be included in the study; lines can also be drawn to indicate ways in which the various disciplines, lessons, and activities relate to one another. The web design serves as a reminder of the brainstormed ideas so that, later, complete lesson and activity plans can be written for the ideas that are needed when the unit is taught.

When the web design is complete, it will also suggest how long the unit may take to complete. An interdisciplinary unit may vary in length from only a few days in primary classes to 4 to 6 weeks or more in the upper elementary grades and middle school. The web design is also useful for making decisions later about the essential questions that the unit will address as well as how the various lessons and activities will need to be sequenced after the unit is introduced.

The design shown in Figure 5.4 shows a few ideas that the teacher has charted as the brainstorming step begins in planning a hypothetical second-grade unit on the topic *Spring*. At this point, the teacher is just beginning to plan, so only a few activities are listed in the web. The main topic is centered, with several disciplines listed around it. So far, the teacher plans to take the students on a walking field trip in the local neighborhood to look for signs of spring. Students will use their observational skills to search for the signs they already know, and their teacher will encourage them to look for signs they have not yet observed. They will record their observations by drawing individual pictures; some of the pictures will later be transferred to a mural. The purpose of the mural is to help the students summarize the signs of spring they observed while on their walk. The teacher will read aloud stories about spring and will give a

FIGURE 5.4
Initial stage in developing the design for an interdisciplinary unit called *Spring*.

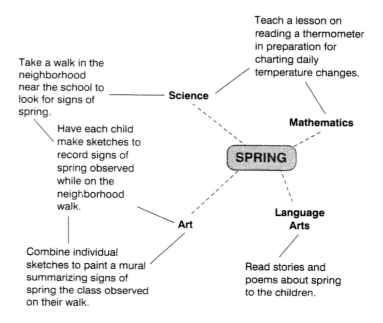

lesson on reading a thermometer. This lesson is in preparation for recording daily temperature changes throughout the unit.

Several academic disciplines and intelligences have been considered at this point in the unit development: making drawings of observations (spatial), having a planning discussion in preparation for the field trip (linguistic; interpersonal), learning to read a thermometer (logical–mathematical), and working together on a mural (interpersonal). Only the teacher's basic idea for each lesson or activity appears in the web design, just enough information to use as a reminder if the idea is used.

The brainstorming step and construction of the web design help to set parameters for the unit and provide an overview of its possible development. As the *Spring* web continues to grow with further brainstorming, more ideas are charted. Interconnecting lines are added to indicate some of the interdisciplinary relationships that the teacher has considered. Interconnecting lines indicate that the teacher has already thought about how some activities are related to more than one discipline or other lessons and activities in the unit. As indicated in Figures 5.5 additions (dotted boxes) to the original web design indicate that the students will keep a record and prepare a graph of daily temperature readings. Additions to the original design also show that the students will listen to musical selections having spring as a topic; the same musical selections will be used for a movement activity. These activities address two other cognitive areas or intelligences. Social studies will include lessons about any spring holidays that occur while the students are involved in the unit. (Additional ideas are included in the web design for the complete *Spring* unit plan in the Instructional Resources section at the back of this book. Also, see other examples of interdisciplinary unit plan web designs on other topics in the Instructional Resources section.)

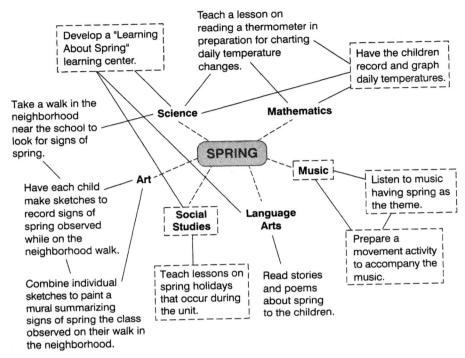

FIGURE 5.5
Additions to the initial design for an interdisciplinary unit called *Spring*.

Step 3: Planning the Introductory Lesson

The design of the first lesson or activity is a key factor in determining the success of a unit. Before beginning to plan the lesson, the teacher should consider the students' background knowledge, academic skill levels, and developmental characteristics as well as the social makeup of the class. The introductory lesson informs students of the unit topic and attempts to engage their interest in the new study. General principles of teaching and learning can help to guide the lesson design. Three especially important principles follow:

1. To be adapted, new information must build the students' existing knowledge base.
2. Students need to construct their own knowledge, using their different cognitive strengths, through direct experiences whenever possible and through opportunities to interact with adults and competent peers.
3. Motivation is stronger if unit activities and lessons capitalize on the students' interests, working styles, and learning styles.

An idea for the first lesson or activity has been selected from the *Spring* web design. The teacher has chosen an idea that appears likely to motivate and engage interest. (If none of the ideas in the web seemed suitable, the teacher would have generated a new one specifically to introduce the unit.) The suggestion for a walk through the neighborhood to look for signs of spring—a field trip—was selected for the first activity in the *Spring* unit.

The field trip activity will take more than one class session; the introductory session or lesson introduces the topic of the new unit and prepares the students for their trip. One learning standard, one general objective, and one essential question are addressed in the lesson:

Learning Standard

Students will develop plans for data-gathering explorations.

General Objective

Students will be prepared for a field excursion during which they will observe signs of spring in their school neighborhood.

Essential Question

What are some of the main signs of spring that are found in our local neighborhood? (This is the main question that will be answered as a result of the field excursion for which this introductory lesson is preparing the students.)

In the introductory lesson, the teacher has decided to elicit from the students several signs of spring that they will then keep in mind and look for during the field trip. When they take their walk, on another day, the teacher will also encourage them to observe carefully and search for other signs they have not noted in the preparatory session.

The first lesson can be described in paragraph form in the unit plan, or it can be written as a sequence of numbered, procedural steps, much as it would in a conventional lesson plan. Only three parts of the first lesson are explained and illustrated in this chapter: (a) the essential question of the lesson, (b) the procedure, and (c) the behavioral objective. (The lesson plan appears in its complete form in the Instructional Resources section at the back of the book.)

The procedure for the introductory lesson in the *Spring* unit includes 11 steps; the first 7 are given next to illustrate how the sequence looks as the teacher begins planning the lesson. Note that, following some steps in the procedure, the teacher has included—in italics—some anticipated student responses to the questions that will be raised during the lesson. Also note that two of the critical elements of the procedure—outlined in chapter 3—are included in the first 7 steps.

Procedure

1. Select a day for the field trip in advance, and secure the necessary permissions. Invite two adults from the list of parent volunteers to assist with supervision on the walk. The field trip will be taken after this introductory lesson, which is designed to prepare the students for their walk.

2. The first lesson begins with a class meeting in the early afternoon during the time regularly devoted to unit studies.

3. Begin the lesson by reminding the children that they have studied their neighbor-hood this year and that their last unit was called *Our School*. Ask the children to recall some activities from that unit.

   Children may say that they remember drawing a map of the school and visiting and interviewing several people who work in the school: the nurse, the school principal, and a custodian. They may also remember that they learned about these people's jobs, that they saw where the people do their work, and that they were given a chance to see some materials used in these jobs. The children may also recall drawing and labeling pictures of school helpers.

4. Ask the children if they have noticed that the school custodians are beginning to do some work they have not been able to do all winter.

   The children may have noticed that the school custodians are working outside on the grounds.

5. Ask the children if they can think of any reasons why work is beginning outside at this time of year.

   Children may say that it is because the grass is growing and it is warmer. They may also say it is now spring.

6. Tell the children that they will be studying this new season and that spring is the topic of their new unit.

7. Ask the children what they already know about the spring season. Write their responses on the board. Use a concept web to record what the children say. (See Figure 5.6 for a concept web showing the children's initial concepts of spring.)

   Responses may include that it is a special time of the year, a time when the weather gets warmer and they no longer have to wear heavy clothing. They may say the grass and some flowers begin to grow in spring and that the trees have buds. Some children may remember that some important holidays occur during the spring season.

FIGURE 5.6
Students' concept web for the
Spring unit.

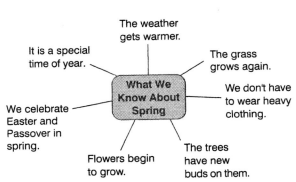

In Steps 3 through 6 of the procedure, the teacher helps the children make a connection between what they studied recently (their school and the people who work in it) and their new unit on the season of spring. The children are asked to recall their interviews with people who work in the school and then to think why the school custodians are beginning to work outside on the school grounds. This conversation will help the children make the transition to the new unit topic and focus their thinking on the spring season.

The lesson procedures are well detailed, clear, and written so that another teacher could easily follow the sequence and know precisely what to do in teaching the lesson. When the teacher is writing the procedures, he or she may want to include, as this teacher has, some possible student reactions—thoughts about what the students may do or say or how they may respond to the teacher's directions and questions. Although anticipating every response is impossible, putting oneself in the students' place and envisioning their reactions and responses to questions and directions can help to minimize the times when an unusual or a distracting response upsets the instructional session. Another value of this exercise is that the teacher is compelled to consider the students' different thinking abilities as an integral part of the lesson planning process.

The final steps in the procedure determine whether the students have understood the point of the lesson; that is, whether the intended purpose of the introductory lesson has been realized. **Closure** is a critical step that must included in any lesson plan. This step is usually at the end of the lesson procedure to provide students with a summary of what they learned (or for this lesson, what the group decided). In this lesson, the teacher needs to raise a final question focusing the children's attention on what they will look for during their walk. This step in the procedure is included intentionally to leave students with a plan in mind for their field trip. In this step, the specific objective—the behavioral objective—of the lesson is assessed. Following is the behavioral objective for this introductory lesson in the *Spring* unit:

Behavioral Objective

In response to the question What signs of spring might we look for as we walk in our school neighborhood? the students will name at least three items—flowers, animals, budding trees, and so on. (Teachers who prefer to use a separate assessment section in their lesson plans instead of behavioral objectives can include the techniques that will be used to assess the students' ability to respond sufficiently to the essential question of the lesson.)

In the behavioral objective, the main point of the introductory lesson is to have the children prepared with a purpose for their field trip, with some specific signs of spring to look for while on their neighborhood walk. Asking the question stated in the objective and listing the children's responses on the board enables the teacher to assess the behavioral objective. This is the final step in the procedure; it not only tests the behavioral objective but also brings closure to the lesson.

Although the main purpose of the lesson is to elicit a list of signs of spring that the children already know, the teacher will expect the children to observe additional signs when they are on the field trip. Otherwise, the activity does not add substantially to the children's existing knowledge.

Step 4: Describing Other Lessons and Activities

Most of the lesson and activity ideas shown in the web design are stated so succinctly that the teacher may later have difficulty remembering exactly what he or she had in mind. Therefore, each idea should be described in a separate section of the unit plan, where the general plan of the lesson activity, its main purpose, and the MIs it addresses are stated in more detail. Three detailed descriptions of ideas shown in the *Spring* web follow. One idea is for painting a mural and several other activities following the children's walk in their neighborhood. A description for a lesson on reading a thermometer and one for preparing a learning center are included.

Descriptions of Lessons and Activities

1. On the day of the students' field trip (walk) through their neighborhood to look for signs of spring, stop occasionally and encourage them to draw or paint one or more sketches showing the signs of spring: animals, birds, insects, and so on. Collect specimens of plants and samples of water to take back to the classroom. After returning to the classroom, have some of the sketches transferred (and enlarged) to a large sheet of mural paper and involve the students in selecting and arranging the pictures on the mural. Some children may use resources in the classroom to determine the names of the plant specimens and to learn more about their growth patterns and needs. One of several learning center activities could be having students use a microscope to examine the water samples brought back from the field trip.

   Sketching their observations and collecting samples during the field trip offers the children opportunities to be involved in the work of scientists. Using art media to prepare the mural will help students develop a visual summary of the signs of spring that they observed. [*linguistic, naturalist, and spatial intelligences*]

2. Teach the students how to read an outdoor thermometer. A thermometer should be installed outside a classroom window, and students should be given opportunities to practice reading the temperature.

   The purpose of this lesson is to prepare the students for keeping a daily temperature record for 2 weeks during the spring. [*logical–mathematical and linguistic intelligences*]

3. Prepare a learning center with at least 10 activities for the students to complete independently. Activities for the learning center may include examining samples of water taken from various sources during their neighborhood walk and writing about or drawing a picture of what they observe. If frogs' eggs are available during the spring, samples may be collected and placed in the learning center for the children to observe. They should have an opportunity to read books about the changes involved as the eggs develop into tadpoles and adult frogs. Suggestions in the center should include creative writing of poems and stories about how spring weather

affects our feelings. A listening activity, including environmental sounds and musical selections, should also be located in the learning center, along with mathematical problem-solving activities related to the daily temperature charts that the students are maintaining. Students should be given the option of submitting any responses or records required for the activities in either written or pictorial form. Each activity should have a task card to explain directions.

The learning center provides students with independent work to extend practice with the concepts that they are studying during the unit in the areas of science, music, language arts, and mathematics. [*most intelligences*]

Figure 5.7 shows one way to organize the learning center.

The preceding lesson and activity descriptions add to basic information provided in the web design and facilitate preparing complete plans for the ideas later. (Additional descriptions can be found in the sample *Spring* unit plan in the Instructional Resources section.)

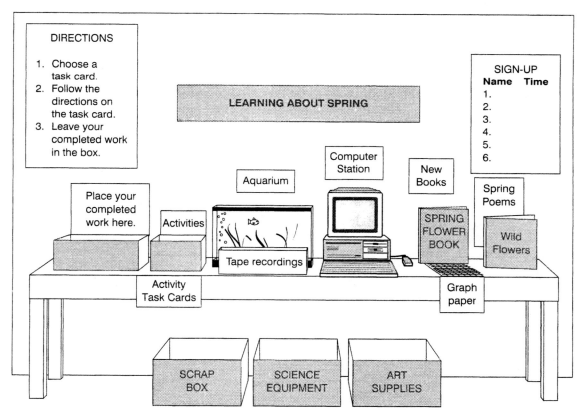

FIGURE 5.7
A model for a *Learning About Spring* learning center.

Step 5: Listing the Unit Learning Standards, General Objectives, and Essential Questions

For each lesson or activity, the teacher lists the learning standards, general objectives, and essential questions it addresses. However, for the unit plan, the teacher must list the major learning standards, general objectives, and essential questions that the unit as a whole addresses. Learning standards and general objectives are the overall, or long-term, goals toward which the unit is expected to contribute. They suggest the major purposes for which the *Spring* unit has been designed and suggests its content as well as its affective and process goals. The essential questions of the unit help to define more specifically what students should gain from their unit. Examples of learning standards and each type of general objective—content, attitudinal, and process—and several examples of essential questions for the *Spring* unit follow:

Learning Standards

- Students will describe their observations.
- Students will develop plans for data-gathering explorations.

General Objectives

Content

- Students will become more aware of the changes going on around them in their environment and learn more about specific changes during the spring season.

Attitudinal

- Students will appreciate that works of art, music, and literature can be inspired by feelings people associate with seasons of the year.

Process

- Students will gain experience in using media—art, music, and movement—to express feelings, attitudes, and ideas.

Essential Questions

- What are some of the main signs of spring that are found in our local neighborhood?
- How can our observations of our natural environment be recorded?
- What techniques can be used to determine whether our weather is changing?
- What important holidays occur during spring, and what is the significance of these holidays?
- In what ways do changes in the seasons affect the ways people feel?

(Additional learning standards, general objectives, and essential questions for the *Spring* unit are included in the sample unit plan in the Instructional Resources section.)

Step 6: Listing Unit Assessment Methods and Techniques

Learning standards, general objectives, and behavioral objectives are starting points in the assessment process. Unit assessment methods and techniques are then planned to assess the achievement of these goals. Usually such assessment involves a combination of teacher observation, authentic assessment, and traditional testing. Directly observing the students helps the teacher evaluate their ability to work together, to use equipment properly, and to assess their own work. Authentic techniques are especially useful because teachers and children can assemble in a student portfolio an authentic record of work that the student has produced or is involved in developing. A portfolio can include a journal, samples of written work, records of science experiments, and pieces of art produced by the student. Examinations are also useful, especially when added to informal teacher observations and authentic measures, for assessing each student's progress toward developing the conceptual knowledge that the unit has been designed to foster. Descriptions of several evaluation techniques planned for the *Spring* unit follow:

Assessment Techniques

- Periodically observe the students during group activities, particularly while they are working on the mural and during planting activities. Watch specifically for their ability to share materials and space. Note these observations in a journal.
- Have each student maintain a unit portfolio. Involve individuals in selecting the following materials for their portfolios:
  - Samples of written work or work in progress, including creative writing pieces and any written reports
  - Examples or photographs of the student's art projects or projects in progress
  - A journal maintained by the student, including any observations or notes
  - Records of observations and notes made by the teacher
  - Records or notes on any individual pupil–teacher conferences
  - Records of science experiments
  - Unit examinations
- Maintain anecdotal records of observations made about each student's general work habits, working and learning style preferences, cooperation when working with others, and ability to learn through experiential activities.
- Keep a journal throughout the unit of work. Include observations of activities and lessons that appear to be most helpful in developing the unit objectives. Also, note the need for revisions in the unit plan—areas that need to be strengthened and additional activities that may be offered to meet students' individual learning styles.
- Administer an examination at the conclusion of the unit to assess facts, concepts, and generalizations developed in the study. The examination may be given orally for students who have difficulty reading the questions. Students should achieve a minimum passing grade of 75 percent.

Step 7: Listing Unit Materials

In the Unit Materials section of the unit plan, only the most important instructional materials and informational resources for the teacher need to be listed. Detailed information on some materials and their sources may be important to keep on record for future reference, particularly if they have proved especially useful or effective. The names of people who have been helpful as consultants or as guest speakers can also be included in this list. Most of the usual art and other consumable materials need not be listed. Each time the unit is taught, new materials will be available and should be added to the list. However, when the teacher is initially preparing a unit, the materials list can be brief and include only the most important materials. Several examples follow:

Materials for Students

- Videotapes of NOVA nature programs (from the school media center) and programs recorded from Instructional Television (ITV) services
- A teacher-prepared computer slide presentation or a filmstrip on planting seeds (from the school media center)
- Recordings of music and environmental sounds
- James Smith (consultant with the local weather TV channel)
- A selection of children's books on spring from the school and public libraries
- Computer software and CD-ROM titles featuring information on the seasons and nature

Information Resources for the Teacher

- Bobick, J. E., & Balaban, N. E. (Eds.). (2002). *The handy science answer book* (Rev. & expanded ed.). Canton, MI: Visible Ink Press.
- *The vernal equinox.* (1997). Retrieved from http://condor.stcloudstate.edu/ ~physcrse/astr106/emapspring.html

Step 8: Deciding on the Unit Title or Designing a Method of Involving the Students in Creating a Title

Deciding on the unit title is important and can usually be accomplished easily. *Spring* could be the title of this sample unit. However, children can probably think of a title they like better. Offering the children a chance to suggest their own title is a good way to stimulate their interest and help them become invested in their unit. In reality, the unit belongs to the children, so their feeling of some sense of ownership is important. The children can also create artwork for the title so that it can be displayed in their classroom throughout the study. The title can be made from cutout letters, be written with crayon, be painted on a long strip of paper, or be made from other suitable materials.

Title

Possible Titles

Spring

Signs of Spring

Spring Is Here

Spring Changes

Method of Involving Students in Selecting a Title

- The students can suggest other titles during a class meeting, or individuals can write suggested titles on slips of paper and put the slips in a suggestion box. A class vote can be taken to select the final title.

- Two or three volunteers can be asked to cut letters for the title that will then be displayed at the top of a large bulletin board.

The eight-step process described in this chapter has generated the material needed to write a formal unit plan and to complete the unit plan outline illustrated in Figure 5.1 at the beginning of this chapter. That outline only reorders the material produced in the eight-step process and provides a logical organizational framework for the plan. The complete *Spring* unit plan can be found in the Instructional Resources section at the back of this book.

▓ ACTIVITIES

1. Consider the physical, social, and intellectual characteristics of development in early childhood. Discuss the implications of each characteristic for planning interdisciplinary units for students in the primary grades.

2. Consider the physical, social, and intellectual characteristics of development for students in middle childhood. Decide on specific ways in which these characteristics can assist teachers in planning interdisciplinary units for students at upper elementary and middle school levels.

3. When teachers plan interdisciplinary units, their web designs offer clear indications of how they conceptualize the interrelationships among the various lessons and activities. Multidirectional designs suggest greater interdisciplinarity in a teacher's concept of a unit than unidirectional web designs do. Examine the various designs provided in the Instructional Resources section. Decide which of the designs are multidirectional and which are more unidirectional.

4. Think of five possible activities to include in an interdisciplinary unit called *Inventions*. Make a list of the activities and ask five students in an upper elementary or a middle school class to rank their preferences for these activities from most to least preferred. Decide what the results suggest.

5. Try to recall a memorable highlight when you studied a topic in social studies or another discipline in elementary or middle school. Describe what you remember about this experience. Explain why you think you can recall this experience in particular.

6. Talk to several students in an elementary or a middle school classroom about the kinds of activities they particularly enjoy. Discuss specific ways this information can be helpful to teachers in planning interdisciplinary units.

7. One suggestion in this chapter is that students need to become "invested" in their unit work. Only two suggestions for doing so were included in the sample interdisciplinary unit plan called *Spring*. Try to think of several other practical ways a teacher can involve students in planning and other decision-making activities that will give them a feeling of ownership of their unit studies.

8. Select a grade level and a topic commonly taught in an elementary or a middle school grade. Work alone or with one or two other students or teachers to plan an interdisciplinary unit on this topic. Follow each of the eight steps in the planning process outlined in this chapter. Consult the examples given at each step in the process as well as the sample lesson plan provided in chapter 3 to help with the planning process. After completing the unit plan, ask other students or classroom teachers to review and critique it for application of the planning recommendations at each step included in this chapter.

REFERENCES

Armstrong, T. (2000). *Multiple intelligences in the classroom* (2nd ed.). Alexandria, VA: Association for Supervision and Curriculum Development.

Berk, L. E. (2002). *Infants, children, and adolescents* (4th ed.). Boston: Allyn & Bacon.

Bruner, J. (1963). *The process of education.* New York: Vintage Books.

Bruner, J. (1990). *Acts of meaning.* Cambridge, MA: Harvard University Press.

Case, R. (1985). *Intellectual development: Birth to adulthood.* Orlando, FL: Academic Press.

Charbonneau, M. P., & Reider, B. E. (1995). *The integrated elementary classroom: A developmental model of education for the 21st century.* Needham Heights, MA: Allyn & Bacon.

Checkley, K. (1997). The first seven . . . and the eighth. *Educational Leadership*, 55(1), 8–13.

Ellis, A. K. (2002). *Teaching and learning elementary social studies* (7th ed.). Boston: Allyn & Bacon.

Flavell, J. H. (1985). *Cognitive development* (2nd ed.). Upper Saddle River, NJ: Prentice Hall.

Forman, E. A., Minick, N., & Stone, C. A. (1993). *Contexts for learning.* New York: Oxford University Press.

Furth, H. G. (1971). *Piaget for teachers.* Upper Saddle River, NJ: Prentice Hall.

Gardner, H. (1991). *The unschooled mind: How children think and how schools should teach.* New York: Basic Books.

Gardner, H. (1993). *Multiple intelligences: The theory in practice.* New York: Basic Books.

Gardner, H. (1995, January 6). Creating creativity. *The Times Educational Supplement*, No. 4097, p. 15.

Jacobs, H. (Ed.). (1989). *Interdisciplinary curriculum: Design and implementation.* Alexandria, VA: Association for Supervision and Curriculum Development.

Kauchak, D. P., & Eggen, P. D. (2003). *Learning and teaching: Research-based methods* (4th ed.). Boston: Allyn & Bacon.

Lillard, P. (1972). *Montessori: A modern approach.* New York: Schocken Books.

McNeil, J. D., & Wiles, J. (1990). *The essentials of teaching: Decisions, plans, methods.* New York: Macmillan.

Montessori, M. (1964). *The Montessori method.* New York: Schocken Books.

NCSS Task Force. (1989). Social studies for early childhood and elementary school children preparing for the 21st century: A report from NCSS Task Force on Early Childhood/Elementary Social Studies. *Social Education, 53*, 14–23.

Pappas, C. C., Kiefer, B. Z., & Levstik, L. S. (1999). *An integrated language perspective in the elementary school* (3rd ed.). NY: Longman.

Phillips, J. L. (1981). *Piaget's theory: A primer.* San Francisco: Freeman.

Piaget, J. (1955). *The language and thought of the child.* New York: Meridian.

Piaget, J. (1966). *Judgment and reasoning in the child.* Totowa, NJ: Littlefield, Adams.

Piaget, J. (1970). *Science of education and the psychology of the child.* (D. Coltman, Trans.). New York: Orion Press.

Piaget, J. (1973). *To understand is to invent.* New York: Grossman.

Piaget, J. (1974). *Understanding causality.* New York: Norton.

Piaget, J. (1976). *The grasp of consciousness.* Cambridge, MA: Harvard University Press.

Piaget, J., & Inhelder, B. (1969). *The psychology of the child.* New York: Basic Books.

Ravich, D. (1988). Tot sociology. *American Educator, 12*(3), 38–39.

Roberts, P. L., & Kellough, R. D. (2004). *A guide for developing interdisciplinary thematic units* (3rd ed.). Upper Saddle River, NJ: Prentice Hall.

Santrock, J. W. (2003). *Children* (7th ed.). Boston: McGraw-Hill.

Standing, E. M. (1957). *Maria Montessori: Her life and her work.* New York: New American Library.

Stephens, L. S. (1974). *The teacher's guide to open education.* New York: Holt, Rinehart & Winston.

Vygotsky, L. S. (1986). *Thought and language* (New rev. ed.). Cambridge, MA: MIT Press.

Wadsworth, B. (1996). *Piaget's theory of cognitive and affective development* (5th ed.) White Plains, NY: Longman.

Wertsch, J. V. (1985). *Vygotsky and the social formation of the mind.* Cambridge, MA: Harvard University Press.

▓ Suggested Readings

The supplemental readings listed next provide additional background material on the unit planning process as discussed in this chapter.

Katz, L., & Chard, S. C. (2000). *Engaging children's minds: The project approach* (2nd ed.). Stamford, CT: Ablex.

Messick, R. G., & Reynolds, K. E. (1992). *Middle level curriculum in action.* White Plains, NY: Longman.

Post, T. R., Ellis, A. K., Humphreys, A. H., & Buggey, L. J. (1997). *Interdisciplinary approaches to curriculum: Themes for teaching.* Upper Saddle River, NJ: Prentice Hall.

Wadsworth, B. J. (1978). *Piaget for the classroom teacher.* New York: Longman.

6

Designing Research-Oriented Interdisciplinary Units

▓ OVERVIEW

This chapter covers an eight-step procedure for planning a research-oriented interdisciplinary unit for students in the upper elementary grades and middle school.

The focus of this chapter is on the following:

- An introduction to the design of research-oriented interdisciplinary units that differentiates them from other interdisciplinary units
- The relationship of child development in middle childhood and early adolescence to the design of interdisciplinary instruction and the research-oriented interdisciplinary unit—an alternative design for the upper elementary grades and middle school
- The reasons why research-oriented interdisciplinary units offer a developmentally appropriate alternative type of interdisciplinary study for older students
- A detailed outline for a research-oriented interdisciplinary unit plan
- An eight-step procedure for planning a research-oriented interdisciplinary unit
- An explanation of each step in the planning process, with examples from a unit called *Deserts of the United States,* which is being planned for students in fifth grade
- A method for modifying research-oriented interdisciplinary units for a departmentalized upper elementary or middle school program

▓ INTRODUCTION TO RESEARCH-ORIENTED INTERDISCIPLINARY UNITS

An alternative to the interdisciplinary unit described in chapter 5 is the **research-oriented interdisciplinary unit.** This type of unit is appropriate for students in the upper elementary and middle school grades. Research-oriented interdisciplinary units differ from interdisciplinary units in several ways:

- The research process guides the development of the unit and its procedures.
- Students are always actively involved in developing questions and suggesting areas to be researched in their study.
- The topic of the unit is separated into subtopics for committee research.
- Students work individually; in small, cooperative groups; and on committees.
- Each student on a committee assumes responsibility for researching a specific part of the committee's subtopic.
- Written research reports—or alternative methods of reporting—are prepared by individual students and committees.
- Each committee summarizes its part of the research for the entire class in an oral presentation.

During research-oriented interdisciplinary units, students work on individual or group projects and have opportunities to continue improving their research and other academic skills. They gain insights into the ways of knowing inherent in the different disciplines used as they investigate their topic. Students work independently, in small cooperative groups, or as members of committees to complete their research.

In middle childhood and early adolescence, students thoroughly enjoy participating in group activities with their peers. Therefore, the committee work in a research-oriented interdisciplinary unit is appealing and naturally motivating. Practical guidance on the type of cooperative grouping involved in committee work at upper elementary and middle school levels can be found in the writings of Chard and Flockhart (2002), Johnson (1999), and Johnson, Johnson, and Holubec (1994) and in two helpful publications from the National Education Association (Lyman, Foyle, & Azwell, 1993; Rottier & Ogan, 1991).

Most students at the upper elementary and middle school levels have developed adequate research, reading, and writing skills for the academic work required by research-oriented interdisciplinary units. At these levels, teachers can usually find more independent-level reading and other resource materials prepared on topics for their students' research. However, an important point to note is that not all older students may be ready for the work involved in this type of unit. The decision about which of the two unit types—interdisciplinary or research-oriented interdisciplinary— is more appropriate for a particular class should be based on the teacher's perception of the students' developmental and academic abilities. Therefore, teachers who know that their students have difficulty with reading and writing skills should follow the procedure outlined in chapter 5 for interdisciplinary units, mainly because these studies do not demand the same level of independence in reading and writing.

The organizational structure of a particular school will also influence the decision about which unit type to use. This is especially true if the school uses a departmentalized plan.

▪ DESIGN OF RESEARCH-ORIENTED INTERDISCIPLINARY UNITS FOR MIDDLE CHILDHOOD AND EARLY ADOLESCENCE

Interdisciplinary units for students in the upper elementary grades and middle school may follow the same basic structure as the units designed for younger students. However, they differ in both the quantity and the level of work that is required; substantially more reading and reporting activities can be added. Most students at the upper elementary and middle school levels will have already achieved what Piaget and Inhelder (1969) described as **concrete operational thought.** This pattern of thinking and reasoning allows students to deal with more abstract concepts and systems of concepts if they can relate these concepts to a personal or direct experience.

Piaget believed that some students approach **formal operational thought** in their early adolescent years. This type of thought involves genuine hypothetical thinking. However, Piaget gave less attention to the importance of individual differences, culture, and instruction on cognitive development. Post-Piagetian researchers are revising his estimates of development in middle childhood and the early adolescent period (as with the challenges to Piaget's early childhood theory). For example, one likelihood is that many young adolescents do not achieve the formal operational thinking patterns that Piaget found from his studies (Santrock, 2003).

Ordinarily, older students can read better, and teachers can provide them with more suitable independent reading and other resource materials. These students' improved skills also enable them to make increasing use of computer technology and, if available, local and distance networking, online, and Internet services. In the upper elementary grades and middle school, students continue to need opportunities to acquire knowledge by using their individual working and learning styles and multiple intelligences (MIs). In an interesting model program called the *Key School*, teachers apply the principles of an MI curriculum. According to Gardner (1993), students in the program participate

on a regular basis in the activities of computing, music, and "bodily–kinesthetics," in addition to topic-centered curricula that embody the standard literacies and subject matter. . . . Each student participates in an apprenticeship-like "pod," where he works with peers of different ages and a competent teacher to master a craft or discipline of interest. (p. 113)

Students at the Key School investigate several topics each year, including those with titles such as *Patterns, Connections, The Renaissance—Then and Now,* and *Mexican Heritage*. These interdisciplinary investigations are research oriented.

Research-Oriented Interdisciplinary Units

Educators can approach research-oriented interdisciplinary studies in the upper elementary and middle school grades by using a variation of the interdisciplinary unit planning structure: the research-oriented interdisciplinary unit plan. This type of unit is an alternative that can, on occasion, be developed with students, often beginning as early as the second half of Grade 3. In middle and late childhood, most students can read independently for information, and they are becoming more proficient at applying the ways of knowing in the various disciplines to which they were exposed in their early years of school. Because they can cooperate better with one another, they enjoy cooperative group activities and committee work. Older students can also participate fully with the teacher in helping to design their units of study; they can plan their research by raising questions and suggesting problems to solve.

Planning and Organizing Research

The teacher plans and introduces a research-oriented interdisciplinary unit to the students. Then, while the teacher is guiding them through the planning phase for their research, students are encouraged to suggest general areas to be investigated and to raise the essential questions to be answered.

Socially, older children usually enjoy working on committees, in which they share tasks and become involved in making group decisions. Under teacher direction, the students next become involved in organizing their research topic into manageable subtopics. To complete the planning phase of the unit, the teacher appoints students to research committees that will investigate each subtopic. Finally, each committee outlines specifically what the group needs to research, and each student assumes responsibility for a specific aspect of the committee's work.

The care and skills needed for organizing any type of cooperative group work also apply to the organization of a research committee. Extensive discussions on cooperative learning can be found in a number of other publications (Arends, 2004; Kauchak & Eggen, 2003; Slavin, 1995; Slavin et al., 1985). Numerous practical suggestions are offered in these and other sources about the design and structure of cooperative learning activities. Also of interest is Dembo's (1994) comprehensive summary of research on the use of cooperative learning in the classroom.

Completing Committee Reports

Committee work continues until each member has contributed his or her findings to the small group and the committee members have decided how they will report to the whole class. When committees begin to complete their work, the teacher schedules group presentations during which they will report their findings to the class. To help maintain interest and to prevent monotony, teachers should help students vary their form of reporting. Students can be encouraged to use alternatives to conventional, individual oral reports, such as the following:

- Panel discussions
- Music and dance performances
- Computer presentations
- Puppet shows and skits
- Experiments
- Demonstrations
- Displays of artifacts, maps, constructions, and art projects

As each committee reports its findings, other students in the class are encouraged to take notes about what they learn from the report and to raise any questions they may have for the committee to answer. After each committee report, the teacher engages the students in a discussion and helps them to prepare an outline of the most important information contained in the report.

Throughout the unit, the teacher is responsible for outlining tasks clearly, providing opportunities for students with different learning styles to gain the information that they are seeking, ensuring that the research process guides students' work, and, in general, encouraging responsible, productive work from everyone. The teacher may arrange field trips and online conferences using the Internet and networking services. Video, DVD, film, filmstrip, and computer presentations may be shown at appropriate points during the development of the unit. Relevant computer software and CD-ROM programs and other suitable media can be suggested for students to use in completing their research. Lessons are always needed in the important locational and note-taking skills.

Teachers usually require some form of report from both individual students and committees. Reporting techniques can respect individual learning preferences; for example, one student may present an art project, another may perform a movement or dance presentation, and others may complete written reports or be part of a panel discussion. Teachers must give clear instructions about forms to be followed for any written or oral reports. Rubrics that indicate how the students' work will be evaluated should be shared with students before the research activities begin.

In the upper elementary grades, a committee report may be a simple compiling of the written reports, demonstrations, or presentations prepared by each member. In the middle school, teachers may ask groups to compile a single written report that reflects the entire group's research. Students may be asked to maintain a "unit portfolio" that includes samples of their individual written work, art projects, photographs, and other materials, such as a log or journal reflecting on their experiences during the unit of study.

Assessing the Unit

To conclude a research-oriented interdisciplinary unit, teachers may want to prepare, as part of the assessment process, an examination based on notes generated from the committee reports. Each committee can be asked to develop several questions about its work. The questions can then be used for a review of concepts developed in the unit; after careful editing by the teacher, some committee questions may become part of a final examination.

The remainder of this chapter covers three important topics. First, a research-oriented interdisciplinary unit plan outline is provided. Second, an eight-step procedure for designing research-oriented interdisciplinary unit plans is discussed in detail. Third, a way to organize a research-oriented interdisciplinary unit plan for interdisciplinary instruction in departmentalized schools is suggested.

▓ A RESEARCH-ORIENTED INTERDISCIPLINARY UNIT PLAN OUTLINE

The eight-step procedure explained and illustrated in the next section provides the information needed for teachers to design a research-oriented interdisciplinary unit plan. The outline for this plan is shown in Figure 6.1.

The outline includes learning standards, general objectives, essential questions, behavioral objectives, possible research committees, procedures representing phases

FIGURE 6.1
A research-oriented
interdisciplinary unit plan
outline.

Topic:

Title:

Level:

Estimated Unit Length:

Learning Standards:

General Objectives:

Essential Questions to Guide Students' Research:

Web Design of the Unit:

Possible Research Committees:

Possible Unit Lessons and Activities:

Introductory Lesson Plan:

    Topic:

    Level:

    Estimated Time:

    Learning Standards:

    General Objectives:

    Essential Questions:

    Behavioral Objectives (or Assessment Techniques):

    Procedure:

    Materials:

Description of the Remainder of the Plan:

Description of the Research Phase:

Description of the Reporting Phase:

Unit Assessment Methods and Techniques:

Unit Materials:

of the research process, unit assessment techniques, and unit materials. In addition, several specific elements required only for this type of interdisciplinary unit plan are included. Major headings, along with statements indicating the kind of information needed for each section, are as follows:

Topic

State the topic of the unit.

Title

List suggestions for a title and possible ways to involve students in selecting a title for the unit.

Level

State the grade or grades for which the unit is intended, keeping in mind the students' background and readiness for the unit, their social and developmental characteristics, and their academic abilities.

Estimated Unit Length

Estimate the amount of time needed to teach the unit.

Learning Standards

Learning standards for research-oriented units are gleaned from lists at national, state, and local levels. Unit standards include those that the unit addresses in significant ways.

General Objectives

As in interdisciplinary unit plans, general objectives address other content, concepts, skills, affective goals, and learning processes that you hope to promote throughout the study with a specific group of students.

Essential Questions to Guide Students' Research

Prepare lists of questions for the various disciplines to help guide students' committee research. These questions are posed mainly to help you prepare a framework for the unit. Encourage students to generate their own questions and problem statements for their research, but your questions may be added if students fail to consider certain important areas.

Web Design of the Unit Plan

Construct a web design that includes the three major areas in research-oriented unit plans: research activities, skills lessons, and other related activity ideas. Different options for web designs are explained in chapter 5.

Possible Research Committees

List anticipated subtopics of the unit that may be assigned to groups of students for committee research.

Possible Unit Lessons and Activities

Describe several possible research and reporting alternatives that students may use in connection with their committee or individual research. List and describe the lessons to be taught—those included in the web design—in this section. Try to make provisions for students' differing working and learning styles as well as their MIs. Finally, indicate in brackets the main MI areas involved in each lesson or activity.

Introductory Lesson Plan

The introductory lesson plan outlines a procedure for the first session in the study with the students. Design the lesson to introduce the planning phase of the research process, to assist students in raising relevant questions and problems, and to help them organize for their study. Although other lesson plan formats can be substituted for the one given next, the plan should accommodate the information included in the following outline:

Topic: State the unit topic and the main topic of the lesson.

Level: State the age levels or grades for which the lesson is designed.

Estimated Time: Estimate the amount of time needed for the first session.

Learning Standards: List the learning standards that the lesson addresses.

General Objectives: State any general objectives for the lesson.

Essential Questions: State one or more essential questions for the session. Often, the introductory lesson in the planning phase addresses only one major question. Any essential questions that are listed should be capable of being assessed in the lesson. The essential question sets the main purpose of the lesson; it is the question that will be answered as a result of instruction.

Behavioral Objectives (or Assessment Techniques): State the specific objectives for the initial procedure in the planning phase of the unit. These objectives are then assessed at steps in the procedure. Optionally, you may prefer to eliminate behavioral objective statements and describe techniques that will be used to assess the lesson in a separate section of the lesson plan.

Procedure: Write a paragraph or a sequential list of steps detailing the procedure for the initial session in this phase. The procedure should include all the critical elements outlined in chapter 3.

Materials: List the principal materials needed for the lesson.

Description of the Remainder of the Planning Phase

Describe how to complete the planning phase after the initial session. This phase ends with the formation of committees, outlines of each committee's intended research, and each committee member's research responsibilities.

Description of the Research Phase

Describe activities that will take place as students pursue their individual projects and committee research.

Description of the Reporting Phase

Explain the procedure and describe possible reporting alternatives for the students' committee reports. Keep in mind the students' different learning and working styles, and provide for some variety in reporting methods.

Unit Assessment Methods and Techniques

List unit assessment techniques in addition to the assessment techniques described in the behavioral objectives or assessment section of lesson and activity plans. Unit techniques may include portfolios to be assembled during the study and examinations to be administered.

Unit Materials

List the major instructional materials needed for the unit and informational resources that may be helpful for the teacher. Include general kinds of materials, such as texts and trade books, computer software, teacher-prepared presentations, DVD and videotaped programs, films and filmstrips, and magazines and newspapers. Each time the unit is taught to a new group of students, add to this list new titles found to be especially valuable, along with notes or descriptions of their content. Some materials may need to be updated or deleted from the list each time the unit is used with a new group.

AN EIGHT-STEP PROCEDURE FOR DESIGNING A RESEARCH-ORIENTED INTERDISCIPLINARY UNIT PLAN

Topics selected for students in the upper elementary grades and middle school should be kept broad to increase opportunities for student participation. Excellent planning guides developed by the National Council for the Social Studies can help in the selection process. Interdisciplinary topics can also be selected from disciplines other than those included in the social studies curriculum. Post, Ellis, Humphreys, and Buggey (1997) recommended selecting topics with an environmental focus. Environmental topics are interesting to most students in the upper elementary grades and middle school and always involve several disciplines.

In long-term planning, teachers should consult statewide and local curriculum guides and lists of learning standards to assist them in making decisions about the topics to be taught throughout the academic year. Often, a prescribed course of study must be met, especially for the middle school (Kellough & Kellough, 2003). Regardless of the source of topics, several criteria may be helpful in making final decisions about topics to teach:

- The topic should be broad and inclusive. However, time constraints for teaching the unit, if any, should be considered because they may influence the type of topic that can be investigated (Criteria for Selection of Class Research Topics, 1966).

- Topics that address specific learning standards and are required by the state should be included where they fit most naturally.

- The availability of resource materials needed by students to investigate the topic should be considered. Required reading materials should be selected according to the students' independent reading levels.

- The unit topic should involve as many disciplines as possible.
- To be sufficiently motivating, the topic selected should be of inherent interest to the students whenever possible. The scope of the study should also be flexible enough to allow for differences in individual interests, intelligence areas, and learning styles.
- A topic should help to broaden students' understanding of the multicultural world and strengthen their sense of social responsibility.

After selecting a topic, the teacher can follow these eight steps for planning a research-oriented interdisciplinary unit:

1. Consider the students' developmental abilities and their background for the topic.
2. Brainstorm to develop four lists: essential questions to help guide students' research, possible research committees, other unit lessons and activities, and skills lessons to be taught during the unit. A web design can be constructed that indicates the committees, activities, and lessons.
3. Plan the initial lesson to be held with students. This first lesson introduces the critical planning phase in the research process.
4. Write a description of the general procedure for completing the three phases of the study: planning, researching, and reporting.
5. List the learning standards, general objectives, and essential questions for the unit.
6. List tentative unit assessment methods and techniques.
7. List the major unit materials required for students and resource materials for the teacher.
8. Decide on the unit title, or develop a method of involving the students in selecting a title.

In addition to drafting a web design of ideas, the second step in designing a research-oriented interdisciplinary unit involves preparing resource lists of the following:

- Committees that might be formed to investigate the topic
- Essential questions to help guide students' research
- Brief descriptions of activities
- Specific skills lessons to be taught during the unit

The same chart of disciplines, study areas, and techniques used in interdisciplinary unit planning can also be helpful when teachers are preparing these four lists (see Table 5.1).

An explanation of the eight-step procedure for planning a research-oriented interdisciplinary unit follows. The examples given at each step are from an upper elementary grade research unit plan called *Deserts of the United States*. Although the unit is designed for fourth grade, the same topic can be addressed at other grade levels, and the unit plan can be modified for teaching at both the upper elementary and middle school levels.

Only a few examples from the complete unit plan are given for each of the eight steps. However, the complete unit plan is included in the Instructional Resources section at the back of this book.

Step 1: Considering Students' Developmental Abilities and Background for the Topic

In the upper elementary grades and middle school, most students like to work together, their thinking has matured, and their academic skills have developed so that they can do more of their work independently. This information will be important as planning begins for the unit. The following class description includes a number of important points about this particular group of students:

> *The students in this heterogeneous group of fourth graders should have opportunities for direct experiences whenever possible to help them develop concepts to be fostered in their Desert unit. Independent reading levels in the class range from second to eighth grade; the students vary in their individual learning and working styles. Several students are especially talented in art. The class has had previous committee experiences; they work well in these cooperative groups when the tasks are clear and well outlined and when there is some leadership in each group. They need guidance when using the school library or media center for research, and they are still learning about taking notes when reading for information. The class includes the usual personality conflicts that occasionally emerge in a group at this level, and minor behavioral problems occur at times. These problems are less pronounced when the students become interested and involved in their work. Three students with special needs are in the class; one cannot read well enough independently for information, another has been diagnosed with minimal brain damage, and another has only residual hearing. Although they all can participate in committee work, these students require more time for their work and need opportunities to learn through alternative strategies. Interviews, drawings, tape recordings, videotape programs, teacher-prepared computer presentations, and computer software may be helpful. Recently, the class completed a unit on their local Long Island and New York City coastal region. These students are beginning to realize how geographic location can affect people. They are also learning more about the concept of interdependence.*

The description reviews group and individual student characteristics as well as their academic and social skills. While planning and introducing the unit, the teacher will keep in mind the previous unit topic, the students' background, and their academic strengths and limitations.

Step 2: Constructing a Web Design of the Unit Plan; Brainstorming for Essential Questions, Possible Research Committees, Unit Lessons, and Activities

A unit plan web design, which is similar to the web designs used for interdisciplinary units, can be constructed for research-oriented interdisciplinary units. If a web design is constructed for the unit, the topic should be clearly stated, with brief descriptions of research committees, activities, specific skills lessons, and other related class activities radiating from the topic. Lines are then drawn to show how the disciplines, lessons, and activities interrelate in a multidirectional design.

There is no single correct way to design the web. (Different web designs, including those that are both unidirectional and multidirectional, were discussed in chapter 5.) Each design type is appropriate for research-oriented interdisciplinary unit plans; examples appear in Charbonneau and Reider (1995); Ellis (2002); Jacobs (1989); Pappas, Kiefer, and Levstik (1999); and Roberts and Kellough (2004). A partially completed web design for the *Deserts* unit is shown in Figure 6.2.

Teachers may prefer to develop lists in addition to—or perhaps instead of—drafting a web design, mainly because the web design for a research-oriented interdisciplinary unit can become crowded and is time consuming to construct.

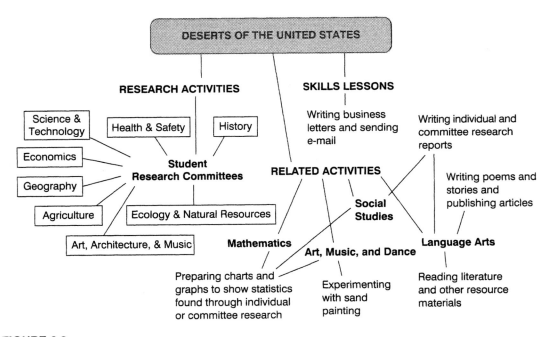

FIGURE 6.2
A partially completed web design for the research-oriented interdisciplinary unit called *Deserts of the United States*.

Four lists should be developed during the brainstorming step, even when a web design is constructed. The following examples show the kinds of information that have been prepared for the *Deserts* unit. (*Note*: None of these lists is complete; see the *Deserts* unit plan in the Instructional Resources section at the back of this book for complete lists.)

Essential Questions to Guide Students' Research

Following are some questions that students may investigate as they research the topic. Although the teacher prepares this list when planning the unit, students should be encouraged to formulate the essential questions of their study during the planning phase. During planning, the questions are usually separated by discipline or domain. From an interdisciplinary perspective, the separation is somewhat artificial, mainly because the disciplines and questions relate to one another and should be considered in combinations by the students during the actual inquiry. Following are examples of questions that the teacher prepares in advance:

Geography

- How do we define a *desert* region?
- What are common features of deserts?
- How were our deserts formed?
- How old are they, and how can their ages be determined?
- Where are deserts in the United States located, and what factors have determined their locations?
- What are the sizes of deserts in the United States?
- Are all deserts in the United States alike in some ways? In what ways do they differ from one another?

History

- Who were the first settlers in U.S. deserts? Why did these people initially settle in these areas?
- How have historians and other social scientists learned about early people who lived in U.S. desert regions?
- How have artifacts found in U.S. deserts contributed to our understanding of early desert civilizations?
- Which Native American tribes currently live in U.S. desert areas?

Science and Technology

- What animals and plants live in desert areas? Do the same kinds of animals and plants live in all deserts?
- What are the reasons for any variations found in wildlife in the different deserts?

- How are desert plants and animals adapted to desert living conditions?
- How have people used technology to provide water for raising crops in a desert and to improve the quality of life in desert areas?

Economics
- What minerals and other natural resources are found in desert areas? What effects do these resources have on desert society?
- How do people in desert areas earn a living?

Agriculture
- Is farming possible in desert areas? If so, what kinds of farms are found in these regions?
- What problems do farmers face in desert areas?

Art, Architecture, and Music
- What famous artists have lived and worked in desert areas? Why do they live there? How can their art be distinguished?

Health
- What kinds of health care are available to people living in sparsely populated desert regions?
- What are the effects of the desert climate on the health of people who live in these areas?

Possible Research Committees

Art, Architecture, Music	Geography	History
Ecology/Natural Resources	Health/Safety	Science/Technology

Possible Unit Lessons and Activities

The following lesson and activity examples provide an outline that will be helpful as the unit proceeds. Along with each suggestion is the main intelligence area it addresses—indicated in brackets.

Lessons and Instructional Activities
- *Form research committees.* A committee should be formed for each area shown in the web design. Each committee should have four to six student members. After completing their research, the committees will be responsible for reporting their findings to the class. [*interpersonal intelligence*]
- *Provide for individual inquiry.* Some students may be interested in subtopics that do not relate well to any committee's work. Encourage these individuals to

pursue their interests, and provide opportunities for them to report their findings to the class. *[intrapersonal intelligence]*

- *Clarify reporting requirements for committees and individuals.* Require each student to prepare a report of his or her committee research. Students who can should prepare their reports in writing. Provide a form to guide the writing process. *[linguistic intelligence]*

- *Teach lessons on letter-writing and note-taking skills. [linguistic intelligence]*

- *Teach lessons on using the Internet for research and communicating by e-mail. [linguistic intelligence]*

- *Offer individuals and committees suggestions for alternative research and reporting activities.* The list should include suggestions that can be made to committees and individual students as the unit progresses. Activities should address students' differing working and learning styles. *[intrapersonal and interpersonal intelligences]*

Student Activities

- Compose and send a letter by e-mail to the students in a fourth-grade class in a desert region. Ask them what living in a desert region of the United States is like. *[linguistic intelligence]*

- Choose a story or poem on desert life from the classroom collection or from the school media center. Prepare to read it to a group of students in kindergarten or first grade. *[linguistic intelligence]*

- Publish an article on the school Web site, comparing living in a desert area with living in our area. *[linguistic intelligence]*

- Organize a panel discussion to present information that your group has gained from its research. *[interpersonal and linguistic intelligences]*

- Develop a time line to display in the classroom. Use TimeLiner, if you would like, to prepare it. The time line should indicate the average rainfall each year for the past 10 or more years in a specific desert area. *[linguistic and logical–mathematical intelligences]*

- Develop a plan for an ideal desert house. Make a drawing of the plan. Write a description of your design and include reasons for its special features. *[spatial and linguistic intelligences]*

- Create a graph showing some statistics, such as population changes, elevations, or average daily temperature readings, about one of the desert areas that you or your committee has been studying. *[logical–mathematical intelligence]*

- Try sand painting. The art teacher can help those of you who would like to try this unique art form. *[spatial intelligence]*

- Invite several classmates to design and paint a mural on life in the desert. (The mural topic can involve animal and plant life, types of homes, typical desert scenes, or other ideas suggested by the students.) *[interpersonal and spatial intelligences]*

- Build a model of a Native American community found in one of the desert areas studied. *[spatial intelligence]*

- Prepare a puppet show or present a skit for the class that includes information about some of the effects that new settlers had on Native Americans who were living in a desert area. *[spatial intelligence]*

- Collect several recordings that have been written about desert living. Present the music to the class. *[musical intelligence]*

- Create a musical instrument made from materials that are found in a desert. Demonstrate the instrument for the class. *[musical and spatial intelligences]*

- Work with several others to plan a classroom "museum" display of all the projects that students in the class have created during the unit. Invite all students in the class to contribute their projects for the display. We can arrange to have other classes in the school visit the museum. *[interpersonal and spatial intelligences]*

- Throughout the unit, maintain a journal in which you record your thoughts and feelings related to our study of deserts. *[linguistic intelligence]*

Step 3: Planning the Introductory Lesson

The procedure for a research-oriented interdisciplinary unit is outlined clearly in three phases. In the **planning phase,** the teacher introduces the topic and provides students with opportunities to participate in organizing for their research. This phase is completed after small research committees are formed to investigate each subtopic of the study. Second, a **researching phase** gives the students time to do their research. During this phase, the teacher oversees each committee's work to ensure that each student is contributing to the group and that students have the materials needed for their research and projects. Finally, the unit culminates in a **reporting phase,** when committees report their findings to the class. Following each committee report, the class outlines the concepts contributed by the group, with the teacher's assistance.

The procedure for the introductory lesson in the planning phase includes the critical elements reviewed in chapter 3. The first lesson introduces the topic of the unit and assists students in beginning to plan for their study. It also helps them form connections between what they studied previously and the new topic to be researched. Each step in the lesson procedure should be well detailed and carefully sequenced.

In this lesson, the teacher intentionally poses questions to stimulate interest and establish a need for the new research. The lesson plan procedure should include specific questions to be raised, along with anticipated student responses. The essential question, the behavioral objective, and part of the procedure for the first lesson in the *Deserts* unit follow.

Essential Question

What kind of information can we expect to learn about desert regions of the United States from the research sources that are available?

Behavioral Objective

After the teacher introduces the topic of the new unit and directs students' attention to research materials in the classroom, each student will begin to develop a list of the kinds of information about U.S. deserts to be found in available materials.

Procedure

1. Before introducing the unit, contact the school librarian, local community children's librarian, and art and music teachers to let them know the topic of the new unit and to invite their help during the study.

   Librarians can probably assign blocks of books or other media to the class for use during the unit. The community librarian may be able to arrange a display of materials and reserve them for the students in the class during the researching phase. The art and music teachers may be able to develop lessons related to the desert topic.

2. In addition to introducing the computer software, applicable audiovisual aids, and textbooks in social studies, science, and mathematics that are available in the classroom, display a sampling of library books, magazines, charts, maps, and other resources that have been brought from the two libraries. Keep the display small so that the students will be motivated to locate other materials themselves.

3. At the first class session, remind students of the unit that they recently completed on their local region and the Atlantic Coast, and ask for some of the major concepts they gained from that study.

   The students should recall that coastal areas are important contributors to U.S. inland areas. The natural harbors along the coast have served for many years as major sites for importing goods from across the world—especially New York Harbor in the students' immediate area. They should mention the fishing industry and recall that there is a concentration of population along the Atlantic Coast.

4. Explain that the new unit will be a study of deserts in the United States and that it will focus on life in desert areas and the ways in which people are affected by desert living.

5. Ask the students what they know about deserts, and construct a concept web with which to record their responses on the chalkboard. Later, transfer the responses to a chart. (See Figure 5.6 for an example of a concept web.) The chart

can be modified as students gain new information; they may need to delete inaccuracies in their original ideas and add other concepts discovered through their research.

6. Tell the students that they will be helping to plan the study and that the first step is to skim available research materials to learn the kinds of information they will be able to find by using available resources.

7. Direct the students' attention to the small classroom display of books, magazines, and other materials on deserts in the United States. Explain that these materials have been brought into the classroom for use during the unit and that additional sources will need to be located, some of which are available in the school library or media center.

8. Ask for three or four volunteers to go to the school library to meet with the librarian, who will assist them in locating other materials for the classroom. Ask the class secretary to keep a list of volunteers' names. Ask one of the volunteers to go to the library to speak to the librarian about a suitable time.

9. Ask the class if anyone can think of sources other than libraries where information about U.S. deserts may be found.

The students will probably mention sources such as the Internet, travel agencies, public television programs, computer software, videotapes, DVD programs, state agencies, and chambers of commerce in desert areas.

The lesson begins with a review to help students make the transition from their previous study of the Atlantic Coast to the new unit, called *Deserts of the United States.* They will then develop a concept web to indicate what they know about deserts before beginning their inquiry. Preparing a small display of materials on deserts before beginning the lesson can help to stimulate students' interest in the new topic. Some students may want to look through the books and magazines even before the introductory lesson is given. The teacher must purposefully take only a few materials to the classroom to allow the students opportunities to locate most of their own resources. In creating an ad hoc group to search for more materials in the school library, the teacher has already involved the students in the business of the study. Gradually, the students will take over more responsibilities.

The behavioral objective will be assessed after the students have had several days to examine the resource materials already displayed in their classroom.

Step 4: Describing the Remainder of the Planning, Research, and Reporting Phases

In this step, the teacher describes the procedure that will be followed in completing the planning phase, then writes a description of each of the two phases that follow. These descriptions will guide the remaining procedures for the unit, including its culmination at the end.

Description of the Remainder of the Planning Phase

1. After a composite list of the kinds of information available in the classroom resources has been compiled, duplicated, and distributed to the class, elicit the students' help in organizing general categories from the items on the newly compiled list. For example, *temperature, climate, rainfall,* and *wind* may all be on the list. These items can be combined to form the general category—or subtopic—*weather.* With the students, develop an outline of all the subtopics, and ask the class secretary to copy it for duplication.

2. Duplicate and distribute the outline to each student. Ask each student to list on a slip of paper three choices of subtopics for a committee assignment. Collect the requests and prepare a list of committee assignments.

   Make the committee assignments with consideration for the social makeup, leadership, and heterogeneity of each group. Make sure that individuals work on different kinds of committees throughout the year. For example, a student should not always be assigned to the economics committee or the art committee. You should make the final committee assignments. If an important subtopic is not selected, you can ask several students if they will volunteer to form a committee for it, or you can assume responsibility for this area.

3. Duplicate and distribute the committee assignments to each student, and announce the first meeting of committees. Before committees meet, discuss the meaning of *committee* and how committees should function. Ask the students to list the main tasks that will need to be accomplished when the committees first meet. Guide students to include the following tasks:

   • Select a chairperson and a recorder

   • Prepare a list of essential questions to guide research on the subtopic

   • Decide on how to divide the committee responsibilities

When the committees meet, the recorder should be instructed to record this information for you. In this way, you will know what each student in the class is investigating. The planning phase ends after the initial committee meetings.

Research and Reporting Phases

This part of the unit plan is completed after descriptions of the research and reporting phases of the unit are added. (These descriptions can be found in the complete *Deserts* unit plan in the Instructional Resources section of this book.)

Step 5: Listing the Unit Learning Standards, General Objectives, and Essential Questions

Learning standards and general objectives in Step 5 address the development of students' cognitive, affective, and process skills that are fostered in the unit study. As explained in chapter 3, learning standards and general objectives are long term and broad based. Two examples are cited next; one is a content learning standard, and the other is an affective general objective.

Learning Standard

Content

- Students will understand ways in which the climate of a geographic region affects plant and animal life.

General Objective

Affective

- Students will develop a greater appreciation for the struggles that early desert settlers experienced when they were adapting to life in desert areas in the United States.

Step 6: Listing Unit Assessment Methods and Techniques

In chapters 3 and 5, it was explained that behavioral objectives are useful for assessing specific lessons and activities. Most teachers of upper elementary and middle school students are also concerned about the students' ability to cooperate with one another, especially when they are engaged in the kind of committee work typical of research-oriented interdisciplinary studies. This ability can often be assessed through observation. By direct observation, the teacher can also note the students' progress in applying the academic skills that they need for their research. Portfolios, which were discussed in chapter 4 and used as an assessment tool in the interdisciplinary unit called *Spring* in chapter 5, can be especially valuable for assessing individual students' progress throughout a research-oriented interdisciplinary unit. Comprehensive unit examinations, based on committee reports, are usually administered at the end of a research-oriented interdisciplinary unit. Sample evaluation statements for this sixth step are listed next.

Assessment Techniques

- Use observation and maintain a journal during the unit in which to note students' individual progress in organizing, sharing responsibilities, and participating in committee work.
- Take photographs of the students' art projects as they develop during the unit.
- Have each student maintain a unit portfolio that includes the following materials:
  - A file of notes taken for individual research
  - Samples of written work or work in progress, including letters, pieces of creative writing, and written reports
  - Samples or photographs of art projects, constructions, charts or graphs, or works in progress

- A journal reflecting on the student's work during the unit
- Records of experiments that students have designed and completed
- Records or notes on any individual pupil–teacher conferences
- Unit examinations

- Collect students' portfolios and add notes about their work habits and ability to work with others cooperatively.

- Administer a comprehensive examination at the end of the unit to evaluate the students' mastery of major concepts developed in the unit of study.

Step 7: Listing Unit Materials

When planning research units, teachers must keep a list of general categories of available materials, such as types of books, computer software, teacher-prepared computer presentations, videotape programs, films, and filmstrips on the unit topic. Names of consultants who have been especially helpful can be added to this section after the unit has been taught at least once. The materials can be listed in two categories: instructional materials for students and informational resources for the teacher. Following are some examples:

Instructional Materials for Students

- Sufficient quantities of social studies and science textbooks from a variety of publishers (four to six copies of each)

Informational Materials for the Teacher

- Hyde, P. (1987). *Drylands: The deserts of North America.* San Diego, CA: Harcourt Brace Jovanovich.

- Mails, T. E. (1993). *The Pueblo students of the earth mother.* New York: Marlowe.

- *The North American deserts.* (n.d.). Retrieved from http://www.desertusa.com/glossary.html

Step 8: Deciding on the Unit Title or Designing a Method of Involving the Students in Creating a Title

List any title suggestions for the unit. If possible, involve the students in creating the title, and display the title prominently in the classroom during the study as a reminder for the class and to inform visitors. Following are examples of titles:

Title

Possible Titles

Deserts of the United States

Our Unusual Desert Areas

Method of Involving Students in Selecting a Title

• Prepare a suggestion box during the first week of the planning phase of the unit. Ask students to contribute title suggestions written on slips of paper. The class officers (president, vice president, and secretary) will choose three title suggestions to present to the class for a vote at the end of the week.

After completing the eight steps just detailed, the teacher will be able to use the material that has been generated to estimate the length of the unit. Research-oriented interdisciplinary units often last from 4 to 6 weeks or more. The information developed in the eight-step procedure can then be reordered and written according to the formal unit plan outline shown in Figure 6.1.

Clearly, planning a new research-oriented interdisciplinary unit is a highly professional task involving a great deal of time, thought, and effort. Each time the same unit is used with a new group of students, it should be updated and perhaps modified. New activities and resources can be added, and others found to be ineffective in the past can be eliminated from the plan. The complete research-oriented interdisciplinary unit plan called *Deserts* can be found in the Instructional Resources section of this book.

◼ MODIFYING A RESEARCH-ORIENTED INTERDISCIPLINARY UNIT PLAN FOR A DEPARTMENTALIZED SCHOOL

Nearly any topic that is taught in a departmentalized upper elementary or middle school curriculum can be approached from an interdisciplinary perspective. Although teachers in departmentalized schools may work independently from one another much of the time, one growing trend is toward a teaming organization in middle schools and some upper elementary grades. With or without teaching teams, teachers can develop a unit plan in which all of them who work with the same group of students address a common topic for at least part of their class time.

In the middle school, topics are more comprehensive than in the lower grades. The topics vary somewhat from school to school, depending on state and local learning standards, departmental guidelines, or other requirements. Topic studies range considerably in Grades 5 through 8 and may include studies of the pre-Columbian period to present-day America as well as the social, economic, and geographic studies of the United States, Canada, Latin America, Africa, Asia, Western and Eastern Europe, the Mediterranean, and other regions. Some topics focus on our emerging nation and its governmental processes and structures.

Because the *Deserts* unit has already been developed in some detail in this chapter, the same topic is used to illustrate how a research-oriented interdisciplinary unit plan can be reorganized for instruction in a departmentalized school. The adaptation will continue to foster valuable connections among disciplines with minimal disruption to the departmental structure of the school.

Interdisciplinary units usually summon contributions from all or most departments—science, social studies, mathematics, English, reading and language arts, health, physical education, art, and music—as well as the school nurse or nurse–teacher. Ideally, participation should be voluntary, and when plans for the unit are being prepared, input should be invited from everyone who will be involved. As an initial step, an organizational meeting can be arranged for the teachers who will participate in teaching the unit. Administrative support may be needed to help set aside a convenient time for the meeting, especially in schools without scheduled team planning time.

The basic unit plan outline for the *Deserts* topic can be used as the team decides how to organize the study. Responsibility for student committee work can be divided among several teachers according their individual specialties. The teachers need to decide where the committee work can best be organized and supervised—that is, which teacher or teachers will assume primary responsibility for beginning the unit and assigning students to their committees. For some topics, this may be the social studies teacher; for others, the science, reading, English, language arts, mathematics, or other specialist may be the most appropriate teacher to organize the student committees.

For a departmentalized approach to the *Deserts* unit, the web design is modified to suggest each department's responsibilities. The web design shown in Figure 6.3 suggests each teacher's role in the unit development.

The main areas of responsibility have been distributed among the teachers. Each teacher will operate both independently and as part of an instructional team to develop the unit. Most of the time, the teachers will be able to complete their part of the instructional plan separately or with minimal consultation with the other teachers. In the web design, some collaborative efforts are indicated, such as those between the art and science teachers, who will develop a plan and assist the students in constructing a model desert village. The science and social studies teachers will cooperate for the field trip. The English/reading/language arts teacher will take a central role in reinforcing the skills that students will need to take notes and write their reports.

This model is only one way to organize for an interdisciplinary study in a departmentalized situation; teachers and administrators who believe the interdisciplinary approach is valuable for students in their schools should search for creative ways to implement it in the context of their school programs. To be viable, interdisciplinary, interdepartmental teaching requires both administrative support and collaboration among teachers. The need for systemwide support for interdisciplinary instruction is emphasized further in chapter 7.

ACTIVITIES

1. Select a topic for a research-oriented interdisciplinary unit of study in an upper elementary or middle school grade. Work alone or with one or two others to plan a unit on this topic. Follow the eight-step process outlined in this chapter to design the plan. Study the examples at each step in the process, and review the web designs provided in the Instructional Resources section for ideas during the planning process.

2. Select a topic for an upper elementary or middle school grade. Work through Steps 1 and 2 of the research-oriented unit planning process. Next, convert the

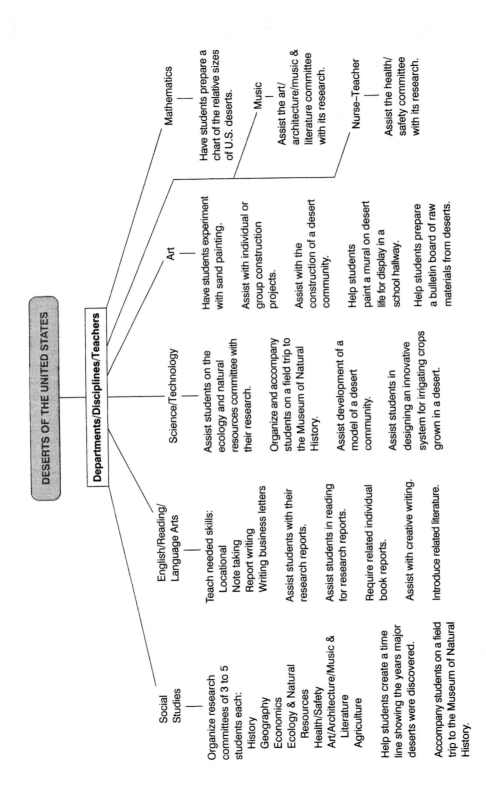

FIGURE 6.3
Plan for a research-oriented interdisciplinary unit in a departmentalized school.

129

design of the unit so that it is suitable for a group of students in a departmentalized middle school program with several teachers working together as a team.

3. Form a group of four to six students who will simulate a middle school team of teachers. Each person should then assume the role of one of the team members—social studies, English, language arts, mathematics, science, and so on. Work together to plan a research-oriented interdisciplinary unit on a topic commonly taught in a middle school. Decide how to delegate responsibilities for the activities and lessons the unit will require.

■ REFERENCES

Arends, R. (2004). *Learning to teach* (6th ed.). New York: McGraw-Hill.

Charbonneau, M. P., & Reider, B. E. (1995). *The integrated elementary classroom: A developmental model of education for the 21st century.* Needham Heights, MA: Allyn & Bacon.

Chard, S. C., & Flockhart, M. E. (2002, November). Learning in the park. *Educational Leadership, 60* (3), 53–56.

Criteria for selection of class research topics. (1966, April 28). *Our 3 C's—Characteristic curricular concepts, 12*(12). (Union Free School District No. 25, Merrick, NY)

Dembo, M. H. (1994). *Applying educational psychology in the classroom* (5th ed.). New York: Longman.

Ellis, A. K. (2002). *Teaching and learning elementary social studies* (7th ed.). Boston: Allyn & Bacon.

Gardner, H. (1993). *Multiple intelligences: The theory in practice.* New York: Basic Books.

Jacobs, H. (Ed.). (1989). *Interdisciplinary curriculum: Design and implementation.* Alexandria, VA: Association for Supervision and Curriculum Development.

Johnson, D. W. (1999). *Learning together and alone: Cooperative, competitive, and individualistic learning.* Boston: Allyn & Bacon.

Johnson, D. W., Johnson, R. T., & Holubec, E. J. (1994). *Cooperative learning in the classroom.* Alexandria, VA: Association for Supervision and Curriculum Development.

Kauchak, D. P., & Eggen, P. D. (2003). *Learning and teaching: Research-based methods* (4th ed.). Boston: Allyn & Bacon.

Kellough, R. D., & Kellough, N. G. (2003). *Middle school teaching: A guide to methods and resources* (4th ed.). Upper Saddle River, NJ: Merrill/Prentice Hall.

Lyman, L., Foyle, H., & Azwell, T. (1993). *Cooperative learning in the elementary classroom.* Washington, DC: National Education Association.

Pappas, C. C., Kiefer, B. Z., & Levstik, L. S. (1999). *An integrated language perspective in the elementary school* (3rd ed.) New York: Longman.

Piaget, J., & Inhelder, B. (1969). *The psychology of the child.* New York: Basic Books.

Post, T. R., Ellis, A. K., Humphreys, A. H., & Buggey, L. J. (1997). *Interdisciplinary approaches to curriculum: Themes for teaching.* Upper Saddle River, NJ: Prentice Hall.

Roberts, P. L., & Kellough, R. D. (2004). *A guide for developing interdisciplinary thematic units* (3rd ed.). Upper Saddle River, NJ: Prentice Hall.

Rottier, J., & Ogan, B. J. (1991). *Cooperative learning in middle-level schools.* Washington, DC: National Education Association.

Santrock, J. W. (2003). *Children* (7th ed.). Boston: McGraw-Hill.

Slavin, R. (1995). *Cooperative learning.* New York: Longman.

Slavin, R., Sharan, S., Kagan, S., Hertz-Lazarowitz, R., Webb, C., & Schmuck, R. (Eds.). (1985). *Learning to cooperate, cooperating to learn.* New York: Plenum.

▒ SUGGESTED READINGS

The supplemental readings listed next provide additional background material on the research-oriented unit planning process as discussed in this chapter.

Davies, I. K. (1976). *Objectives in curriculum design.* London: McGraw-Hill.

Dick, W., & Carey, L. (1996). *The systematic design of instruction.* New York: Harper Collins.

Gronlund, N. E. (2000). *How to write and use instructional objectives* (6th ed.). Upper Saddle River, NJ: Merrill/Prentice Hall.

Grosvenor, L. (1993). *Student portfolios.* Washington, DC: National Education Association.

Kibler, R. J., Cegala, D. J., Barker, L. L., & Miles, D. T. (1981). *Objectives for instruction and evaluation* (2nd ed.). Boston: Allyn & Bacon.

Mager, R. (1997). *Preparing instructional objectives: A critical tool in the development of effective instruction* (3rd ed.). Atlanta, GA: Center for Effective Performance.

Mason, E. (1972). *Collaborative learning.* New York: Agathon Press.

Messick, R. G., & Reynolds, K. E. (1992). *Middle level curriculum in action.* New York: Longman.

O'Neil, J. (1993, September). The promise of portfolios. *Update, 35*(7), 1–5.

Reigeluth, C. M. (1987). *Instructional theories in action: Lessons illustrating selected theories and models.* Hillsdale, NJ: Erlbaum.

Stevenson, C., & Carr, J. F. (Eds.). (1993). *Integrated studies in the middle grades.* New York: Teachers College Press.

Wadsworth, B. J. (1978). *Piaget for the classroom teacher.* New York: Longman.

Weinland, T. P., & Protheroe, D. W. (1973). *Social science projects you can do.* Upper Saddle River, NJ: Prentice Hall.

7

Interdisciplinary Instruction and the Change Process

▓ Overview

This chapter covers the challenges involved when schools adopt an interdisciplinary approach to teaching.

The focus of this chapter is on the following:

- The process of change involved in moving toward an interdisciplinary program
- The kinds of support that teachers need from their school systems so that they can develop an interdisciplinary instructional program
- The need to involve parents in any significant changes in a school program
- The main points presented in support of the interdisciplinary method and its major values for students

▓ Moving Toward an Interdisciplinary Program

The thrust toward interdisciplinary instruction is not the only challenge confronting teachers and schools in recent years.

> Teachers are told that they have to set higher standards for all students, eliminate tracking, tailor lessons to kids' individual needs (including those with various disabilities), adopt small-group and cooperative learning techniques, design interdisciplinary and multicultural curricula, work in teams with other teachers, promote "critical" and "creative" thinking instead of rote learning, attend to children's social and emotional needs, rely on "performance assessment" instead of multiple-choice tests, get with the latest technology, encourage active learning in "real-life" contexts, use fewer textbooks, and, on top of everything else, become "agents of change" in their schools. (Miller, 1995, p. 2)

Recommendations come from many sources both inside and outside the teaching profession. Sometimes, teachers have inspired other teachers to make changes. At times, teachers have written about methods that they have developed or that have grown from their personal teaching experiences and observations. Well-known teacher–authors of the past include Ashton-Warner (1963), Barth (1972), Channon (1970), Dennison (1969), Kohl (1967), Montessori (1964), and Richardson (1964). Some authors have advocated more humanistic approaches in educating children (Hentoff, 1966; Holt, 1964, 1967, 1969). Occasionally, educational critics have pressed for radical school reforms (Gross & Gross, 1969; Kozol, 1975; Pines, 1967; Postman & Weingartner, 1969; Silberman, 1970).

Why Teachers Are Reluctant to Change Methods

Each year, new voices add their criticisms of and recommend modifications to U.S. educational programs. Yet, in practice, most changes evolve slowly.

A number of years ago, Leonard (1968) cited several major reasons for the reluctance of teachers to act rapidly on any changes that are recommended. Leonard's thinking is logical, and it is applicable today:

> A certain caution in educational matters is quite understandable. A school child is far more complex, embodying far more variables, than NASA's entire satellite communications network. Baffled by this complexity and inhibited by a reluctance to "experiment" with children's lives, educators feel justified in clinging to methods that have been developed, hit or miss, over the centuries—even when they are shown to be inefficient. (p. 214)

Leonard's reasoning makes the cautious acceptance of changes in teaching understandable, especially if the changes suggested are extensive or if evidence from research supporting their effectiveness is insufficient. However, reluctance about the interdisciplinary method is not as easy to understand, mainly because the method is not new or revolutionary. An integrated approach to curriculum is no longer considered experimental, and some teachers have used it for many years.

Nevertheless, educators have little information on the success of the interdisciplinary method from schools where it has been tried. Therefore, the lack of both documented evidence of its success and information from practical applications may contribute to a general reluctance to try it.

Research and the Interdisciplinary Method

Some materials that can help promote the interdisciplinary approach are available. For example, the videotape presentation *Cross-Subject Teaching* (1993) demonstrates the benefits of interdisciplinary instruction in schools where it has been implemented. The video shows ways in which music was integrated into other disciplines across a school curriculum in an Appalachian school.

Formal reports on interdisciplinary programs in schools are relatively rare. In 1968, Roland Chatterton, a school district administrator in a suburban community on Long Island in New York State, produced and directed two unique documentary films illustrating a *multidisciplinary*, unit-centered instructional program that the teachers in his schools had developed. The films show a master teacher, Joyce Schonberger Mills, guiding a group of fifth-grade students through two research-oriented interdisciplinary units. Special area teacher–consultants in art, music, library and media, and health are observed assisting the classroom teacher and students with their research, projects, and reports.

The Chatterton films follow the students and teachers engaged in various lessons and activities throughout a 5- to 6-week interdisciplinary unit. The films intentionally leave the value of the interdisciplinary approach for the viewer to decide. Although the documentaries are both inspiring and convincing, and the method's positive results are inferred by the film director, neither film reports any research that may have been undertaken by the school system to document the value of this approach.

Therefore, viewers are left to wonder if any objective evidence was collected that indicated that the approach was more effective than other methods. (Some colleges and universities have copies of these unusual films, but, unfortunately, the film company that produced them no longer exists.)

Current lists of learning standards clearly indicate that many state departments of education are advocating the interdisciplinary approach. However, until more serious research studies and formal reports on the method's actual use in schools are available, movement toward interdisciplinary instruction will probably continue slowly, and teachers may continue to be reluctant to try the method in their classes.

The Need for System Support

The slow pace of change toward interdisciplinary instruction is especially disturbing when its potential values for students are considered, particularly those discussed in chapter 1. It is likely that, as state departments of education continue to add their support and recommend the method, more school systems will be encouraged to introduce an interdisciplinary approach. In the future, schools that do so will need to undertake studies of its value and issue formal reports of their experiences. However, any change will take time and commitment from school systems, as well as from the teachers who implement it.

How to Effect Curricular Change

A number of important factors are involved in making any systemwide curricular change. Initially, an orderly process for instituting any change must be outlined. A completely new procedure for instituting curricular change does not have to be invented because a number of excellent models exist. For example, Fullan (2002) and Wiles and Bondi (1998) provided insights and suggestions for educators contemplating curricular revisions. These writers offered valuable outlines of the tasks involved and leadership requirements for a successful change process.

Oliva (1997) explained several alternative models useful in making curricular changes. He also proposed his own model, which appears to be well suited for the shift from traditional to interdisciplinary programs. The Oliva model begins with an outline of program aims and philosophical and psychological principles on which the new curriculum is to be based. Other steps involve analyzing community and student needs and stating goals and objectives. Listing steps toward implementation of the new program and evaluation procedures completes the process. Oliva's model is flexible, and his suggestion that "the faculty may develop school-wide, interdisciplinary programs that act across areas of specialization" (p. 176) indicates that the model not only is applicable for elementary programs, but also is applicable for introducing interdisciplinary instruction in departmentalized middle schools.

Earlier, Frymier (1973) had outlined a six-phase process for curricular change in schools. Even though Frymier was talking to educators of the 1970s, the same phases—or steps—that he proposed are still useful for school systems intending to move toward an interdisciplinary curricular program. Frymier explained his six-phase plan as an "awareness of the need for change; conceptualizing a range of alternatives; exploration and consideration of the alternatives; commitment and institutionalization of the proposal for change; preparation of staff; implementation, evaluation, and modification of the change" (p. 289).

Adequate planning, staff preparation, and systemwide support are strongly inferred from this list. In fact, preparation and support may be the keys to success in the interdisciplinary curricular change process. Any methodological change can place heavy demands on a school system; this fact is especially true of the interdisciplinary approach because both in-service preparation and new instructional materials may be needed.

Teacher and Classroom Needs

If any progress toward interdisciplinary instruction is to last, teachers will need not only preparation for their new role, but also support throughout the transitional period. The teachers who will use the new approach should be consulted and involved in the change process from the outset. Whenever teachers are not included in the initial decision-making steps or when administrative support is weak, the movement toward an interdisciplinary program—or any other instructional modification—is unlikely to succeed. Lack of consultation with teachers is described as the principal reason for the failure of an innovative primary program (Wood, 1977).

The teaching staff should also be involved in selecting the topics they will be teaching in their interdisciplinary units, and they should be given time to share their unit plan designs with one another. Opportunities should be scheduled for teachers to complete these tasks during the school day.

In addition to having support from the school system, teachers need to have opportunities to form networks in which they can work together to effect the changes they believe are appropriate for the students in their schools (Miller, 1995). Again, such collaboration cannot occur without adequate time and administrative backing.

The teaching staff may also need new materials. Both the kind and the quantity of instructional materials will change with interdisciplinary methods. For example, instead of having a textbook from one publisher for each child in a class, a teacher should have a collection of five or six copies of social studies and science textbooks from each of several publishers. This approach gives students access to more than one viewpoint as they research their unit topics. Purchasing the new materials will involve additional funding.

All classrooms should be equipped with computers, Internet access, and an adequate supply of computer software. Teachers should have access to software catalogs from various suppliers so that they can study new programs that are continually being produced. Computer networking opportunities with college and university libraries and other community resources should be carefully explored and added if found to be valuable and feasible. Carlitz and Lentz (1995) offered an especially helpful list and discussion of the standards that educators should consider when they are making decisions about these networking opportunities.

Teachers also need a supply of trade books on unit topics. Some of these books should be kept in individual classrooms; others can be centrally located in the school library or media center. The school media center should house enough books and magazines, DVD and videotape programs, films and filmstrips, and other resource materials so that students from different classrooms who are studying similar topics at the same time will have an adequate, up-to-date supply of resource materials.

INVOLVING PARENTS AND THE COMMUNITY IN THE CHANGE PROCESS

Any commitment to major changes in a school curriculum must involve parents and the community. Parents are usually included in some aspects of school life, but often their participation has been limited to routine matters, such as field trip supervision, fund-raising, and involvement in parent–teacher organizations. A somewhat more important role for parents is one that is "best interpreted to mean being consulted, having one's opinion taken seriously, and becoming part of the equation when vital decisions are made" (Marsh & Horns-Marsh, 1999, p. 152).

To support the idea of parent and community participation in the decision-making process, the National Parent–Teacher Association has included among its six Standards for Parent/Family Involvement Programs "parent involvement in school decision making and advocacy" (Sullivan, 1999, p. 43). Parents and other members of the community should be invited to join the educational staff for any discussions about a move toward an interdisciplinary instructional program in their school. Parents also need to understand the underlying theory so that they can help their children at home with the kinds of work that an interdisciplinary method entails.

Bryk and Schneider (2003) have emphasized the need to build a trusting relationship among members of the teaching staff, administration, and parents to reduce "the sense of risk associated with change" (p. 43). Any movement toward instituting an interdisciplinary approach will require cooperation, support, and mutual trust on the part of those involved. Working together, a team composed of teachers, administrators, and parents can effect changes that endure.

ACTIVITIES

1. Interview two or three teachers who have taught for at least 5 years. Ask them whether their methods have changed, and if so, how. Ask if they have tried to integrate disciplines or to teach interdisciplinary units. If they have, ask them to tell about their experience. If they have not, ask them to explain why they have not done so. Try to relate the teachers' responses to the conditions for the process of change discussed in this chapter.

2. Ask several parents if they are involved in their schools, and, if so, in what ways they participate. Decide if the parents who are interviewed are part of a decision-making group on curriculum matters.

▨ REFERENCES

Ashton-Warner, S. (1963). *Teacher*. New York: Simon & Schuster.

Barth, R. S. (1972). *Open education and the American school*. New York: Agathon Press.

Bryk, A. S., & Schneider, B. (2003, March). Trust in schools: A core resource for school reform. *Educational Leadership*, 60(8), 40–44.

Carlitz, R. D., & Lentz, M. (1995, April). Standards for school networking. *T.H.E. Journal*, 22(9), 71–74.

Channon, G. (1970). *Homework*. New York: Outerbridge & Dienstfrey.

Chatterton, R. (1968). *The multidisciplinary teaching of class research topics*. Merrick, NY: Merrick School District No. 25.

Cross-subject teaching [Film]. (1993). West Haven, CT: National Education Association. (Episode No. 4, NEA Professional Library)

Dennison, G. (1969). *The lives of children: The story of the First Street School*. New York: Random House.

Frymier, J. R. (1973). *A school for tomorrow*. Berkeley, CA: McCutchan.

Fullan, M. (2002, May). The change leader. *Educational Leadership*, 59(8), 16–20.

Gross, B., & Gross, R. (1969). *Radical school reform*. New York: Simon & Schuster.

Hentoff, N. (1966). *Our children are dying*. New York: Pitman.

Holt, J. (1964). *How children fail*. New York: Delta.

Holt, J. (1967). *How children learn*. New York: Pitman.

Holt, J. (1969). *The underachieving school*. New York: Pitman.

Kohl, H. (1967). *36 children*. New York: Signet.

Kozol, J. (1975). *The night is dark and I am far from home*. Boston: Houghton Mifflin.

Leonard, G. B. (1968). *Education and ecstasy*. New York: Delacorte Press.

Marsh, F. E., & Horns-Marsh, V. (1999). For the record. *Kappa Delta Pi Record*, 35(4), 152.

Miller, E. (1995, January/February). The old model of staff development survives in a world where everything else has changed. *The Harvard Education Letter*, 11(1), 1–3.

Montessori, M. (1964). *The Montessori method*. New York: Schocken Books.

Oliva, P. F. (1997). *Developing the curriculum*. New York: Addison-Wesley.

Pines, M. (1967). *Revolution in learning: The years from birth to six*. New York: Harper & Row.

Postman, N., & Weingartner, C. (1969). *Teaching as a subversive activity*. New York: Delacorte Press.

Richardson, E. S. (1964). *In the early world*. New York: Pantheon Books.

Silberman, C. E. (1970). *Crisis in the classroom: The remaking of American education*. New York: Random House.

Sullivan, P. (1999). The PTA's national standards. *Educational Leadership*, 55(8), 43–44.

Wiles, J., & Bondi, J. (1998). *Curriculum development: A guide to practice* (5th ed.). Upper Saddle River, NJ: Merrill/Prentice Hall.

Wood, K. E. (1977). *Open education experiments: What really causes them to fail?* Washington, DC: Clearinghouse on Urban Education, Institute for Urban and Minority Education. (ERIC Document Reproduction Service No. ED166387)

▨ SUGGESTED READINGS

The supplemental readings listed next provide additional background material on the challenges faced by schools that adopt an interdisciplinary instructional program.

Fraser, H. W. (1985). Microcomputers in schools. *The Educational Forum*, 50(1), 87–100.

Herndon, J. (1968). *The way it spozed to be*. New York: Simon & Schuster.

Hertzberg, A., & Stone, E. F. (1971). *Schools are for children: An American approach to the open classroom*. New York: Schocken Books.

Knirk, F. G., & Gustafson, K. L. (1986). *Instructional technology: A systematic approach to education.* New York: Holt, Rinehart & Winston.

Kohl, H. R. (1969). *The open classroom: A practical guide to a new way of teaching.* New York: New York Review/Random House.

Parker, R., & Parker, B. J. (1994). A historical perspective on school reform. *The Educational Forum, 59*(3), 278–287.

Peterson, D. (Ed.). (1984). *Intelligent schoolhouse: Readings on computers and learning.* Reston, VA: Reston.

Postman, N., & Weingartner, C. (1973). *The school book.* New York: Delacorte Press.

CONCLUSION

Interest in interdisciplinary instruction has increased, and the demand for information about it is growing. This book has provided preservice and in-service teachers and administrators with an introduction to the theoretical and developmental foundations of interdisciplinary instruction, as well as with practical lesson planning suggestions and procedures for designing two types of interdisciplinary unit plans.

Features of the interdisciplinary method that distinguish it from other educational approaches have been discussed. One primary characteristic of interdisciplinary instruction involves a unique, interdisciplinary (or research-oriented interdisciplinary), unit-centered approach to the study of social studies or other topics. Another is that teachers who use the method are able to help students develop the processes and the skills they need for learning throughout life.

▓ SKILLS REQUIRED OF TEACHERS

Teachers who use interdisciplinary instruction find it professionally demanding. To be successful, they need to become secure in the unit planning process and in classroom management. As an aid to individuals who are unfamiliar with the unit planning process, both interdisciplinary and research-oriented interdisciplinary units have been explained in this book. Step-by-step instructions, along with examples, have been given to help teachers begin the unit planning process.

This book has also emphasized that interdisciplinary teachers need to have an extensive fund of general knowledge. They must also be able to apply their understandings of child development and must consider the fundamental learning theories and principles when planning their units. Individual differences in students also require teachers to study students' diverse learning styles and to adapt instruction to the ways in which their students are best able to learn.

▓ BENEFITS TO STUDENTS

The discussion in this book has also attempted to emphasize what is most beneficial to students who are taught to use an interdisciplinary approach to their studies. In particular, students gain experience with the research process, the scientific method, and the ways of knowing inherent in different disciplinary areas as they investigate their unit topics. Students find many natural opportunities to practice their academic skills as they study a topic and prepare reports of their findings. Students are encouraged to develop higher level thinking skills and to recognize that several disciplines and subcategories within the disciplines must usually be examined when they are investigating a topic. They discover that their inquiries are often open ended and continuing rather than finished or complete.

Interdisciplinary units provide students with specific, individual responsibilities, and students can work at their personal ability levels. Whenever they work with others in cooperative research groups or serve on committees, they learn how to work together and share responsibilities.

Holistic studies of topics help students note the interrelationships among the disciplines. Such studies also help students realize that they often need to apply the skills from more than one discipline whenever they study a topic or need to solve a problem in real life.

When compared with more conventional approaches to education, this alternative approach is more suitable for students with special needs because it permits greater flexibility in scheduling. It also supports the use of alternative research methods and reporting techniques. Students can be given the extra time and help they need so that they are better able to participate along with their peers in standard classrooms.

Students are exposed to a greater variety of resources than with traditional, disciplinary approaches, which usually involve the use of a single textbook as a resource. This variety offers them a more rounded, less biased viewpoint, which is especially important in the social studies and science disciplines. Discovering that a great variety of resources can be consulted whenever they undertake research helps them not only while they are in school, but also as they continue to learn throughout life.

Instructional Resources

■ OVERVIEW

The resources in this section include examples that may be useful for further study of the planning processes involved in planning lessons and interdisciplinary units. Samples include the following:

- Lesson plans that follow the planning protocols introduced in chapter 3
- A lesson plan that includes preparation of a computer presentation
- The complete interdisciplinary unit plan on spring for students in second grade that is introduced in chapter 5
- The complete interdisciplinary research-oriented unit plan on deserts for students in fifth grade that is introduced in chapter 6
- Sample web designs for interdisciplinary units at different instructional levels

■ SAMPLE LESSON PLANS

This section includes six sample lesson plans. Five of the plans follow protocols outlined in chapter 3, including directed reading, directed listening, directed viewing, the KWL (know, want to know, learned) technique, and the five-step protocol for a skills lesson. The sixth sample lesson plan includes the use of a teacher-prepared computer presentation.

Example 1

A Lesson Plan Following a Directed Reading Activity (DRA) Protocol

The Louisiana Purchase

Topic:	The Louisiana Purchase
Level:	Grade 5
Estimated Time:	35–40 minutes

Learning Standard

Students investigate and interpret key turning points in U.S. history and explain why these events or developments are significant.

General Objective

Students will improve their comprehension of materials they read for information.

Essential Question

Why was the purchase of new territories—particularly Louisiana—historically important to the growth of the United States?

Behavioral Objective

After reading a selection on the Louisiana Purchase, students will state at least three reasons why this purchase was significant in the history of the United States and support their responses by orally reading appropriate sections from the text.

Procedure

1. Remind the students that they have been studying the early growth of the United States and that they have learned that several large land purchases contributed to the westward expansion of U.S. borders. Explain that they are now ready to learn more about some of these purchases.

2. Ask the students if they can recall the names of some of the purchases.

   Students may recall the names of several that they have heard about, such as Texas, Louisiana, Alaska, and others.

3. Tell the students that today they will be reading about the purchase of the Louisiana Territory and that a short selection from a book on the purchase has been duplicated for them to read.

4. Explain that the selection is the introductory chapter from the book *The Louisiana Purchase,* by James A. Corrick.

5. Explain that the selection will help them to understand why the Louisana Territory purchase was so important in U.S. history.

6. Ask students whether they know the meaning of the word territory.

   Students may respond that it means land *or something that belongs to someone. Explain if needed.*

7. Ask the meaning of *real estate.*

   Students should suggest that this has to do with land or the value of land. Explain if necessary.

8. Write the word *impact* in a sentence on the chalkboard: "The purchase of the Louisiana Territory had a considerable impact on the expansion of the United States." Ask students what they think the word *impact* means in this sentence.

   Students should indicate that it means an effect *on the expansion.*

9. Distribute the reading selection to each student.

10. Ask the students to read the boldface headings silently so that they will have a general idea about the kinds of information the selection includes.

11. When students are finished examining the headings, say, "Now, I would like you to read the selection. As you read, try to note some of the reasons why the Louisiana Purchase had such a significant impact on U.S. history. You can take notes if doing so will help you to recall the reasons you find in the text. Turn the selection over on your desk when you have finished reading so that I will know when most of you have completed the reading."

12. When most students have completed the reading, ask the class for the reasons they found. Note these reasons on the chalkboard. As students offer their contributions, ask them also to locate and read orally a sentence or two that supports what they contributed.

    The major reasons provided by the students should include the following:

    - *This was the first purchase of new territory by the United States, and because no provision was made for such purchases in the Constitution, the purchase of Louisiana established the right of the federal government to acquire new property. This right also strengthened the power of the federal government.*

    - *The purchase nearly doubled the size of the United States.*

    - *It opened the way for thousands of people to begin exploring the West.*

    - *The territory was rich in ores for mining, and the land provided an expanse of farmland for agricultural development.*

    - *It gave the United States complete control of the Mississippi River.*

13. Raise other related questions, such as the following:

    - Why was control of the Mississippi River important?

      Students should respond with the idea that the river was needed for economic reasons, for transportation, and for exploration.

    - What were the borders of the Louisiana Territory?

      Students should reply that the exact borders were not clear.

    - What groups of people lived in the new territory?

      Students should say that Native Americans, Blacks, and White settlers lived there.

    - What are some of the states that were part of the Louisiana Territory?

      Students should include Oklahoma, Colorado, North and South Dakota, Wyoming, Kansas, Iowa, Minnesota, Missouri, Montana, and Louisiana.

14. Bring the lesson to closure by asking the students what they believe they learned from this reading.

    Students will include the idea that the purchase of the Louisiana Territory was exceptionally important to the westward expansion of the United States.

15. Ask students to copy the reasons listed on the chalkboard into their notebooks for future reference.

Materials

Corrick, J. A. (2001). *The Louisiana Purchase*. San Diego, CA: Lucent Books. (Copies of pages 10–14 will be needed for each student.)

Example 2

A Lesson Plan Following a Directed Listening Protocol

An Eskimo Story

By Audrey Asaro and Smithe Jean-Baptiste
(*Note:* See Figure A.25 for the web design of an interdisciplinary unit on Alaska that includes this lesson.)

Topic:	Eskimos of Alaska (This lesson is a directed listening activity that introduces students to a research-oriented interdisciplinary unit on the study of Alaska.)
Level:	Grade 4
Estimated Time:	30–45 minutes

Learning Standards

* Students will understand why people and places are located where they are located and the patterns that can be perceived in these locations.
* Students will describe the relationship between people and environments and the connections between people and places.

General Objective

Students will be familiar with the culture of the Eskimos of Alaska.

Essential Questions

How does the lifestyle of Alaskan Eskimos differ from ours? In what ways is it similar?

Behavioral Objective

After listening to the book *The Seasons and Someone*, students will each suggest one new fact that they gained about Alaskan Eskimos or their lifestyle.

Procedure

This lesson will introduce a new interdisciplinary unit on Alaska. In preparation for the lesson, maps of the United States and the world should be displayed, and a small collection of materials on this topic should be available for students. Have the students meet in a section of the classroom conducive to listening, where you will read to them *The Seasons and Someone,* by Virginia Kroll. This book is about a young Eskimo girl and her family.

1. When ready for the lesson, ask students if they know who the Eskimos are.

   Students will probably reply that Eskimos are people who live in the cold weather of the North, that they live in igloos, and that they are people of the snow.

2. Ask if students know the part of the United States where Eskimos are living.

   Some students may know that Eskimos live in the state of Alaska.

3. Ask if students know any other parts of the world where Eskimos are living.

   Some students may cite the North Pole and Canada. Some may not know.

4. Ask for volunteers to point out Alaska, Greenland, Canada, and the parts of Asia where Eskimos live. Assist students as needed in finding these locations.

5. Before beginning to read the story, ask students to listen carefully to learn about the family's living environment, what their homes are like, the kinds of clothing they wear, and the kinds of animals they have. List these purposes on the board or on a chart for student reference during the reading.

6. Begin the oral reading with the author's note. The note explains that Eskimos inhabit the northernmost areas of the world, areas that have the coldest and most bitter weather. The note also gives some information about Eskimo beliefs, customs, and homes. Ask students if they have any questions. Respond as needed; then continue.

7. During the reading, stop occasionally to show students the beautiful illustrations of Eskimo life and the Eskimo environment. Also, ask for any questions, and remind students about the list of purposes for listening.

8. After the story is completed, begin assessing what students have gained from the listening activity by asking each student to take a few minutes to write what he or she learned about Eskimos in Alaska. Refer to the list on the board as an outline.

9. After students have made a list of their understandings, bring closure to the lesson by asking each student to tell one thing he or she learned about this Eskimo family from listening to the story.

   Students will most likely reply that the Eskimos in the story live in a very cold climate, in igloos, and near high mountains. Some students will suggest that Eskimos wear warm, furry clothing; that they gather nuts and berries; and that many animals live in their environment, such as oxen, seals, birds, and polar bears.

10. To conclude the lesson, do the following:

    - Tell the students to keep in mind all they learned from this story about one Eskimo family, and explain that this lesson begins a new study during which they will be working in committees to complete research on Alaska for the next several weeks.

- Direct students' attention to the materials that have been collected on Alaska for their use. Explain that they may look at these materials to get some ideas about what they may be able to learn about Alaska.
- Ask students to begin thinking about what they would like to learn about Alaska as they begin the study. Explain that after they have had a few days to look over the materials and to think about what they would like to learn, they will prepare an outline to help guide their research.

Materials

- Kroll, V. (1994). *The seasons and someone*. San Diego, CA: Harcourt Brace.
- A collection of materials on Alaska and Eskimos
- Large maps of the United States and the world

Example 3

A Lesson Plan Following a Directed Viewing Protocol

The Space Age

Topic:	Exploring Space, a lesson that introduces an interdisciplinary unit on the exploration of outer space
Level:	Middle school—Grades 6–7
Estimated Time:	30–40 minutes

Learning Standard

Students will know the major turning points in the world history of space exploration and the factors that brought about significant changes.

General Objective

Students will be introduced to the unit theme, and student interest in the history of space exploration will be generated.

Essential Questions

What were some of the most critical events that occurred during the Space Age (1947–1961) that brought about advances in the exploration of outer space? Why did the exploration of space take such a long time before it began?

Behavioral Objective

After viewing a DVD documentary presentation on the Space Age (from 1947 to 1961), students will orally list at least three significant events in the history of space exploration and infer that considerable failure occurred before success.

Procedure

In preparation for this lesson, have all equipment ready in advance—a computer with a DVD-ROM drive, an LCD projector, and a chart on which to record students' contributions following the presentation.

1. Say, "You know that U.S. scientists have been exploring outer space." Ask if students know some of the accomplishments of the U.S. space program.

   Students are likely to recall that U.S. astronauts landed on the moon, that satellites have been launched, and that we have a space shuttle.

2. Ask students if they know when the first satellite was launched.

   Some students may know that it was Sputnik in 1957. Others may not know.

3. Explain that we are beginning a new study about the exploration of outer space and that, today, students will view a DVD presentation that includes information about the Space Age in the 20th century.

4. Explain that in the presentation, they will see film clips of significant events that occurred during the Space Age.

5. Introduce the DVD presentation. Say, "As you view the presentation, look for some of the most significant events—the turning points—that took place during the Space Age.

6. Explain that the presentation has a great deal of information and that students may ask to have it paused at times so that they can take notes.

7. Show the presentation. Remind students to watch carefully and to take notes about the events they see. (Pause the presentation when students need more time to take notes.)

8. After the presentation, hold a discussion about information the students gained. On the chart prepared beforehand (such as the one shown in Figure A.1), record the students' contributions.

9. Ask the following questions:

   • What were some of the most important events that occurred during the Space Age?

   The students will suggest most of the events given in the presentation, including Sputnik in 1957 and the first U.S. satellite in 1958. They may also recall that Gargarin was the first human to travel in space in 1959.

   • What living things were sent into outer space before any humans rocketed into orbit?

   Students should mention rats, dogs, and monkeys.

   • Why do you think it took such a long time for the first U.S. satellite to be launched?

   Students should have noticed that failures occurred in the space program before the first successful satellite was launched.

Space Age Exploration: 1947–1961

Important events:

First living things in space:

Why launching the first satellite took so long:

Other information:

FIGURE A.1
Chart on which to record student contributions after a DVD presentation on the space age (1947–1961).

- Do you recall any other information that was included in the presentation?
  Students may have noted that outer space begins at 250 kilometers above the earth and that the temperature in outer space is −273°C.
10. Summarize the lesson by reviewing the students' contributions recorded on the chart.
11. Remind students that their new study will include conducting research on space exploration, and ask what the first step will be in conducting their research.
    Responses should indicate the need for questions to guide their research.
12. Conclude the lesson by asking students to prepare at least two questions to guide their research before the next session.

Materials

- *A century to remember: The great events of the 20th century* [DVD CD-ROM]. (1999). St. Laurent, Quebec, Canada: Mendacy Entertainment Group.
- LCD projector and screen
- Chart paper

Example 4

A Lesson Plan Following a Know, Want to Know, Learned (KWL) Protocol

Dolphins

By Carla Cardoso, Donna Fuchs, and Evelyn Kaszuba

(*Note*: A web design for the complete unit plan on dolphins appears in Figure A.8.)

Topic: Dolphins

Level: Grade 3

Estimated Time: 30–40 minutes

Learning Standard

Students will raise questions necessary for scientific inquiries.

General Objective

Students will learn to use know, want to know (or learn), learned (KWL) charts to guide studies of specific topics.

Essential Question

What are the most important questions that need to be answered when you are learning about life in the sea, particularly about dolphins, which are unusual animals?

Behavioral Objective

Students will complete the first two sections of a KWL chart to guide their study of dolphins.

Procedure

In preparation for the lesson, three sections of the chalkboard—or large charts—will be needed for the three columns. Use vertical lines to separate the columns, and leave a space at the top on which to write headings for the KWL, as shown in Figure A.2. Because this lesson will involve a discussion, before beginning the lesson, remind students about rules for participation.

1. Display a large picture of a dolphin on an easel.
2. Ask, "What do you notice in this picture?"

   Some students may say that the picture is of an animal, some sea animal or fish; others will know that it is a picture of a dolphin.

3. Say, "Today, we are going to begin to study about dolphins." Then raise the following questions:
   - Has anyone ever seen a dolphin?

WHAT WE *KNOW*	WHAT WE *WANT* TO KNOW	WHAT WE HAVE LEARNED

FIGURE A.2
Chalkboard or large chart preparation for an introductory lesson involving a KWL (know, want to know, learned) chart.

- Where have you seen dolphins?

  Some students may say that they have seen dolphins on television or in an aquarium, such as at Sea World. Other students may not have seen dolphins.

- What do you think dolphins eat?

  Some students will say that dolphins eat fish or seaweed. Others may not know.

4. As the discussion progresses, suggest that a good idea would be to create a KWL chart.

5. Ask the students if they know what a KWL chart is and, if so, if they know how to create one.

   Many students will have had experience with KWL charts, although some will not have.

6. Explain what the letters *KWL* indicate, and review with the students the kinds of information that should be included in each section. Write headings for the sections of the chart on the board, using different colored chalk for each.

7. Begin to complete the Know section of the chart. On the *K* section of the chart, include what students suggested about what they believe dolphins eat and where dolphins live. Write the students' contributions in complete sentences.

8. Ask students if they think they know anything else about dolphins. If so, add these ideas to the *K* section, or ask individual students to write their own ideas.

If students write their ideas, first ask them to say what they will write to help ensure clarity of the written information.

Note that some of the students' ideas may be incorrect. At this point, include these ideas; as the study progresses, students will determine the accuracy of their ideas. Be sure to explain that they will need to check whether each idea is correct.

9. After the students list all they know about dolphins, review the list by reading it to the students.

10. Begin the *W* section by asking students to think about what they would like to learn about dolphins. Write the questions students raised in the *W* section on the board, or have volunteers write their own questions.

Students may be interested in learning information such as how big dolphins grow, how long they live, or in what parts of the ocean they are usually found.

11. If the students fail to include any important questions, add these questions at this point.

12. Review the *W* section by reading all the questions listed.

13. Provide time for students to copy the first two sections of the KWL chart into their notebooks.

14. To bring closure to the lesson, explain that the first two sections of the KWL chart will help the class as they study dolphins, that the *L* section will be completed as answers to their questions are found, and that ideas listed in the *K* section will be checked for accuracy during the study.

Materials
- Large picture or poster of a dolphin
- Easel
- Colored chalk

Example 5

A Lesson Plan Following the Five-Step Protocol

Learning How to Outline

Topic:	An introduction to outlining
Level:	Grade 4
Estimated Time:	30 minutes

Learning Standard
Students prepare outlines of information needed for research.

General Objective

Students will learn to use outlining to assist them in preparing written reports.

Essential Question

What is the process followed in outlining information found in reading materials?

Behavioral Objective

After a demonstration and guided practice in outlining paragraphs from a social studies textbook, each student will outline the main ideas and supporting details from a five-paragraph textbook selection.

Procedure

1. Ask the students what they do when they are researching a topic and want to remember information they find in books or other reading materials.

   Students are likely to say they copy some of the sentences from the readings into their notebooks.

2. Explain that the purpose of this lesson is to help them to learn more about how to record such information without copying it, that they will be learning how to outline information they find in a book, in an article, or in a document on the Internet.

3. Invite the students to watch as you demonstrate a way to outline paragraphs in a reading selection. (Using an LCD or an overhead projector, project a selection that includes three or four paragraphs of content material, preferably a page from the students' social studies textbook. The topic should be one that students are currently investigating.)

4. Direct students' attention to the title and first paragraph of the selection. Have students read the first paragraph silently; then ask one student to read it orally for the class. (Note that although you are demonstrating at this point in the lesson, students should be involved in the thought process as much as possible.)

5. Hold a brief discussion of the content of the paragraph. Ask students what they think is the main point of the paragraph. Phrase the main idea for the students, and demonstrate how to begin the outline by writing the main idea on the chalkboard next to a Roman numeral *I*.

6. Ask students to suggest other important points they recall from the paragraph. Phrase these points, and write each under the main idea, using uppercase letters—*A*, *B*, *C*, and so on.

7. Continue demonstrating how to outline each succeeding paragraph in the projected sample, following Steps 4 and 5.

8. Ask students to look at the outline and to explain how the outline differs from the text selection.

   Students should note that the outline is shorter than the selection, that it includes the most important information, that the wording is different, and that nothing from the text has been copied directly.

9. If necessary, demonstrate the process with a second projected selection.

10. If students appear to understand what has been demonstrated, continue by helping them to apply the skill to a new selection.

    a. Ask the students to read the selection silently.

    b. Ask the students to decide on the main idea and other related information for each paragraph in the projected selection.

    c. Guide the students in their wording of the outline.

    d. Continue to guide students as they outline additional projected selections if needed.

11. Direct students to a selection in their social studies textbooks. Follow the same procedure outlined in Step 10 to guide students through the outlining procedure. Use more than one selection if needed. If students appear to understand the process, continue with Step 12.

12. Ask students to individually outline a new five-paragraph selection from their textbooks.

13. Collect the students' outlines after they have had sufficient time to prepare them so that you can assess their success and understanding of the process.

14. After the outlines have been collected, ask the students to explain the process involved in outlining information they locate in reading materials.

    Students should explain that the process begins with a careful reading of the selection. Next, each paragraph is analyzed for its main idea and important information related to that idea. Finally, the students should explain that they need to write the outline of these points in their own words and without copying directly from the text.

15. Tell the students they will have further practice with outlining but that the most important practice will be the outlining they need to do when they are researching the topics they are studying.

Materials

- Several three- to five-paragraph selections of content material prepared for overhead or LCD projection
- Copies of the students' social studies textbooks
- An LCD projector and a computer, or an overhead projector with transparencies prepared in advance

Example 6

A Lesson Plan Using a Teacher-Prepared Computer Presentation

Endangered Animals

The following lesson plan is an example of one use of presentation software to create a slide show. The teacher follows a directed viewing protocol to introduce the slide show, providing students with purposes for viewing pictures of several endangered animals. This lesson assists students in planning for individual research on an endangered animal of their choice.

Examples of 9 of the 40 slides that make up the presentation are shown in Figure A.3. Each example indicates some suggestions for the possible layout, text, pictures, and animation. Pictures of endangered animals—which do not appear in Figure A.3 but make up most of the slides to be included—should be carefully selected for their clarity and color. Animal pictures can be downloaded from many sources on the Internet; they can also be scanned from print sources or from photographs taken by the teacher.

Topic:	Endangered Animals
Level:	Upper elementary—Grades 4–6
Estimated Time:	35–45 minutes

Learning Standards

- Students will describe some survival behaviors of common living specimens.
- Students will engage in the research design process.

General Objectives

- Students will develop skills needed for research.
- Students will understand that many animal species are endangered.

Essential Question

What are the important questions to raise in the investigation of an endangered animal?

Behavioral Objective

After viewing a presentation slide show of several animals currently on the list of endangered animals, each student will (a) prepare a list of three animals he or she would like to study, and (b) write at least one question to guide research on any endangered animal.

Procedure

This lesson introduces a study of endangered animals. In preparation for the lesson, collect a variety of materials on this topic. Although some books and other resources

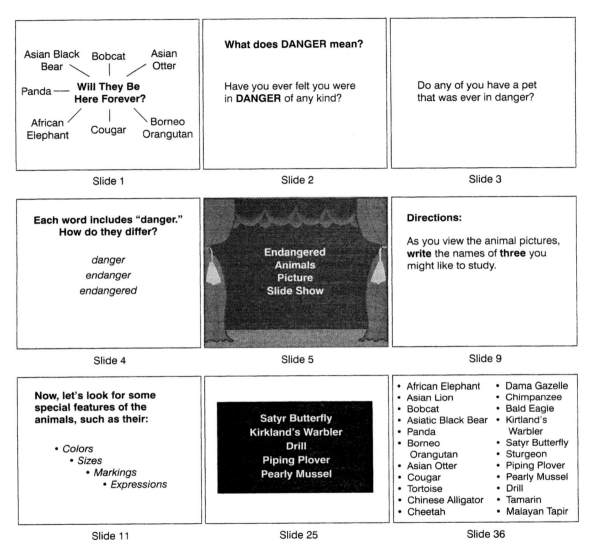

FIGURE A.3

Possible layouts for nine slides in a presentation for an introductory lesson plan on the study of endangered animals.

can be displayed prior to the lesson, these materials should be limited so that students will need to use the school media center, the community library, and the Internet to locate additional sources as they conduct their research.

Prepare a slide-show presentation in advance for this directed viewing activity. Collect photographs of approximately 25 endangered animals from the Internet or other sources. A computer, presentation program software, and an LCD projector will be needed. (As an alternative, use 35-mm slides and a slide projector.)

1. *Slide 1:* Before beginning the lesson, project the first slide in the presentation, which should show a composite of pictures of several endangered animals. Leave this slide on the screen until the class is ready to begin. Some soft music can be added from a CD. If music accompanies the first slide, fade it out before projecting the second slide. (Figure A.3 shows a possible layout for Slide 1. Small pictures of endangered animals surround the question Will they be here forever? Animation can be used to add the connecting lines and pictures—one by one—to the slide.)

2. *Slide 2:* When ready for the lesson, project the second slide. Ask the students whether they have ever been in a situation in which they believed they were in some kind of danger. (Figure A.3 shows a possible layout for Slide 2. A small illustration, clip art, or another picture can be placed between the two sentences on the slide. The word *DANGER* should appear in boldface.)

   The students will probably suggest a variety of situations, such as having been left alone too long in a strange place, having been in a very dark place, being stranded in some way or in a deserted location, having a car break down in a remote location, or possibly having been in a situation where they could not get any food to eat for a long time.

3. *Slide 3:* Ask if anyone having a pet at home has ever thought his or her pet was in danger of some kind. (Figure A.3 shows a possible layout for Slide 3. Several small pictures of pets should be added, surrounding the text on the slide.)

   It may be possible to elicit a situation in which a pet has been left alone for a long time without care or food, perhaps when the family was delayed while returning from a trip. It is also possible that one of the students has had a pet that strayed from home and did not return for a long period.

4. *Slide 4:* Ensure that students understand the meanings of *danger, endanger,* and *endangered.* (Figure A.3 shows a possible layout for Slide 4. The prefixes and suffix should be emphasized with boldface.)

   The word endangered will probably be associated with danger. However, you may need to clarify. If so, write the following sentence on the board: "Some animals on our planet have become endangered because of a lack of food in their natural surroundings."

5. *Slide 5:* Project a title slide. (Figure A.3 shows a possible layout for this slide. Select contrasting colors for the background, frame, and text on the slide.)

6. *Slides 6–11:* Read the text on each slide aloud, and respond to any questions. Explain to students that you will provide them with some questions or suggestions about what to look for during the slide show that may help them as they view the pictures. Possible text for this group of slides follows:

   Slide 6: "All of the animals, birds, and insects you will see in this slide show are endangered."

Slide 7: "They are in danger of becoming extinct. Do you know what it means to become extinct?"

Slide 8: "Our new unit will be a study of endangered animals. During our study, each person will need to research and report on one endangered animal."

Slide 9 (see Figure A.3): This slide provides the main purposes for viewing the presentation: "As you view the animal pictures, write the names of three you might like to study." Bold colors can be used for words to be emphasized.)

Slide 10: Include two sentences to clarify the procedure: "I will collect your choice lists tomorrow. Then, you will be assigned one of your choices to research."

Slide 11 (see Figure A.3): Now, let's "look for some special features of the animals, such as their colors, sizes, markings, and expressions." Alternate colors for the bulleted list, and use animation to have the words in the list appear one at a time.)

7. *Slides 12–24:* Each of these slides presents a picture of a different endangered animal. Using animation, have each slide first show only the name of the animal or bird. Before bringing the picture forward, which will cover the name and the entire slide, raise a question about or make a suggestion for studying the picture. After the picture appears, add text after a few seconds to stimulate additional discussion about the animal or bird. The text can be added with animation features in presentation software. Show the slides, stopping to read the name of each animal, raise questions, and offer suggestions to stimulate students' thinking and to focus on research possibilities. Finally, ask the following question after projecting: "What special characteristics or features do you see as you look at this animal, bird, or insect?"

Students are likely to notice distinguishing markings, unusual physical features, or size.

Remind the students occasionally that as they view the pictures, they will need to consider some animals they may want to study.

8. *Slide 25* (see Figure A.3): This slide is a brief pause in the show to introduce the names of the remaining endangered animals to be viewed in the presentation. The animals listed on the slide are examples. Because many other possibilities exist, list only those that will appear in the remainder of the presentation.

9. *Slides 26–34:* Complete the slide show, and remind students to note their choices as they view the endangered animal pictures.

10. *Slides 35–40:* The last six slides need to bring closure to the lesson and provide for a review of the endangered animals shown in the presentation. Ask students to raise a question to help guide their research. Possible text follows:

Slide 35: Include a question and a comment: "Have you chosen three animals to study?" and "Here are their names again." An arrow with animation can be added to this slide.

Slide 36 (see Figure A.3): List all the animals previously shown. For clarity, alternate between two colors for the animal names. Use animation and timing to bring the names forward individually.

Slide 37: Include two sentences on this slide: "Try to make your final choices by tomorrow. If you haven't seen an animal today that you would like to study, there are other endangered animals you may choose." Add an endangered animal picture to the slide.

Slide 38: Raise two questions for discussion: "After everyone chooses an animal, what will we need to do next? What is the next step in the research process?"

Students should respond that they need some questions to guide their research before they can begin.

Slide 39: Bring up this slide after students have responded. The text can read as follows: "YES, all research begins with one or more QUESTIONS."

Slide 40: Write the following statement: "Take a few minutes now to write one or two questions you think will be important for us to answer about each animal."

11. While students are writing their questions, open a blank word-processing document that has been prepared in advance and formatted with a large, clear font. When students are ready, ask them to contribute some of their questions. Listen to several questions, then choose several to type for the class to view. Invite the students to help select the most important questions everyone should try to answer about his or her endangered animal. Explain that individual students can add other questions for their endangered animals if they think doing so is necessary, but that everyone should first try to find information on the essential questions decided by the class.

Possible questions

- Why is the animal endangered? (*analysis*)
- Where does this animal live? (*comprehension*)
- What does the animal eat? (*knowledge*)
- What can be done to save the animal? (*synthesis*)

12. Summarize the research task:

- Explain again that the new unit on endangered animals will begin with each person selecting and studying one endangered animal from the slide show. If some students know of other endangered animals and prefer to study one that was not presented during the slide show, allow them to choose alternatives.
- Indicate that the questions they listed will help guide their research project, although some of them may find other important questions about the animals they selected to study.
- Explain that their animal choice lists will be collected the next day and that you will try to assign each student his or her first choice. Explain that you may

need to assign some students their second or third choice if the same animal has been chosen too often.

- Explain that the class will need to discuss some ways to find information about the animals, and ask students to begin thinking about possible research sources before the next class session.

13. Have each student copy the questions for research—those decided on by the class—into their notebooks, and remind the students that their animal choice lists will be collected tomorrow.

Materials

Resource materials for students to use in researching endangered animals—textbooks, magazines, current newspapers, trade books, encyclopedias, CD-ROM encyclopedias, and environmental programs

A collection of pictures of animals currently on the endangered animals list (*Note*: If the needed equipment is available, the pictures should be prepared as a slide show presentation for computer and LCD projection so that they can be viewed easily. Presentation software, such as Microsoft PowerPoint, can be used to prepare the slides.)

A computer with presentation viewing software installed

An LCD or a slide projector and a screen

▓ SAMPLE UNIT PLANS

Spring: An Interdisciplinary Unit Plan

Topic: Spring

Title:

Possible Titles: Spring, Signs of Spring, Spring Is Here, Spring Changes

Method of Involving Students in Creating a Title

- The students can suggest other titles during a class meeting, or individuals can write suggested titles on slips of paper and put the slips in a suggestion box. A class vote can be taken to select the final title.
- Two or three volunteers can be asked to cut letters for the title that will then be displayed at the top of a large bulletin board.

Level: Grade 2. This unit plan is designed specifically for students in the second grade, but it can be adapted for students in Grades 3 or 4.

Estimated Unit Length: 3–4 weeks

Learning Standards

Students will do the following:

- Develop plans for data-gathering explorations
- Describe their observations

- Explain how knowledge can be gained by careful observation
- Explain why keeping accurate and detailed records is important
- Use direct observations and measurements of temperature to explore phenomena
- Develop tentative explanations of what they observed
- Experiment and create artwork in various media.
- Describe patterns of daily, monthly, and seasonal changes in their environment
- Use simple instruments to measure such quantities as distance, size, weight, and temperature, and look for patterns in the data
- Construct tables, charts, and graphs to display and analyze real-world data
- Interpret graphs
- Collect and display data
- Discover patterns in nature, art, music, and literature
- Describe the major stages in the life cycles of selected plants and animals
- Demonstrate appropriate audience behavior, including attentive listening in a variety of musical settings
- Understand the roles and contributions of individuals and groups to social, political, economic, cultural, scientific, technological, and religious practices and activities
- Create their own stories, poems, and songs using the elements of the literature they have read and appropriate vocabulary
- Observe the conventions of grammar and usage, spelling, and punctuation
- Engage in technological design and use a variety of materials to design and construct examples of what they learned

General Objectives

Content

Students will do the following:

- Become more aware of the changes going on around them in their environment and learn more about specific changes during the spring season
- Understand basic Earth processes
- Understand that all plants need varying amounts of air, sunlight, and water to thrive
- Know how to construct and use graphs
- Understand that all sound is produced by vibrating objects
- Increase their knowledge of the various holidays that occur during the spring season and develop their understanding of the many ways people in U.S. society celebrate these occasions
- Understand that seasonal changes bring about some of the events they can observe in their own community

Attitudinal

Students will do the following:

- Appreciate that works of art, music, and literature can be inspired by feelings people associate with seasons of the year
- Be aware that various phenomena, including the weather and seasonal changes, can affect our feelings and attitudes, and that we may experience changes in feelings because of seasonal changes in our environment
- Appreciate that scientific experimentation demands preciseness and patience

Process

Students will do the following:

- Gain experience in using media—art, music, and movement—to express feelings, attitudes, and ideas
- Develop and refine their observational skills
- Gain experience with using instruments and in preparing graphs to record changes they observe
- Apply the scientific method in experimenting with plants
- Realize that even though scientific investigations may fail to support their hypotheses, they can always learn from the inquiry
- Learn how to record data to show the results of their investigations

Essential Questions

- What are some of the main signs of spring that are found in our local neighborhood?
- How can our observations of our natural environment be recorded?
- What techniques can be used to determine whether our weather is changing?
- How can we use weather instruments, such as a thermometer or a rain gauge, to help us study seasonal changes?
- How can information from weather instruments be charted?
- How can we determine the basic needs of plant life?
- What are the most important factors in the care of plants?
- In what ways do changes in the seasons affect the ways people feel?
- How are sounds produced?
- What important holidays occur during spring, and what is the significance of these holidays?
- What activities in our community are specifically related to changes in the seasons?
- How can art media be used to represent the seasons of the year?

- How can the design of a birdhouse be related to observations of birds in their natural environment?
- How is the spring season represented in our literature and writing?

Web Design of the Unit See Figure A.4.

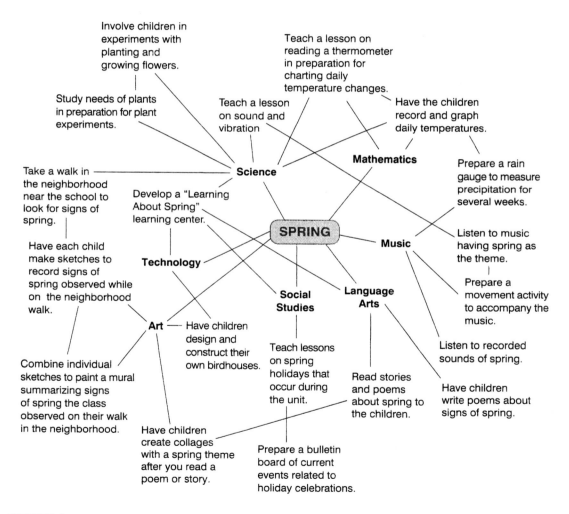

FIGURE A.4
Web diagram for a complete interdisciplinary unit plan called *Spring*.

Introductory Lesson Plan

Topic: *Spring*, a lesson to prepare children for a walk in their neighborhood to observe the signs of spring

Level: Grade 2

Estimated Time: 20–25 minutes

Learning Standard

Students will develop plans for data-gathering explorations.

General Objective

Students will be prepared for a field excursion during which they will observe signs of spring in their school neighborhood.

Essential Question

What are some of the main signs of spring that are found in our local neighborhood?

Behavioral Objective

In response to the question What signs of spring might we look for as we take our walk in the neighborhood? the students will name at least three items—flowers, animals, budding trees, and so on.

Procedure

1. Select a day for the field trip in advance, and secure the necessary permissions. Invite two adults from the list of parent volunteers to assist with supervision on the walk. The field trip will be taken after this introductory lesson, which is designed to prepare the students for their walk.
2. The first lesson begins with a class meeting in the early afternoon during the time regularly devoted to unit studies.
3. Begin the lesson by reminding the children that they have studied their neighborhood this year and that their last unit was called *Our School*. Ask the children to recall some activities from that unit.

   Children may say that they remember drawing a map of the school and visiting and interviewing several people who work in the school: the nurse, the school principal, and a custodian. They may also remember that they learned about these people's jobs, that they saw where the people do their work, and that they were given a chance to see some materials used in these jobs. The children may also recall drawing and labeling pictures of school helpers.

4. Ask the children if they have noticed that the school custodians are beginning to do some work they have not been able to do all winter.

   The children may have noticed that the school custodians are working outside on the grounds.

5. Ask the children if they can think of any reasons why work is beginning outside at this time of year.

   Children may say that it is because the grass is growing and that it is warmer. They may also say it is now spring.

6. Tell the children that they will be studying this new season and that spring is the topic of their new unit.

7. Ask the children what they already know about the spring season. Write their responses on the board. Use a concept web to record what the children say. (See Figure 5.6 for a concept web showing the children's initial concepts of spring.)

   Responses may include that it is a special time of the year, a time when the weather gets warmer and they no longer have to wear heavy clothing. They may say the grass and some flowers begin to grow in spring and that the trees have buds. Some children may remember that some important holidays occur during the spring season.

8. Suggest that all the ideas they noticed are important. Then ask the children if they know that their ideas are actually "signs" of the spring season. Write *sign* on the board, and ask if the children know what it means.

   Children may say that a sign is a signal or an idea of something. Similar responses may be given as well.

9. Tell the children that they may not have noticed other signs of spring, and explain that at the end of the week, the class will take a walk along several streets near the school to look for signs of spring in the neighborhood. Then ask, "What signs of spring might we look for when we take our walk in the neighborhood?" List the signs that the children suggest on a large sheet of paper. Encourage the children to look at the list before they leave the classroom.

   The children may suggest looking for different kinds of flowers and noticing where the grass has begun to turn green. They may also mention looking for birds that have returned after the winter and examining trees and shrubs for signs of new growth.

10. To conclude the lesson, summarize briefly by reviewing the list of signs of spring on the chart.

11. Distribute permission slips and explain that each child must take a permission slip home to be signed. Tell the students that the slips must be returned in 2 days so that the class can take the walk.

Materials

Chart paper
A supply of parental permission slips to distribute to each child in the class

Descriptions of Lessons and Activities

- On the day of the students' field trip (walk) through their neighborhood to look for signs of spring, stop occasionally and encourage them to draw or paint one or more sketches showing the signs of spring: animals, birds, insects, and so on. Collect specimens of plants and samples of water to take back to the classroom. After returning to the classroom, have some of the sketches transferred (and enlarged) to a large sheet of mural paper, and involve the students in selecting and arranging the pictures on the mural. Some children may use resources in the classroom to determine the names of the plant specimens and to learn more about their growth patterns and needs. One of several learning center activities could be having students use a microscope to examine the water samples brought back from the field trip.

  Sketching their observations and collecting samples during the field trip offers the children opportunities to be involved in the work of scientists. Using art media to prepare the mural will help students develop a visual summary of the signs of spring that they observed. *[linguistic, naturalist, and spatial intelligences]*

- Teach the students how to read an outdoor thermometer. A thermometer should be installed outside a classroom window, and students should be given opportunities to practice reading the temperature.

  The purpose of this lesson is to prepare the students for keeping a daily temperature record for 2 weeks during the spring. *[logical-mathematical and linguistic intelligences]*

- Help the students make a rain gauge. Locate the gauge in an outdoor area near the classroom for students to inspect after any precipitation. Then prepare a chart showing the amount of precipitation each week throughout the unit. The different amounts can be used to create addition and subtraction problems to solve in mathematics.

  This activity provides students with opportunities to observe, measure, create a graph, and practice computation skills. *[logical–mathematical and naturalist intelligences]*

- Have students use their daily temperature records for a lesson on graphing. Work with them to prepare a simple graph (either line or bar) to chart the temperature readings they recorded.

  The purpose of this mathematics lesson is to introduce the students to graphing. *[logical–mathematical intelligence]*

- If plant specimens have been collected from the field trip, some students may want to care for these plants. They can determine what each plant needs, care for it, and keep a record to show how the plant changes throughout the spring.

  This activity provides students with experience in caring for plants. *[naturalist intelligence]*

- Give the students opportunities to conduct their own experiments to determine the basic needs of plants. Begin by having them suggest what plants need to live, then help individual students set up their experiments. Students who already know what plants need to live can design scientific experiments to confirm what they believe. Some may fail to control variables when conducting their experiments. When this happens, let the students perform their experiments, then raise questions to help them realize the need to test one variable at a time. Replicate experiments when needed.

This activity not only helps students discover the basic needs of the plants they use, but also gives them opportunities to design and carry out their own scientific investigations. *[naturalist, logical–mathematical, and intrapersonal intelligences]*

- After students determine, experimentally, the basic needs of plants, teach a lesson on planting flower seeds. Use marigold seeds because they will grow rapidly and easily under proper conditions. In this activity, students should decide the conditions needed for growing the seeds and be given time to collect soil and containers for the growing plants. Ask the students to observe the plants each day and keep a record by writing about or drawing the changes that they observe. Students should also measure and chart the height of their plants each week after the seeds have sprouted. Later in the spring, the students can take their plants home when the marigolds are mature enough for transplanting.

  This science activity offers students a concrete experience in raising and caring for growing plants. *[logical–mathematical and naturalist intelligences]*

- Prepare a learning center with at least 10 activities for the students to complete independently. Activities for the learning center may include examining samples of water taken from various sources during their neighborhood walk and writing about or drawing a picture of what they observe. If frogs' eggs are available during the spring, samples may be collected and placed in the learning center for the children to observe. They should have an opportunity to read books about the changes involved as the eggs develop into tadpoles and adult frogs. Suggestions in the center should include creative writing of poems and stories about how spring weather affects our feelings. A listening activity, including environmental sounds and musical selections, should also be located in the learning center, along with mathematical problem-solving activities related to the daily temperature charts that the students are maintaining. Students should be given the option of submitting any responses or records required for the activities in either written or pictorial form. Each activity should have a task card to explain directions.

  The learning center provides students with independent work to extend practice with the concepts that they are studying during the unit in the areas of science, music, language arts, and mathematics. *[most intelligences]*

  See Figure 5.7 for one way to organize the learning center.

- Conduct several lessons on sound. Begin with a listening exercise by having the students listen to a tape recording of spring sounds in their environment. Students should try to identify sounds of birds chirping, children playing outside, water rushing in a stream, and so on. Next, select recordings of music having spring as the theme. Try to include both classical and popular music. Have the students think about the specific feelings that the music evokes in them. Discuss these feelings, and give students the choice of either writing about their feelings in their journals, or creating poetry or drawings to represent their feelings. These listening activities can lead to a lesson on what causes sound.

The main purposes of this activity are to develop students' auditory sense and discrimination, to introduce them the concept that all sound is caused by vibration, and to help them realize that the sounds we hear can stimulate different feelings. *[musical, intrapersonal, and logical–mathematical intelligences]*

- Give lessons on spring holidays that occur during the unit. Select appropriate stories and video, film, and filmstrip presentations about the holidays to use in the lessons. Conduct these lessons as directed listening or directed viewing activities. Provide a purpose for listening or viewing, then raise questions about the reading or media presentation at the end of the activity. Keep the lessons informal, emphasizing the information provided in each about a particular holiday.

  These social studies lessons provide the children with insights about how each holiday originated and the different ways in which people in our multicultural society celebrate these holidays. *[linguistic and spatial intelligences]*

- Prepare a spring holiday current events bulletin board. Invite students to look through the magazines and newspapers in the classroom to find articles and pictures showing spring holiday celebrations. The local newspaper may be most meaningful to the students because it contains items on local events with which they are more likely to be familiar. Invite students to write their own articles or create drawings that describe the current events that are especially important to them. Collect items for the display, and have several students decide how to place them on the bulletin board. Hold a class discussion about the items on the bulletin board.

  The discussion of the events should help the students realize that their community has activities that are related to the changes that occur during spring. *[spatial, interpersonal, intrapersonal, and linguistic intelligences]*

- Have the students prepare collages on the spring theme. They can use the holidays, signs of spring, spring plants, or other ideas they may have to create their art. As an alternative, some students may want to write a song or create a dance to express their feelings or newly gained knowledge about changes that occur during the spring season.

  This activity provides opportunities for creative expression and experience with various art media, music, or movement exercises. *[musical, bodily–kinesthetic, and spatial intelligences]*

- Give students an opportunity to create a design for a birdhouse. This creative activity in technology should follow their observations of birds during their walk in the school neighborhood.

  Creating a design provides an experience involving both technology and art. *[naturalist, spatial, and intrapersonal intelligences]*

- Periodically, throughout the unit on spring, select and read stories, books, and poems to the students that have spring-related changes as a theme. The readings should lead to one or more lessons in which students write their own stories or poems about spring or prepare drawings to express their thoughts.

  These listening and creative activities provide students with opportunities to express themselves by using a variety of forms. [*linguistic, intrapersonal, and spatial intelligences*]

Unit Assessment Methods and Techniques

- Periodically observe the students during group activities, particularly while they are working on the mural and during planting activities. Watch specifically for their ability to share materials and space. Note these observations in a journal.

- Have each student maintain a unit portfolio. Create rubrics for any papers or project work to be included in the portfolio. Involve individuals in selecting the following materials for their portfolios:
  - Samples of written work or work in progress, including creative writing pieces and any written reports
  - Examples or photographs of the student's art projects or projects in progress
  - A journal maintained by the student, including any observations or notes
  - Records of observations and notes made by the teacher
  - Records or notes on any individual pupil–teacher conferences
  - Records of science experiments
  - Unit examinations

- Maintain anecdotal records of observations made about each student's general work habits, working and learning style preferences, cooperation when working with others, and ability to learn through experiential activities.

- Keep a journal throughout the unit of work. Include observations of activities and lessons that appear to be most helpful in developing the unit objectives. Also, note the need for revisions in the unit plan—areas that need to be strengthened and additional activities that may be offered to meet students' individual learning styles.

- Administer an examination at the conclusion of the unit to assess facts, concepts, and generalizations developed in the study. The examination may be given orally for students who have difficulty reading the questions. Students should achieve a minimum passing grade of 75 percent.

Unit Materials

Materials for Students

Videotapes of NOVA nature programs (from the school media center) and programs recorded from Instructional Television (ITV) services

A teacher-prepared computer slide presentation or a filmstrip on planting seeds (from the school media center)

A videotape program or film on the needs of plants (to show after children conduct their own experiments with plants)

Materials for experiments with plants

Recordings of music and environmental sounds

A selection of children's books on spring from the school and public libraries

Computer software and CD-ROM titles featuring information on the seasons and nature

Marigold (or other annual) seeds for planting

Tuning fork for the lesson on vibration

Tape recording of spring sounds (teacher prepared)

Informational Resources for the Teacher

Bobick, J. E., & Balaban, N. E. (Eds.). (2002). *The handy science answer book* (Rev. & expanded ed.). Canton, MI: Visible Ink Press.

Phillips, R. (1978). *Trees of North America and Europe.* New York: Random House.

Smith, James (consultant with the local weather TV channel)

The vernal equinox. (1997). Retrieved from http:// condor.stcloudstate.edu/~physcrse/ astr106/emapspring.html

Vernal equinox quiz. (2004). Retrieved from http://familyeducation.com/quiz/0,1399, 2-5647,00.html

Weinstein, E. W. (1999). *Vernal equinox.* Retrieved from http://scienceworld.wolfram. com/astronomy/VernalEquinox.html

Williams, J. (1997). *The weather book* (2nd ed.). New York: Vintage Books.

■ DESERTS OF THE UNITED STATES

A Research-Oriented Interdisciplinary Unit Plan

Topic:	Desert Areas of the United States
Title:	
Possible Titles:	Deserts of the United States, Our Unusual Desert Areas

Method of Involving Students in Creating a Title

Prepare a suggestion box during the first week of the planning phase of the unit. Ask students to contribute title suggestions written on slips of paper. The class officers (president, vice president, and secretary) will choose three title suggestions to present to the class for a vote at the end of the week.

Level: Grade 4.

This unit plan is designed specifically for students in the fourth grade, but it can be adapted for students in fifth, sixth, or seventh grade.

Estimated Unit Length: 4–6 weeks

Learning Standards

Students will do the following:

- Understand ways in which the climate of a geographic region affects plant and animal life
- Know important events in U.S. history
- Understand cultural and other interactions that occurred among previously unconnected groups of people as a result of early exploration and colonization
- Formulate questions related to geographic problems and issues
- Use research skills to locate and gather information
- Learn about expansion in the United States and its effects on relations with Native Americans
- Understand the history and economics of development in desert areas of the United States; learn how this development affected Native Americans, the first settlers
- Understand the effects of geography, climate, and weather on human, plant, and animal life

General Objectives

Content

- Students will develop an awareness of the effects of the topography and climate in desert areas on the art, architecture, music, and literature of the people who live there.

Affective

- Students will develop a greater appreciation for the struggles that early desert settlers experienced when they were adapting to life in desert areas in the United States.

Essential Questions to Guide Students' Research

Geography

- How do we define a *desert* region?
- What are common features of deserts?
- How were our deserts formed?
- How old are they, and how can their ages be determined?
- Where are deserts in the United States located, and what factors have determined their locations?

- What are the sizes of deserts in the United States?
- Are all deserts in the United States alike in some ways? In what ways do they differ from one another?
- What is the climate like in a desert area?
- Is the climate the same in all our deserts?
- How is the weather in a desert area different from our weather?
- What seasonal changes are found in the different U.S. deserts?
- How do climate and weather patterns in deserts affect the people who live in these areas?
- How populated are the different U.S. deserts?
- What are the reasons for any variations found in population density in different deserts?
- Are U.S. deserts increasing or decreasing in population? What are some of the reasons for these changes?

History
- Who were the first settlers in U.S. deserts? Why did these people initially settle in these areas?
- How have historians and social scientists learned about early people who lived in U.S. desert regions?
- How have artifacts found in U.S. deserts contributed to our understanding of early civilizations?
- Which Native American tribes currently live in U.S. desert areas?
- How and when were the different deserts discovered by immigrants from other countries? What attracted the new settlers to these areas?
- What were the effects of discovery by new settlers on Native Americans who were living in these areas? What changes occurred as a result of contacts among the different cultures?
- Do people living in desert areas live in homes similar to ours? Do they wear similar clothing? Do they have similar beliefs and customs? How can the likenesses and differences be described and explained?
- What governmental structures exist in desert areas? Are they similar to those in our local area?

Science and Technology
- What animals and plants live in desert areas? Do the same kinds of animals and plants live in all deserts?
- What are the reasons for any variations found in wildlife in the different deserts?
- How are desert plants and animals adapted to desert living conditions?

- What are the effects of human-made environmental changes on animals and plants living in U.S. deserts?
- What endangered animals and plants live in desert areas? How are they being threatened? What can be done to protect them?
- How have people used technology to provide water for raising crops in a desert and to improve the quality of life in desert areas?

Economics

- What minerals and other natural resources are found in desert areas? What effects do these resources have on desert society?
- How do people in desert areas earn a living?
- What products are produced in different desert areas? Does a demand exist for these products?
- What objects and materials do we have in our homes that may have come from a U.S. desert?
- What types of industries are found in desert regions? Why are these industries located in a desert?
- Are any of these industries threatened by our emerging technology? In what ways?

Agriculture

- Is farming possible in desert areas? If so, what kinds of farms are found in these regions?
- What problems do farmers face in desert areas?
- What crops are raised in deserts? What conditions would be necessary to raise other crops in the future?
- How has irrigation been used to benefit farming in a desert?

Art, Architecture, and Music

- What famous artists have lived and worked in desert areas? Why do they live there? How can their art be distinguished?
- Do artists who live in desert regions produce special kinds of art or use special kinds of art media?
- How does the geography of desert areas affect the ways houses and other buildings are constructed?
- What kinds of music and musical instruments are found in desert areas?
- What famous musicians have lived and worked in desert areas? Why did they choose to work in these areas?

Health

- What kinds of health care are available to people living in sparsely populated desert regions?

- What are the effects of the desert climate on the health of people who live in these areas?
- What are the safety hazards of life in desert areas?

Language Arts

- What books have been written by authors who live in desert areas?
- What poetry has been written by people living in desert areas?
- In what ways are the books, stories, and poetry written by people in desert areas influenced by the geography, climate, and weather in these areas?
- What languages, other than English, are spoken in U.S. desert areas?

Web Design of the Unit: See Figure A.5.

Possible Research Committees

Agriculture	Economics	History
Art, Architecture, Music	Geography	Science/Technology
Ecology/Natural Resources	Health/Safety	

Possible Unit Lessons and Activities

- *Form research committees.* A committee should be formed for each area shown in the web design. Each committee should have four to six student members. After completing their research, the committees will be responsible for reporting their findings to the class. Students on each committee should be involved in deciding what the committee will investigate and how their findings will be reported to the class.

  Make sure that members of each committee all share in both the research and the reporting. When forming the committees, pay attention to individual student abilities in each group. The composition of the group should be planned carefully, with consideration of factors such as leadership, learning styles, social factors, the students' ability to share responsibilities, and their individual talents, interests, and academic abilities.

  Encourage committee members to use a variety of reporting forms, such as displays, panel discussions, computer slide-show presentations, and skits.

  Develop a "buddy" system in committees that include students with special needs, who often leave the classroom during regular times devoted to research or project activities. Students who leave for special assistance programs can be paired with others in their committee groups who will brief them on the committee's work during their absence. *[interpersonal intelligence]*

- *Provide for individual inquiry.* Some students may have interests in subtopics that do not relate well to any committee's work. Encourage these individuals to pursue their interests, and provide opportunities for them to report their findings to the class. *[intrapersonal intelligence]*

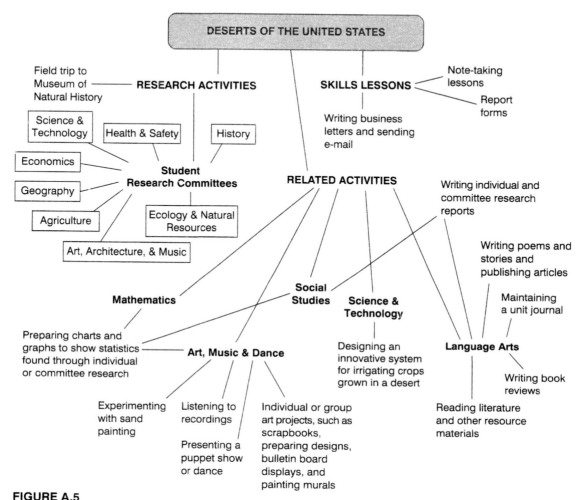

FIGURE A.5
Web diagram for a complete research-oriented interdisciplinary unit plan called *Deserts of the United States*.

• *Clarify reporting requirements for committees and individuals.* Require each student to prepare a report of his or her committee research. Students who can should prepare their reports in writing. Provide a form to guide the writing process. The form should include information about the questions that the student was researching, answers to these questions, and the sources consulted during the research phase. Ask students who write their reports to include the following information in their papers:

Topic: The committee topic and the subtopic for which the student was responsible.

Questions: The ideas the student used to guide his or her research.

Findings: This section will vary in complexity according to the students' abilities. A simple list of findings, written in the student's words, may be adequate for some students. Others will be able to write several paragraphs or pages.

References: Depending on each student's abilities, the documentation format can vary from a simple list of the books and other materials used to a more sophisticated and complete documentation format. *[linguistic intelligence]*

- *Teach lessons on letter-writing and note-taking skills.* Many students will need to write for information. Either give a lesson to all the students to show them an appropriate form for business letters, or assist only those who need to write letters during the unit. Review and then continue the series of letter-writing and note-taking lessons started during the previous units. *[linguistic intelligence]*

- *Teach locational skills lessons.* Ask the school librarian (or media specialist) to assist in teaching a series of lessons on locating reference materials in the library or media center.

- *Teach lessons on using the Internet for research and communicating by e-mail.* Use a classroom computer connected to the Internet and LCD projection to teach lessons on using the Internet for research. Demonstrate searching for information and checking for authenticity of sources. Review the procedure for composing e-mail. *[linguistic intelligence]*

- *Offer individuals and committees suggestions for alternative research and reporting activities.* The list should include suggestions that can be made to committees and individual students as the unit progresses. Activities should address students' differing working and learning styles. The suggestions may also include alternatives, such as making art projects and displays or presenting puppet shows and skits, that are suitable for students with specific disabilities. Students who have difficulty preparing written reports should have alternatives, such as explaining a construction or project or preparing a demonstration for the class. Encourage each student to use art media for a project that reflects understandings gained as a result of the desert study. Several students can elect to work together on larger projects. *[intrapersonal and interpersonal intelligences]*

Suggestions

- Use the Internet to get in contact with a fourth-grade class in one of the desert areas we are studying. Write a story describing your visit to that class.

- Compose and send a letter by e-mail to the students in a fourth-grade class in a desert region. Ask them what living in a desert region of the United States is like.

- Choose a story or a poem on desert life from the classroom collection or from the school media center. Prepare to read it to a group of students in kindergarten or first grade.

- Read a book from the library (either fiction or nonfiction) related to desert life. The book can be either prose or poetry. Write a book review that will encourage other students to read it, or prepare a story map or plot profile for fiction.

- Write a poem about one of the plants or animals that can be found in a specific desert region.

- Publish an article on the school Web site, comparing living in a desert area with living in our area.

- Organize a panel discussion to present information that your group has gained from its research.

- Prepare an oral report on an individual research project that you have undertaken.

- Decide on your own way of reporting the information found through your research.

- Develop a time line to display in the classroom. Use TimeLiner, if you would like, to prepare it. The time line should indicate the average rainfall each year for the past 10 or more years in a specific desert area.

- Develop a plan for an ideal desert house. Make a drawing of the plan. Write a description of your design and include reasons for its special features.

- Create a graph showing some statistics, such as population changes, elevations, or average daily temperature readings, about one of the desert areas that you or your committee has been studying.

- Prepare a scrapbook to show some of the information gained from your research.

- Using other art media, draw or construct a map showing the locations of different U.S. deserts.

- Draw or paint a picture showing how an irrigation project is used to raise plants for food in a desert.

- Paint a picture or design a collage to show typical plants or animals found in one of the desert areas.

- Try sand painting. The art teacher can help those of you who would like to try this unique art form.

- Invite several classmates to design and paint a mural on life in the desert. (The mural topic can involve animal and plant life, types of homes, typical desert scenes, or other ideas suggested by the students.)

- Create a three-dimensional construction showing how an irrigation project works.
- Build a model of a Native American community found in one of the desert areas studied.
- During the unit study, collect newspaper and magazine pictures and articles relating to U.S. deserts. Prepare a bulletin board display of the items collected.
- Prepare a puppet show or present a skit for the class that includes information about some of the effects that new settlers had on Native Americans who were living in a desert area.
- Collect several recordings that have been written about desert living. Present the music to the class.
- Study a Native American dance, and teach the dance to the class.
- Create a musical instrument made from materials that are found in a desert. Demonstrate the instrument for the class.
- Work with several others to plan a classroom "museum" display of all the projects that students in the class have created during the unit. Invite all students in the class to contribute their projects for the display. We can arrange to have other classes in the school visit the museum.
- Throughout the unit, maintain a journal in which you record your thoughts and feelings related to our study of deserts.

Introductory Lesson Plan

Topic: Deserts of the United States

Level: Grade 5

Estimated Time: 45 minutes to 1 hour

Learning Standard: Students use research skills to locate and gather information.

General Objective: Students will develop plans for their research unit on deserts of the United States.

Essential Question: What kind of information can we expect to learn about desert regions of the United States from the research sources that are available?

Behavioral Objective: After the teacher introduces the topic of the new unit and directs students' attention to research materials in the classroom, each student will begin to develop a list of the kinds of information about U.S. deserts to be found in the materials.

Procedure

1. Before introducing the unit, contact the school librarian, local community children's librarian, and art and music teachers to let them know the topic of the new unit and to invite their help during the study.

Librarians can probably assign blocks of books or other media to the class for use during the unit. The community librarian may be able to arrange a display of materials and reserve them for the students in the class during the researching phase. The art and music teachers may be able to develop lessons related to the desert topic.

2. In addition to introducing the computer software, applicable audiovisual aids, and text books in social studies, science, and mathematics that are available in the classroom, display a sampling of library books, magazines, charts, maps, and other resources that have been brought from the two libraries. Keep the display small so that the students will be motivated to locate other materials themselves.

3. At the first class session, remind students of the unit that they recently completed on their local region and the Atlantic Coast, and ask for some of the major concepts they gained from that study.

The students should recall that coastal areas are important contributors to U.S. inland areas. The natural harbors along the coast have served for many years as major sites for importing goods from across the world—especially New York Harbor in the students' immediate area. They should mention the fishing industry and recall that there is a concentration of population along the Atlantic Coast.

4. Explain that the new unit will be a study of deserts in the United States and that it will focus on life in desert areas and the ways in which people are affected by desert living.

5. Ask the students what they know about deserts, and construct a concept web with which to record their responses on the chalkboard. Later, transfer the responses to a chart. (See Figure 5.6 for an example of a concept web.) The chart can be modified as students gain new information; they may need to delete inaccuracies in their original ideas and add other concepts discovered through their research.

6. Tell the students that they will be helping to plan the study and that the first step is to skim available research materials to learn the kinds of information they will be able to find by using available resources.

7. Direct the students' attention to the small classroom display of books, magazines, and other materials on deserts in the United States. Explain that these materials have been brought into the classroom for use during the unit and that additional sources will need to be located, some of which are available in the school library or media center.

8. Ask for three or four volunteers to go to the school library to meet with the librarian, who will assist them in locating other materials for the classroom. Ask the class secretary to keep a list of volunteers' names. Ask one of the volunteers to go to the library to speak to the librarian about a suitable time.

9. Ask for another five volunteers to accompany you on a walk to the local public library to locate more materials on desert living. Have the class secretary keep a

list of their names. Explain that you will meet with them later in the day to make arrangements for their noon walk to the library.

Permission slips can be distributed during the small-group meeting. Allow several days for returning the slips when scheduling the library trip.

10. Ask the class if anyone can think of sources other than libraries where information about U.S. deserts may be found.

    The students will probably mention sources such as the Internet, travel agencies, public television programs, computer software, videotapes, DVS programs, state agencies, and chambers of commerce in desert areas.

11. Explain that during the next several days the students will need to look through the research materials in the room (and those that students will bring from the libraries) to learn about the kinds of information that they can expect to find about U.S. deserts. Ask students to keep a list of the kinds of information found in the materials. Tell them that they will be asked to give their lists to the class secretary after 3 days. The secretary will then choose several people to help compile one list (to eliminate duplicate entries). The final list will be duplicated for the class.

12. Explain that the main point of looking through the materials at this time is simply to get an idea of what information is available. They need not read extensively, only note and record the kinds of information they find.

13. Review with the class the ways to locate information in the various materials available: using the table of contents, index, captions, boldface headings, and so on.

14. Provide 20 to 25 minutes for students to peruse materials available in the classroom. Remind them to start their lists in their notebooks.

15. As the students begin, assist them to be certain that they understand the assignment. Meet briefly with the two ad hoc groups to make arrangements for their library visits. Distribute permission slips to students who will walk to the community library at noon.

Materials

A variety of science and social studies textbooks from several publishers

A selection of books from the media center in the school and from the public library

Magazines and newspapers with relevant articles and pictures

Computer software, CD-ROM encyclopedias, and special programs on the desert theme

Description of the Remainder of the Planning Phase

1. After a composite list of the kinds of information available in the classroom resources has been compiled, duplicated, and distributed to the class, elicit the

students' help in organizing general categories from the items on the newly compiled list. For example, *temperature, climate, rainfall,* and *wind* may all be on the list. These items can be combined to form the general category—or subtopic—*weather.* With the students, develop an outline of all the subtopics, and ask the class secretary to copy it for duplication.

2. Duplicate and distribute the outline to each student. Ask each student to list on a slip of paper three choices of subtopics for a committee assignment. Collect the requests and prepare a list of committee assignments.

    Make the committee assignments with consideration for the social makeup, leadership, and heterogeneity of each group. Make sure that individuals work on different kinds of committees throughout the year. For example, a student should not always be assigned to the economics committee or the art committee. You should make the final committee assignments. If an important subtopic is not selected, you can ask several students if they will volunteer to form a committee for it, or you can assume responsibility for this area.

3. Duplicate and distribute the committee assignments to each student, and announce the first meeting of committees. Before committees meet, discuss the meaning of *committee* and how committees should function. Ask the students to list the main tasks that will need to be accomplished when the committees first meet. Guide students to include the following tasks:

    - Select a chairperson and a recorder
    - Prepare a list of essential questions to guide research on the subtopic
    - Decide on how to divide the committee responsibilities

    When the committees meet, the recorder should be instructed to record this information for you. In this way, you will know what each student in the class is investigating. The planning phase ends after the initial committee meetings.

Description of the Research Phase

1. Once the work of the unit has been divided among committees, each period devoted to research should begin with a progress report from each committee chairperson. Any problems in locating needed information, the need for art materials for projects, and how well the group is doing on its subtopic should be shared with the class. The remainder of the period may involve a variety of activities, all happening simultaneously. For example, some students will be reading and taking notes for their research. One or two may be viewing film-strips or using computers in a corner of the room. Several students may be working on the mural in the hall, two or three students may have signed out for the library, and others may be meeting with the art or music teacher for help with their projects.

2. Throughout the researching phase, you should meet with individual students on a rotating basis to monitor progress and to provide any special help needed. When not meeting with individuals, you should circulate among the committees and

assist students with various projects. Once the committee work is progressing, ask each group to decide how it would prefer to report its findings to the class. You should encourage variety in reporting methods. Make suggestions such as panels, demonstrations, drama, dance, displays, and so on. During the researching phase, you should also give a series of skills lessons in language arts on locating resources, taking notes, and writing for information using a business letter form.

3. The researching phase draws to a close as the committees complete their work. Each committee should then be scheduled to present its report to the class. Not all the committees will finish at the same time, so reports can be spread across several days or a week near the end of the unit.

Description of the Reporting Phase

1. Schedule the committee reports for this phase of the unit—one or two presentations for each day.

2. Before each committee begins its presentation, remind the class about good listening habits and suggest taking notes during the report so that important information will not be forgotten. Explain that the most important material from the committee's report should be outlined after the presentation.

3. After each committee presentation, ask the class to participate in developing an outline of the most important information gleaned from the committee report. Assist the students with the outline, using a conventional (I., A., 1., a.) outline form and writing it on the board.

4. Have all students copy the outline into their notebooks. Explain that the outline will help them when they study for the unit final examination.

5. After all committees have reported and the students have a complete set of outlines for all committee reports recorded in their notebooks, ask committees to meet once again to prepare three or four important questions about their subtopic. Explain that the questions should be based on those that were prepared by the group for its research, that the questions will be used for a review session before the final examination, and that some of their questions may be on the test.

   If any of the committee-generated questions are used for the exam, you should edit them for clarity, grammar, and punctuation.

6. Hold a review session with the class. Have committee chairpersons read some of their questions for the class to discuss. Limit questions to no more than two from any committee during this session.

7. Administer the unit examination. Formats and questions on the examination will depend on the material presented in committee reports. A combination of multiple-choice, true–false, completion, and limited-response essay formats will probably be needed.

8. Return all materials to the students: examinations, research reports (from committees), books reports, and art projects. Hold a drawing of names of interested

students to determine who may take the mural home after it has been displayed for a week or two.

Unit Assessment Methods and Techniques

- Use observation and maintain a journal during the unit in which to note students' individual progress in organizing, sharing responsibilities, and participating in committee work.

- Observe as students take notes for their research projects to determine specific skills that should be stressed in future note-taking lessons.

- Review all written reports to assess the progress that students are making with their writing skills and in organizing their research and book reports.

- Take photographs of the students' art projects as they develop during the unit.

- Examine students' projects to determine the extent to which they reflect the concepts they have studied and to note the progress being made in using various art and construction media.

- Have each student maintain a unit portfolio that includes the following materials:

  - A file of notes taken for individual research
  - Samples of written work or work in progress, including letters, pieces of creative writing, and written reports
  - Samples or photographs of art projects, constructions, charts or graphs, or works in progress
  - A journal reflecting on the student's work during the unit
  - Records of experiments that students have designed and completed
  - Records or notes on any individual pupil–teacher conferences
  - Unit examinations

- Collect students' portfolios and add notes about their work habits and ability to work with others cooperatively.

- Administer a comprehensive examination at the end of the unit to evaluate the students' mastery of major concepts developed in the unit of study.

Unit Materials

Instructional Materials for Students

Sufficient quantities of social studies and science textbooks from a variety of publishers (four to six copies of each)

Trade books from the school and public libraries on U.S. desert areas

Films, filmstrips, and videotapes on U.S. deserts

Computer software and related CD–ROM titles

Computer technological services and consultation on the Internet for sources of information

Travel agency brochures that highlight desert vacation areas

Art materials for projects and report covers

Informational Resources for the Teacher

Butcher, R. D. (1976). *The desert*. New York: Viking Press.

Desert USA. (n.d.). Retrieved from http://www.desertusa.com

Digital desert. (n.d.). Retrieved from http://aeve.com/digitaldesertt/ddpi/lalol.html

Hyde, P. (1987). *Drylands: The deserts of North America*. San Diego, CA: Harcourt Brace Jovanovich.

Mails, T. E. (1993). *The Pueblo students of the earth mother*. New York: Marlowe.

McMahon, J. A. (1997). *Deserts*. New York: Knopf.

The North American deserts. (n.d.). Retrieved from http://www.desertusa.com/glossary.html

Waldman, C. (1985). *Atlas of the North American Indian*. New York: Facts on File.

◼ SAMPLE INTERDISCIPLINARY UNIT PLAN WEB DESIGNS

Web designs for interdisciplinary unit plans may be constructed in a number of ways. The purpose of the sample webs in this section (Figures A.6 through A.25) is to show designs that differ stylistically from one another. Of the 20 samples, 3 were prepared by the author, 11 were prepared by practicing teachers, and 6 were designed by undergraduate students in teacher education. Because the webs vary in detail, number of ideas, and overall quality, the samples are intended only to show alternative ways to construct them.

The essential components are included in all the web designs. Each includes a central theme and related disciplines to be used in exploring the theme; brief statements or phrases describing the planner's ideas for related lessons and activities; and interconnecting lines that indicate the planner's interdisciplinary thinking about the relationships among the various components. Some designs are multidirectional and weblike; others are more unidirectional.

Each sample is the result of the brainstorming step—described in chapters 5 and 6—followed during planning of the initial unit. As explained in this book, interdisciplinary unit diagrams should be designed mainly as a reminder to the teacher of the kinds of activities and lessons that may be included in the unit when it is taught. Therefore, the diagrams do not give detailed information about learning options, materials, processes, or content that the unit will include. In an interdisciplinary unit plan, these details are provided in the Descriptions of Lessons and Activities section; in a research-oriented interdisciplinary unit plan, details are included in these sections: Possible Research Committees, Sample Questions to Guide Students' Research, and Possible Unit Lessons and Activities. Although web designers can include more detail, doing so yields overcrowded designs that are difficult to read.

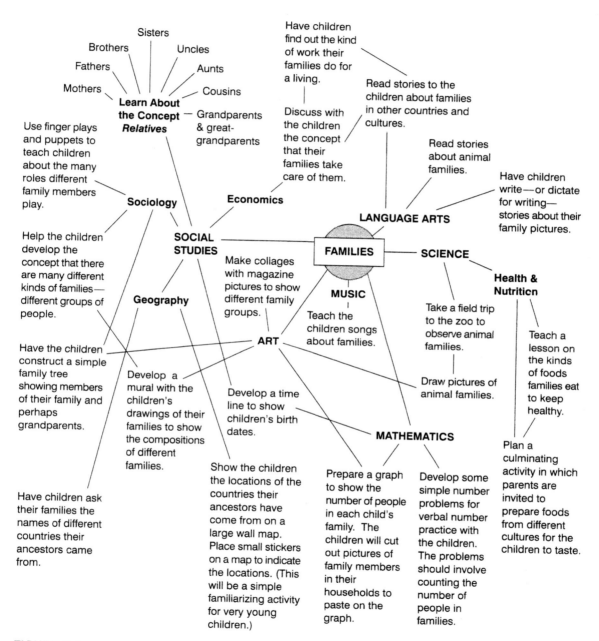

FIGURE A.6
Web design for Families unit (primary grades).

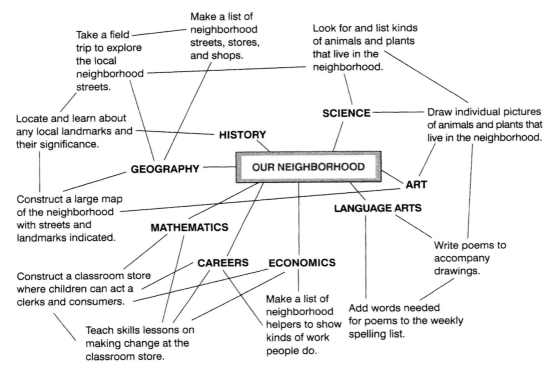

FIGURE A.7
Web design for Our Neighborhood unit (primary grades).

The samples indicate only the general level for which the unit theme is appropriate—primary, upper elementary, or middle school. The plans can always be adapted for more than one grade level by adding or substituting lessons and activities. Designs for upper elementary and middle school levels can be converted to become research-oriented interdisciplinary plans by adding information about student committees. The decision about the most appropriate grade level for any topic always depends on the students' developmental levels, their academic abilities, the materials available for student inquiry, and local and statewide learning standards and curriculum goals.

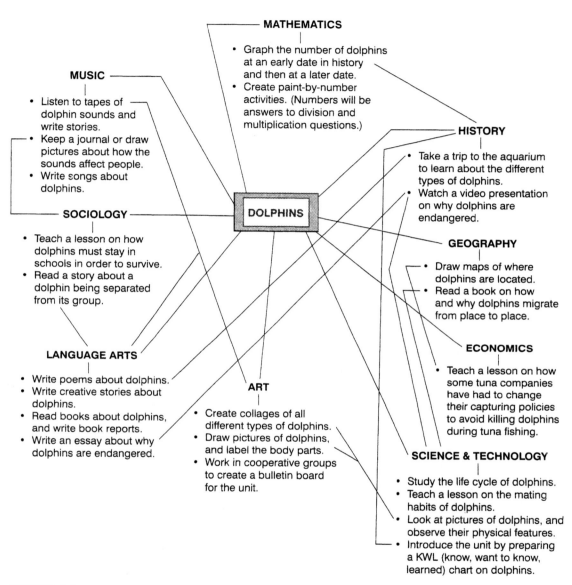

MATHEMATICS

- Graph the number of dolphins at an early date in history and then at a later date.
- Create paint-by-number activities. (Numbers will be answers to division and multiplication questions.)

MUSIC

- Listen to tapes of dolphin sounds and write stories.
- Keep a journal or draw pictures about how the sounds affect people.
- Write songs about dolphins.

SOCIOLOGY

- Teach a lesson on how dolphins must stay in schools in order to survive.
- Read a story about a dolphin being separated from its group.

LANGUAGE ARTS

- Write poems about dolphins.
- Write creative stories about dolphins.
- Read books about dolphins, and write book reports.
- Write an essay about why dolphins are endangered.

DOLPHINS

ART

- Create collages of all different types of dolphins.
- Draw pictures of dolphins, and label the body parts.
- Work in cooperative groups to create a bulletin board for the unit.

HISTORY

- Take a trip to the aquarium to learn about the different types of dolphins.
- Watch a video presentation on why dolphins are endangered.

GEOGRAPHY

- Draw maps of where dolphins are located.
- Read a book on how and why dolphins migrate from place to place.

ECONOMICS

- Teach a lesson on how some tuna companies have had to change their capturing policies to avoid killing dolphins during tuna fishing.

SCIENCE & TECHNOLOGY

- Study the life cycle of dolphins.
- Teach a lesson on the mating habits of dolphins.
- Look at pictures of dolphins, and observe their physical features.
- Introduce the unit by preparing a KWL (know, want to know, learned) chart on dolphins.

FIGURE A.8
Web design for Dolphins unit (upper primary–upper elementary grades).
Note. Courtesy of Caria Cardoso, Donna Fuchs, and Evelyn Kaszuba.

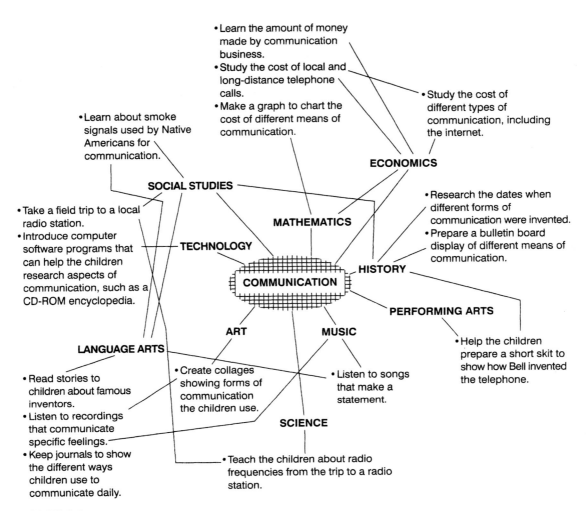

• Learn the amount of money made by communication business.
• Study the cost of local and long-distance telephone calls.
• Make a graph to chart the cost of different means of communication.

• Study the cost of different types of communication, including the internet.

ECONOMICS

• Learn about smoke signals used by Native Americans for communication.

SOCIAL STUDIES

• Take a field trip to a local radio station.
• Introduce computer software programs that can help the children research aspects of communication, such as a CD-ROM encyclopedia.

TECHNOLOGY

MATHEMATICS

COMMUNICATION

HISTORY

• Research the dates when different forms of communication were invented.
• Prepare a bulletin board display of different means of communication.

PERFORMING ARTS

• Help the children prepare a short skit to show how Bell invented the telephone.

LANGUAGE ARTS

• Read stories to children about famous inventors.
• Listen to recordings that communicate specific feelings.
• Keep journals to show the different ways children use to communicate daily.

ART

• Create collages showing forms of communication the children use.

MUSIC

• Listen to songs that make a statement.

SCIENCE

• Teach the children about radio frequencies from the trip to a radio station.

FIGURE A.9
Web design for Communication unit (upper elementary grades).

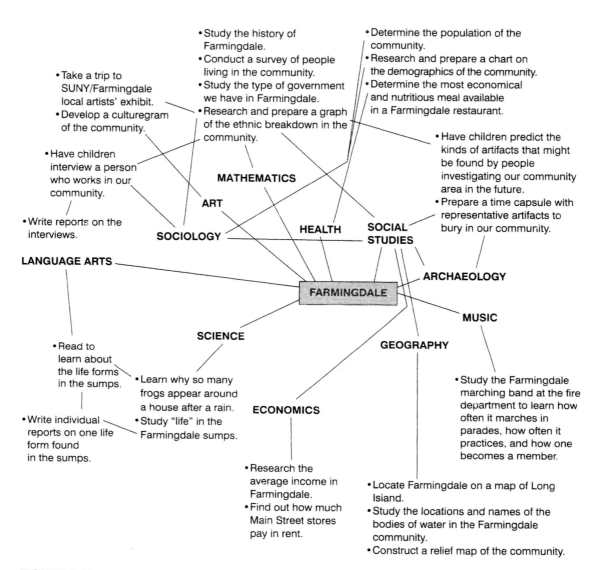

FIGURE A.10
Web design for Farmingdale unit (primary–upper elementary grades).
Note. Courtesy of Shereen Phillips.

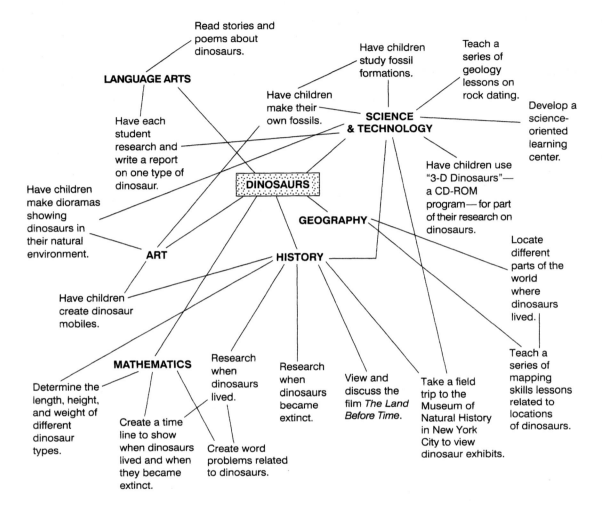

FIGURE A.11
Web design for Dinosaurs unit (primary–upper elementary grades).
Note. Courtesy of Judy Levy.

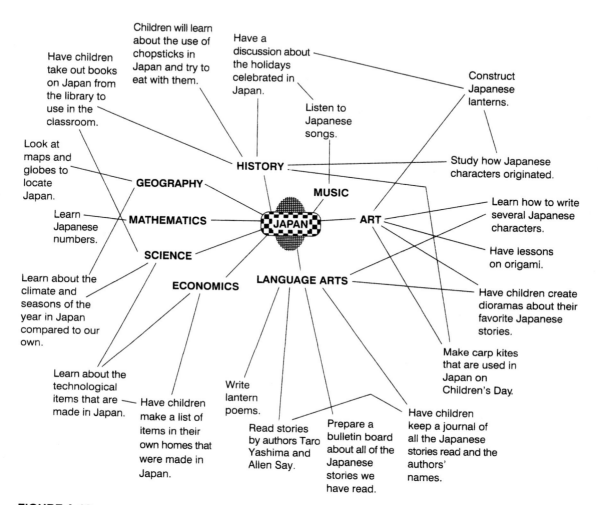

FIGURE A.12

Web design for Japan unit (upper elementary grades).
Note. Courtesy of Jill Thompsett.

- Air, sea, and land: Have students survey machines we use for transportation and their elementary principles of operation.
- The travelers' forecast: Learn why and how weather affects transportation.
- Prepare a lesson on how energy is used in transportation.
- Learn how animals have been used in transportation.

- Study the reasons we choose one means of transportation over another.
- Determine the most affordable way for a family of four to travel to Disney World.

- Have students work in groups and produce constructions of their ultimate fantasy travel machine.
- Assemble a collage of old magazine photos with transportation themes.

ECONOMICS

ART

SCIENCE & TECHNOLOGY

LANGUAGE ARTS

- Read narratives of journeys set in different time periods.
- Write narratives using story elements based on transportation themes.

ENVIRONMENTAL STUDIES

- Study how various forms of transportation can make the air and water dirty.

TRANSPORTATION THROUGH THE AGES

MUSIC

- Learn traditional sea chanteys.
- Listen to songs about train travel.

GEOGRAPHY

HISTORY

MATHEMATICS

- Study places famous in the history of transportation, like the Golden Gate Bridge, the Continental Divide, and the Panama Canal.
- Have students predict the importance of location(e.g., if they had to choose where to put a new amusement park or build a new airport).
- Learn that the shortest distance between two points on the globe is a circle.
- Learn about different types of maps and how they are used.

- Learn about Marco Polo's journey to China.
- Study why and how nomadic cultures travel.
- Study how changes in transportation affected the settlement of the West.
- Prepare a lesson on Ellis Island and the Statue of Liberty.
- From footpaths to freeways: Learn how some crowded highways began as Native American trails.

- Study, through a simple graphing activity, the relationship between speed and time and distance.
- Have students conduct a statistical survey of school employee commuting times and distances, and prepare a graph of the results.

FIGURE A.13
Web design for Transportation Through the Ages unit (upper elementary grades).
Note. Courtesy of David Kennedy.

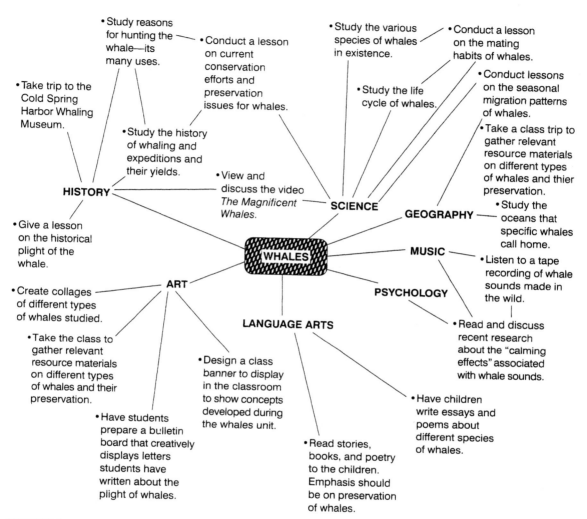

FIGURE A.14
Web design for Whales unit (upper elementary grades).
Note. Courtesy of Toni Keatley.

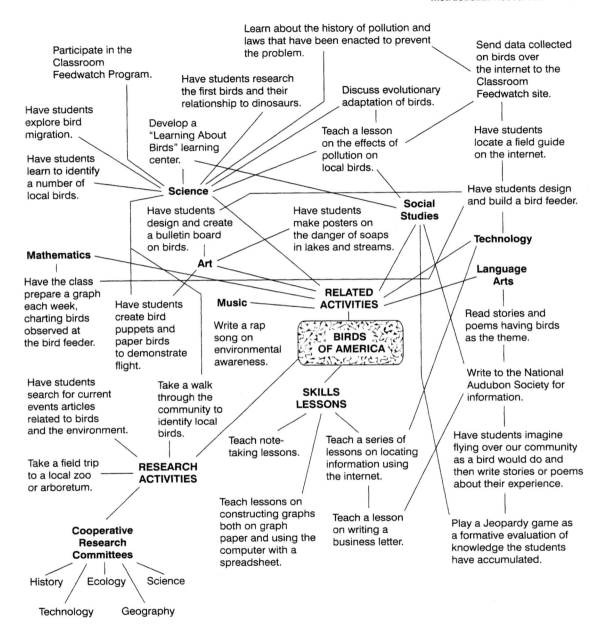

FIGURE A.15
Web design for Birds of America unit (upper elementary grades).
Note. Courtesy of Margaret Kenzie and Sheryl Schuhose.

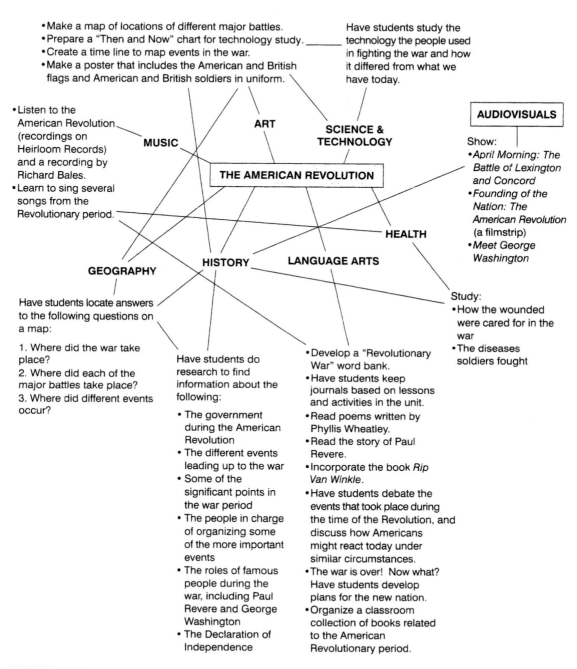

- Make a map of locations of different major battles.
- Prepare a "Then and Now" chart for technology study.
- Create a time line to map events in the war.
- Make a poster that includes the American and British flags and American and British soldiers in uniform.

Have students study the technology the people used in fighting the war and how it differed from what we have today.

- Listen to the American Revolution (recordings on Heirloom Records) and a recording by Richard Bales.
- Learn to sing several songs from the Revolutionary period.

ART

MUSIC

SCIENCE & TECHNOLOGY

THE AMERICAN REVOLUTION

AUDIOVISUALS

Show:
- *April Morning: The Battle of Lexington and Concord*
- *Founding of the Nation: The American Revolution* (a filmstrip)
- *Meet George Washington*

HEALTH

HISTORY   **LANGUAGE ARTS**

GEOGRAPHY

Have students locate answers to the following questions on a map:

1. Where did the war take place?
2. Where did each of the major battles take place?
3. Where did different events occur?

Have students do research to find information about the following:

- The government during the American Revolution
- The different events leading up to the war
- Some of the significant points in the war period
- The people in charge of organizing some of the more important events
- The roles of famous people during the war, including Paul Revere and George Washington
- The Declaration of Independence

Study:
- How the wounded were cared for in the war
- The diseases soldiers fought

- Develop a "Revolutionary War" word bank.
- Have students keep journals based on lessons and activities in the unit.
- Read poems written by Phyllis Wheatley.
- Read the story of Paul Revere.
- Incorporate the book *Rip Van Winkle*.
- Have students debate the events that took place during the time of the Revolution, and discuss how Americans might react today under similar circumstances.
- The war is over! Now what? Have students develop plans for the new nation.
- Organize a classroom collection of books related to the American Revolutionary period.

FIGURE A.16
Web design for The American Revolution unit (upper elementary–middle school grades).
Note. Courtesy of Jennifer Fanno.

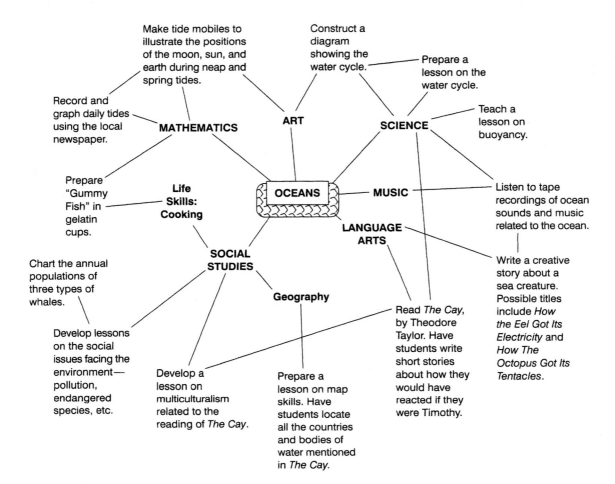

FIGURE A.17
Web design for Oceans unit (upper elementary–middle school grades).
Note. Courtesy of Patrick Morris.

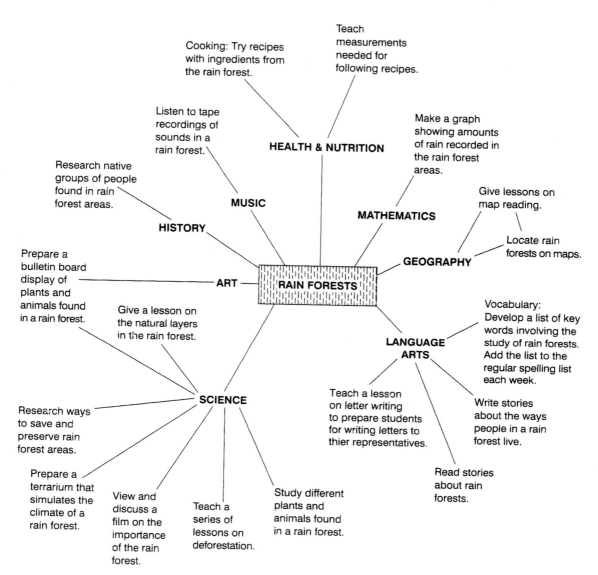

FIGURE A.18
Web design for Rain Forests unit (upper elementary–middle school grades).
Note. Courtesy of Ann Brancale and Katina Paulsen.

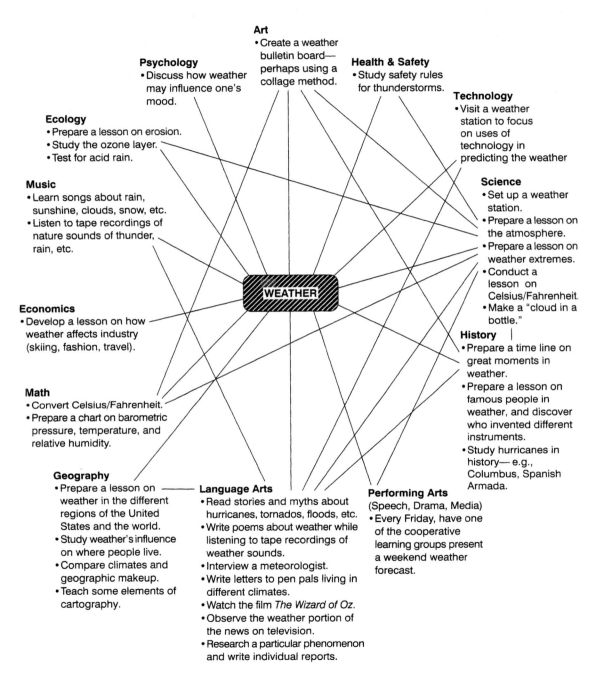

Art
- Create a weather bulletin board—perhaps using a collage method.

Psychology
- Discuss how weather may influence one's mood.

Health & Safety
- Study safety rules for thunderstorms.

Technology
- Visit a weather station to focus on uses of technology in predicting the weather

Ecology
- Prepare a lesson on erosion.
- Study the ozone layer.
- Test for acid rain.

Science
- Set up a weather station.
- Prepare a lesson on the atmosphere.
- Prepare a lesson on weather extremes.
- Conduct a lesson on Celsius/Fahrenheit.
- Make a "cloud in a bottle."

Music
- Learn songs about rain, sunshine, clouds, snow, etc.
- Listen to tape recordings of nature sounds of thunder, rain, etc.

WEATHER

Economics
- Develop a lesson on how weather affects industry (skiing, fashion, travel).

History
- Prepare a time line on great moments in weather.
- Prepare a lesson on famous people in weather, and discover who invented different instruments.
- Study hurricanes in history— e.g., Columbus, Spanish Armada.

Math
- Convert Celsius/Fahrenheit.
- Prepare a chart on barometric pressure, temperature, and relative humidity.

Geography
- Prepare a lesson on weather in the different regions of the United States and the world.
- Study weather's influence on where people live.
- Compare climates and geographic makeup.
- Teach some elements of cartography.

Language Arts
- Read stories and myths about hurricanes, tornados, floods, etc.
- Write poems about weather while listening to tape recordings of weather sounds.
- Interview a meteorologist.
- Write letters to pen pals living in different climates.
- Watch the film *The Wizard of Oz*.
- Observe the weather portion of the news on television.
- Research a particular phenomenon and write individual reports.

Performing Arts
(Speech, Drama, Media)
- Every Friday, have one of the cooperative learning groups present a weekend weather forecast.

FIGURE A.19
Web design for Weather unit (upper elementary–middle school grades).
Note. Courtesy of Margaret Norton.

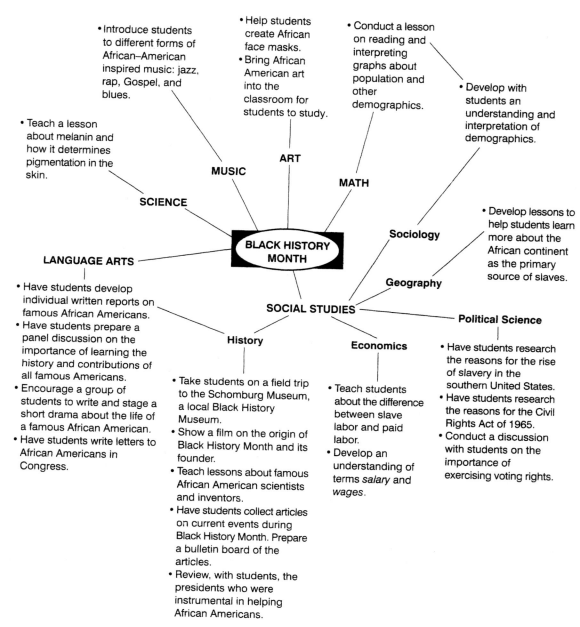

- Introduce students to different forms of African–American inspired music: jazz, rap, Gospel, and blues.

- Help students create African face masks.
- Bring African American art into the classroom for students to study.

- Conduct a lesson on reading and interpreting graphs about population and other demographics.

- Develop with students an understanding and interpretation of demographics.

- Teach a lesson about melanin and how it determines pigmentation in the skin.

ART

MUSIC

MATH

SCIENCE

BLACK HISTORY MONTH

Sociology

- Develop lessons to help students learn more about the African continent as the primary source of slaves.

Geography

LANGUAGE ARTS

- Have students develop individual written reports on famous African Americans.
- Have students prepare a panel discussion on the importance of learning the history and contributions of all famous Americans.
- Encourage a group of students to write and stage a short drama about the life of a famous African American.
- Have students write letters to African Americans in Congress.

SOCIAL STUDIES

History

- Take students on a field trip to the Schomburg Museum, a local Black History Museum.
- Show a film on the origin of Black History Month and its founder.
- Teach lessons about famous African American scientists and inventors.
- Have students collect articles on current events during Black History Month. Prepare a bulletin board of the articles.
- Review, with students, the presidents who were instrumental in helping African Americans.

Economics

- Teach students about the difference between slave labor and paid labor.
- Develop an understanding of terms *salary* and *wages*.

Political Science

- Have students research the reasons for the rise of slavery in the southern United States.
- Have students research the reasons for the Civil Rights Act of 1965.
- Conduct a discussion with students on the importance of exercising voting rights.

FIGURE A.20

Web design for Black History Month unit (upper elementary–middle school grades).
Note. Courtesy of Dearl Topping.

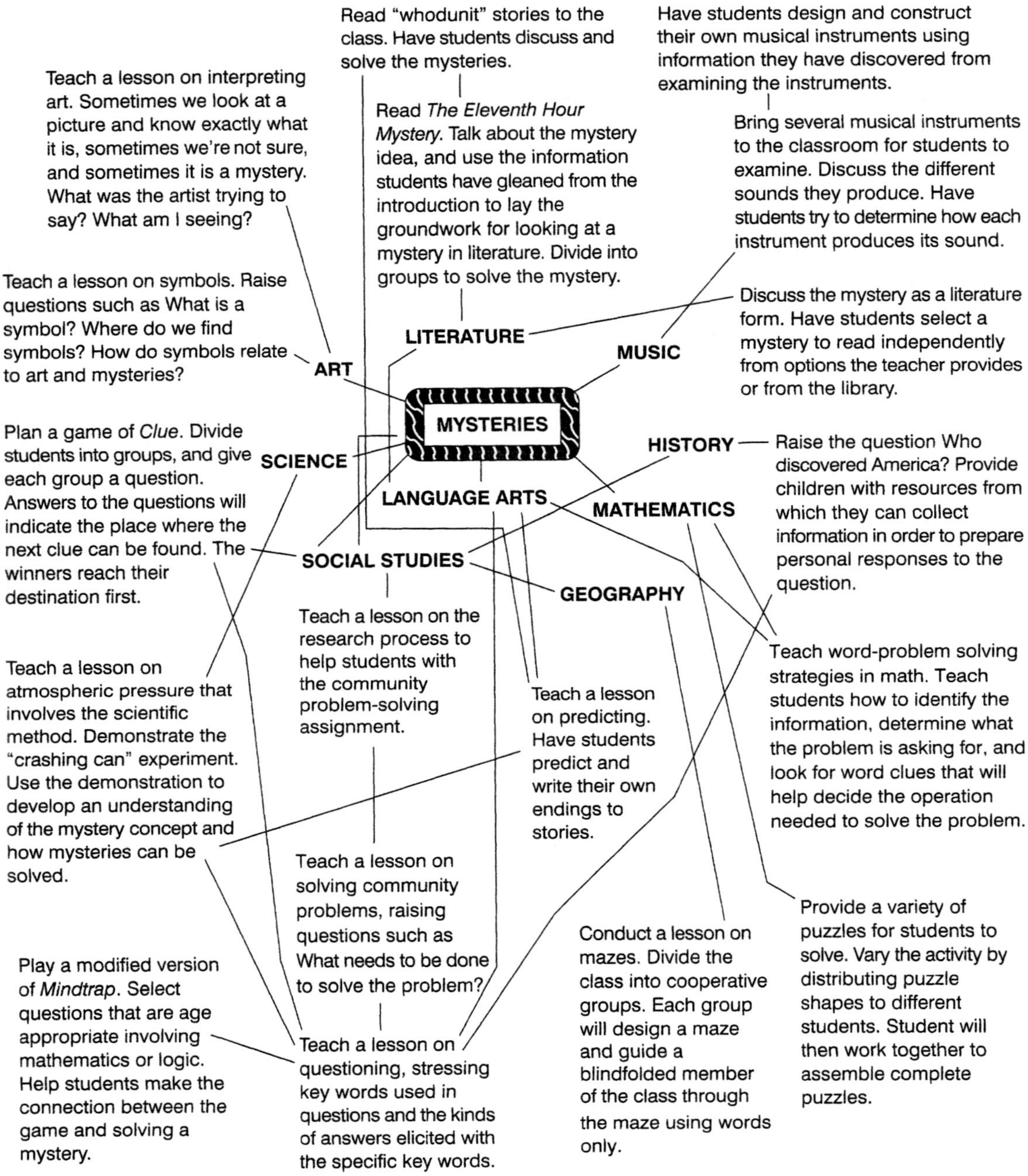

Teach a lesson on interpreting art. Sometimes we look at a picture and know exactly what it is, sometimes we're not sure, and sometimes it is a mystery. What was the artist trying to say? What am I seeing?

Teach a lesson on symbols. Raise questions such as What is a symbol? Where do we find symbols? How do symbols relate to art and mysteries?

Plan a game of *Clue*. Divide students into groups, and give each group a question. Answers to the questions will indicate the place where the next clue can be found. The winners reach their destination first.

Teach a lesson on atmospheric pressure that involves the scientific method. Demonstrate the "crashing can" experiment. Use the demonstration to develop an understanding of the mystery concept and how mysteries can be solved.

Play a modified version of *Mindtrap*. Select questions that are age appropriate involving mathematics or logic. Help students make the connection between the game and solving a mystery.

Read "whodunit" stories to the class. Have students discuss and solve the mysteries.

Read *The Eleventh Hour Mystery*. Talk about the mystery idea, and use the information students have gleaned from the introduction to lay the groundwork for looking at a mystery in literature. Divide into groups to solve the mystery.

Have students design and construct their own musical instruments using information they have discovered from examining the instruments.

Bring several musical instruments to the classroom for students to examine. Discuss the different sounds they produce. Have students try to determine how each instrument produces its sound.

Discuss the mystery as a literature form. Have students select a mystery to read independently from options the teacher provides or from the library.

LITERATURE

MUSIC

ART

MYSTERIES

SCIENCE

HISTORY

LANGUAGE ARTS

MATHEMATICS

SOCIAL STUDIES

GEOGRAPHY

Raise the question Who discovered America? Provide children with resources from which they can collect information in order to prepare personal responses to the question.

Teach a lesson on the research process to help students with the community problem-solving assignment.

Teach a lesson on predicting. Have students predict and write their own endings to stories.

Teach word-problem solving strategies in math. Teach students how to identify the information, determine what the problem is asking for, and look for word clues that will help decide the operation needed to solve the problem.

Teach a lesson on solving community problems, raising questions such as What needs to be done to solve the problem?

Teach a lesson on questioning, stressing key words used in questions and the kinds of answers elicited with the specific key words.

Conduct a lesson on mazes. Divide the class into cooperative groups. Each group will design a maze and guide a blindfolded member of the class through the maze using words only.

Provide a variety of puzzles for students to solve. Vary the activity by distributing puzzle shapes to different students. Student will then work together to assemble complete puzzles.

FIGURE A.21
Web design for Mysteries unit (upper elementary–middle school grades).
Note. Courtesy of Jane Boyd.

TECHNOLOGY

- Using the internet, students will research Francis Scott Key and find a recording of the national anthem.
- Students will design a spreadsheet of the original states, indicating the number of senators, representatives, and electoral votes.

MUSIC

- Students will listen to "The Star Spangled Banner," and discuss what they think it means.
- Students will write a song based on the three branches of government, using the melody of the national anthem or Yankee Doodle.

DRAMA

- Students will study the drama "1776."
- Have students design costumes and sets and reenact part of the debate.

ART

- Have students design a mobile depicting the three branches of government.
- Have students make a collage of images and phrases from the Constitution.
- Students will create a bulletin board of the Preamble.
- Using cardboard boxes (appliance size), students will create mini-museums for artifacts related to the Constitution.
- Teach a lesson on calligraphy. Have students use it in various projects during the unit.

LANGUAGE ARTS

- Students will study, then rewrite the Preamble using their own words.
- Together, have students create a class Constitution that they will illustrate and display.
- Have students write a short biography on a person involved in the making of the Constitution. (Review the research process.)
- Have students keep a journal of current government activities (news articles) and make connections to the Constitution.
- Write a newspaper article covering the 1787 Constitutional Convention.

THE UNITED STATES CONSTITUTION

HISTORY & GOVERNMENT

- Play Constitution Jeopardy with the biographies of famous people the students have researched.
- Teach a lesson on the Great Compromise and discuss the differences between the Senate and the House of Representatives.
- Discuss the original Articles of Confederation and why they did not work well.
- Have a class discussion on how the Constitution affects our daily lives; then have the students write a short related essay.
- Divide the class into three groups to research the three branches of the government and to report back to the class.

SCIENCE

- Students will investigate inventions of the 1700s.
- Have students study the work of Benjamin Franklin.
- Students will conduct experiments on electricity.

MATHEMATICS

- Teach a lesson on time lines. Then have the students create a time line of the ratifications and amendments to the Constitution.
- Teach a lesson on fractions in connection with the 3/5ths compromise.
- Calculate the distance each delegate had to travel to get to the convention.

GEOGRAPHY

- Have students practice their mapping and research skills by creating and labeling a map of the United States in 1787.

FIGURE A.22

Web Design for United States Constitution unit (upper elementary grades and above). *Note.* Courtesy of Virginia Mullis and Lori Oliver.

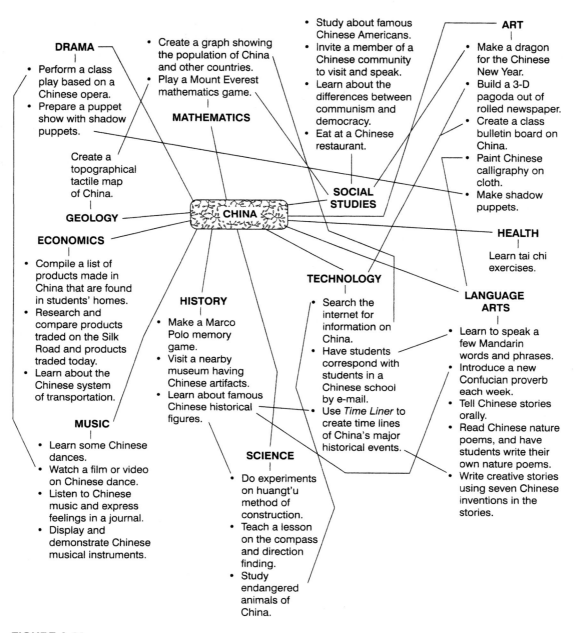

DRAMA
- Perform a class play based on a Chinese opera.
- Prepare a puppet show with shadow puppets.

Create a topographical tactile map of China.

GEOLOGY

ECONOMICS
- Compile a list of products made in China that are found in students' homes.
- Research and compare products traded on the Silk Road and products traded today.
- Learn about the Chinese system of transportation.

MUSIC
- Learn some Chinese dances.
- Watch a film or video on Chinese dance.
- Listen to Chinese music and express feelings in a journal.
- Display and demonstrate Chinese musical instruments.

- Create a graph showing the population of China and other countries.
- Play a Mount Everest mathematics game.

MATHEMATICS

HISTORY
- Make a Marco Polo memory game.
- Visit a nearby museum having Chinese artifacts.
- Learn about famous Chinese historical figures.

SCIENCE
- Do experiments on huangt'u method of construction.
- Teach a lesson on the compass and direction finding.
- Study endangered animals of China.

CHINA

- Study about famous Chinese Americans.
- Invite a member of a Chinese community to visit and speak.
- Learn about the differences between communism and democracy.
- Eat at a Chinese restaurant.

SOCIAL STUDIES

TECHNOLOGY
- Search the internet for information on China.
- Have students correspond with students in a Chinese school by e-mail.
- Use *Time Liner* to create time lines of China's major historical events.

ART
- Make a dragon for the Chinese New Year.
- Build a 3-D pagoda out of rolled newspaper.
- Create a class bulletin board on China.
- Paint Chinese calligraphy on cloth.
- Make shadow puppets.

HEALTH
- Learn tai chi exercises.

LANGUAGE ARTS
- Learn to speak a few Mandarin words and phrases.
- Introduce a new Confucian proverb each week.
- Tell Chinese stories orally.
- Read Chinese nature poems, and have students write their own nature poems.
- Write creative stories using seven Chinese inventions in the stories.

FIGURE A.23
Web design for China unit (upper elementary–middle school grades).
Note. Courtesy of Christine Coyle.

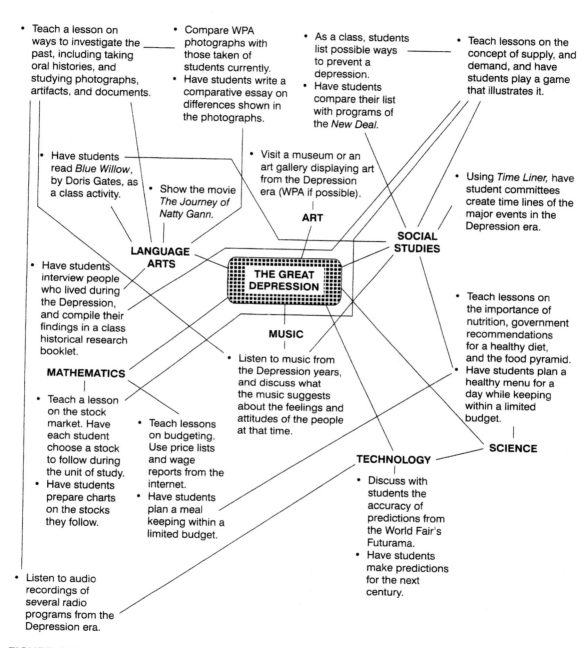

- Teach a lesson on ways to investigate the _____ past, including taking oral histories, and studying photographs, artifacts, and documents.

- Compare WPA photographs with those taken of students currently.
- Have students write a comparative essay on differences shown in the photographs.

- As a class, students list possible ways ——— to prevent a depression.
- Have students compare their list with programs of the *New Deal*.

- Teach lessons on the concept of supply, and demand, and have students play a game that illustrates it.

- Have students read *Blue Willow*, by Doris Gates, as a class activity.

- Show the movie *The Journey of Natty Gann*.

- Visit a museum or an art gallery displaying art from the Depression era (WPA if possible).

ART

- Using *Time Liner*, have student committees create time lines of the major events in the Depression era.

LANGUAGE ARTS

THE GREAT DEPRESSION

SOCIAL STUDIES

- Have students interview people who lived during the Depression, and compile their findings in a class historical research booklet.

MATHEMATICS

- Teach a lesson on the stock market. Have each student choose a stock to follow during the unit of study.
- Have students prepare charts on the stocks they follow.

- Teach lessons on budgeting. Use price lists and wage reports from the internet.
- Have students plan a meal keeping within a limited budget.

MUSIC

- Listen to music from the Depression years, and discuss what the music suggests about the feelings and attitudes of the people at that time.

TECHNOLOGY

- Discuss with students the accuracy of predictions from the World Fair's Futurama.
- Have students make predictions for the next century.

- Teach lessons on the importance of nutrition, government recommendations for a healthy diet, and the food pyramid.
- Have students plan a healthy menu for a day while keeping within a limited budget.

SCIENCE

- Listen to audio recordings of several radio programs from the Depression era.

FIGURE A.24

Web design for The Great Depression unit (upper elementary–middle school grades).
Note. Courtesy of Janice Hedge.

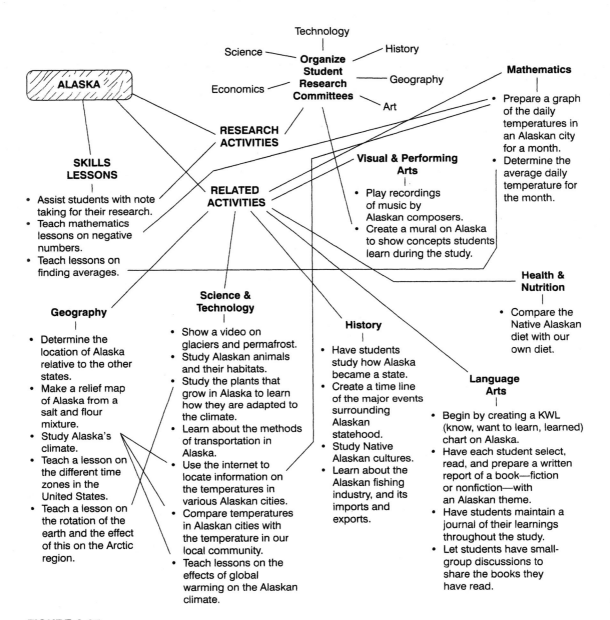

FIGURE A.25
Web design for Alaska unit (upper elementary–middle school grades).
Note. Courtesy of Audrey Asaro and Smithe Jean-Baptiste.

Index